T0271593

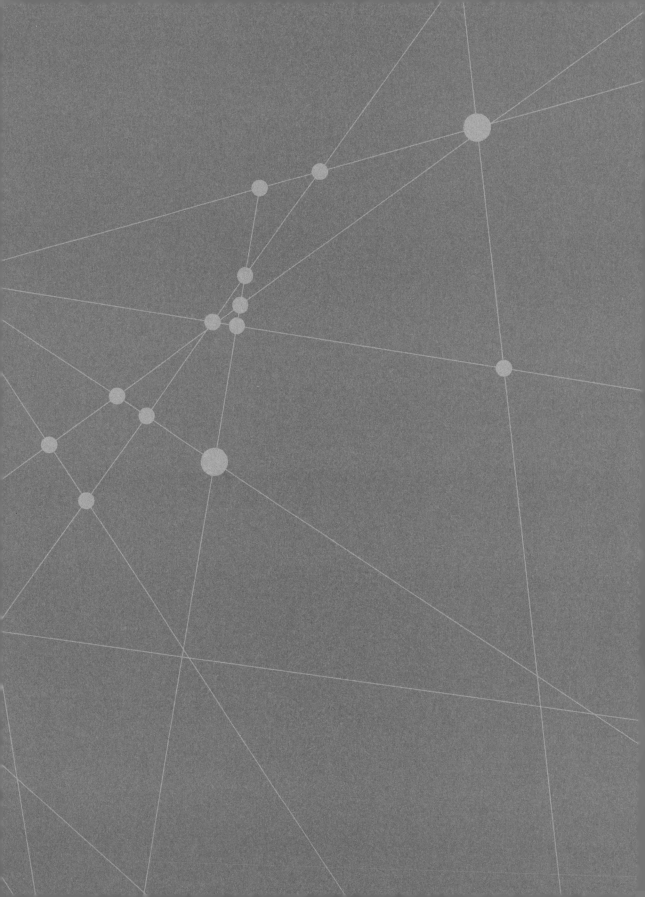

Migration

Above: A child peers from the window of a bus, after arriving at Key West, Florida, as part of the mass exodus from Cuba during the Mariel boat lift in 1980.

THIS IS AN ANDRÉ DEUTSCH BOOK

Published in 2019 by André Deutsch Limited
A division of the Carlton Publishing Group
20 Mortimer Street
London W1T 3JW

Text © André Deutsch Limited, 2019
Design © André Deutsch Limited, 2019

A CIP catalogue for this book is available from the British Library.

ISBN: 978 0 233 00597 3

10 9 8 7 6 5 4 3 2 1

Printed in Dubai

Back cover photographs: (left) AP/Shutterstock & (right) Arsis Messinis/AFP/Getty Images

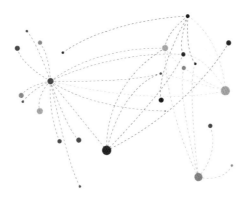

Migration

THE MOVEMENT OF HUMANKIND FROM
PREHISTORY TO THE PRESENT

ROBIN COHEN

ANDRE
DEUTSCH

Contents

———

PART ONE
The Matrix of Migration

———

PART TWO
Migration in Recent History

———

PART THREE
Contemporary Migration

—

PART FOUR
Controversies and Developments

—

Acknowledgements

———

This book could not have been written without the help of Jason Cohen, who checked the references, found many of the illustrations online and generally acted in support. Selina Molteno Cohen read most of the entries and picked up infelicities of style. This task was also shouldered by Alison Moss, who had the difficult responsibility of getting me to stick firmly to the timetable. No slacking was allowed. She liaised with the team at André Deutsch and held the ring between designer, publisher and author with panache. Our talented designer, James Pople, drew maps, constructed graphs and provided an arresting layout. Slav Todorov, the Editorial Manager for reference books at Carlton Books, was supportive and effective. When I was struggling with sources on the partition of India my colleague at Kellogg College, Oxford, Yasmin Khan, handed me a gift of her excellent book on the subject. Finally, I must mention Donald Winchester, my agent at Watson, Little Ltd, who brokered this project. My sincere thanks go to all I have mentioned.

Introduction

How do we address a complex and controversial subject like human migration? Once largely the preserve of palaeontologists, demographers, geographers and sociologists working in academic settings, migration has moved into the limelight and often to the centre of angry political debate and contestation.

This book provides what the French call a *tour d'horizon*, or overview, of the subject, covering 44 topics. In choosing what to cover, many topics suggested themselves. Where did human migration begin and when was the Earth peopled? Why do some people move and others remain? What are the different types of migration? Can migration flows be staunched? Given that this book is conceived on a global scale covering much of the span of human history, these questions are addressed by finding telling and salient cases, which can serve to tell a wider story.

Any general survey of the field can hardly avoid the major examples of forced migration, such as Atlantic slavery, Asian indentured labour and the flight of refugees. It is also essential to include dramatic cases of voluntary migration, such as the substantial movements of Europeans to the Americas from the 1870s to the First World War and the colonization of Australia and other settlements. Political conflict has also played an important role in animating migration and,

consequently, the book contains chapters on the partition of India, on exiled and diasporic communities, and on the ways in which Israel first became a home for the "ingathering" of the Jews, then the place of exile for Palestinians who fled to Gaza and the West Bank. The politics of Cold War migration is, likewise, considered.

Migration is often motivated by the search for work. As large-scale mining and industrialization took root in many countries, workers from further afield were often needed to supplement local workers. At various times this situation applied to the diverse cases of the USA, to factories in Britain, to the South African diamond and gold mines, and to the manufacturing heartlands of China, where millions of rural Chinese found employment. The rapid rebuilding of European economies after the Second World War also necessitated recruiting workers from afar. Britain found its labour recruits in the Commonwealth, seeking surplus workers in the Caribbean, India and Pakistan, while West Germany turned to Turkey, among other sources of supply. The colossal infrastructure commissioned by the oil-rich States of the Gulf from the 1970s, including hospitals, universities, museums and shopping malls, was overwhelmingly built by labour hired in Southeast Asia.

In contrast to the importation of workers recruited by companies or countries is the development of state-sponsored emigration. The pioneer of this model on a large-scale is the Philippines, a country that has developed particular strengths in training mariners and healthcare workers for employment abroad. So successful has this strategy been that the Philippines now provides a quarter of all seafarers worldwide. The core idea is that remittances sent back by workers in foreign countries or on the high seas will more than compensate for the cost of training them at home. India has similarly moved into the training of engineers and IT workers for "export" on a significant scale, with the additional downstream benefits of fostering international enterprises and return investment flows. Despite these positive examples of labour emigration, smaller, poorer, countries often struggle with the loss of educated and skilled workers and consequently some negative cases of "brain-drain" are also considered in this book.

For many citizens and politicians in the countries of immigration, unconstrained migration is seen as deleterious, offering competition to long-standing residents for jobs, housing and other services, while also providing a threat to established ways of life and cultural norms. While these threats are frequently exaggerated, they are keenly felt and it is instructive to consider attempts to control the movement, and particularly the unregulated movement, of migrants.

Beyond the themes already mentioned, there are important definitional issues affecting the field of migration studies. One of the major changes in looking at human migration is the idea that migration is not a distinct phenomenon in itself, but part of a general "mobilities paradigm".[1] The flow of people around the world, it is thought, is comparable to, and often linked with, the flow of goods, resources, money, images, pollutants, drugs, music, data, and many other aspects of contemporary life. For migration scholars, this shift towards looking at many dimensions of mobility has meant abandoning a stricter definition of migration (the movement of people for the purposes of working and settling for a defined period) in favour of movement per se. This shift in outlook is strongly reflected in this book, which includes chapters on music, nomads, missionaries, pilgrims, soldiers, explorers, international students, children, retirees and tourists, among other topics.

I hope that readers will be unperturbed by this more capacious understanding of the subject matter and will find something new and interesting to stimulate them. I have enjoyed selecting the material and have tried to give the cases a sense of immediacy without diminishing the complexity of the subject matter.

Robin Cohen
Oxford, June 2019.

Opposite: Migrants disembark from their ship to start a new life in New York.

وَكَادَ يُزَعْزِعُ الجِمَالَ السَّيْرُ وَالنَّشَدُ

مَا الحَجُّ سَيْرَكَ تَأْوِيبًا وَادْلَاجًا وَلَا اعْتِيَامَكَ أَجْمَالًا وَأَجْدَالًا

الحَجُّ أَنْ تَقْصِدَ البَيْتَ الحَرَامَ عَلَى تَجْرِيدِكَ الحَجَّ لَا تَبْغِي بِهِ جَاحَا

وَسِطْ كَأَهْلِ الإِنْصَافِ مُتَّخِذًا رَدْعَ الهَوَى هَادِيًا وَالحَزْنَ مِنْهَاجَا

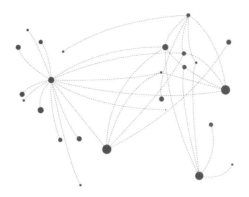

PART ONE

The Matrix
of Migration

1
Out of Africa
Early Humans

Human beings were, from the beginning, a migrating species. As they sought food, warded off enemies and explored their landscapes, humans ranged far from their origins in Africa, eventually populating most of the world's land mass.

——

As paleoanthropologists (scientists who research early humans) dig up more skeletons, different sites are nominated as "the origin" of humankind. Sometimes the fossil remains of early humans look very similar to each other, even though DNA markers may indicate divergence. With new finds the exact evolution of the human species is always under review. Very early specimens, dating back to two million years ago, have been found in the Malapa caves, now rebranded the Cradle of Humankind World Heritage Site, about 45km (28 miles) north-west of Johannesburg, South Africa.

The fossils of "modern humans", as they are called, are often dug up in East Africa. Humans like *Homo habilis*, *Homo erectus* or *Homo ergaster* were later to make way for our best-known ancestor, *Homo sapiens*. Unlike many of the earlier species, *Homo erectus* had shorter arms and, with elongated legs, was bi-pedal, and walked and ran just like us.

From the Rift Valley in East Africa, humans migrated north around 200,000 years ago, and with the continents then conjoined, slowly colonized the earth, reaching the tip of South America as recently as 10,000 years ago. Since 2013 Paul Salopek has been walking the journey (he has to use boats and ferries where the continents have become separated) on behalf of *National Geographic* magazine (see map and feature opposite).

Above: From left to right: *Homo habilis*, *Homo erectus*, *Homo sapiens*.

A walk through time

Roughly 200,000 years ago humans migrated from the East Africa Rift area –"Start" on the map below – into different parts of Africa.

At around 60,000 years ago humans migrated out of Africa to the rest of the world, making it to the tip of South America about 10,000 years ago.

Paul Salopek is literally walking through these "time bands" of human settlement.

Numbers on the map represent thousands of years before present.

Time bands were produced using interpolation from fossil sites with cartographic smoothing applied.

Many theories exist regarding precise dates of human migration. Direction is not true on this map.

For this map the Fuller projection was used to "straighten" this near circum-global route to better emphasize the sheer length of the 34,000km (21,000-mile) walk.

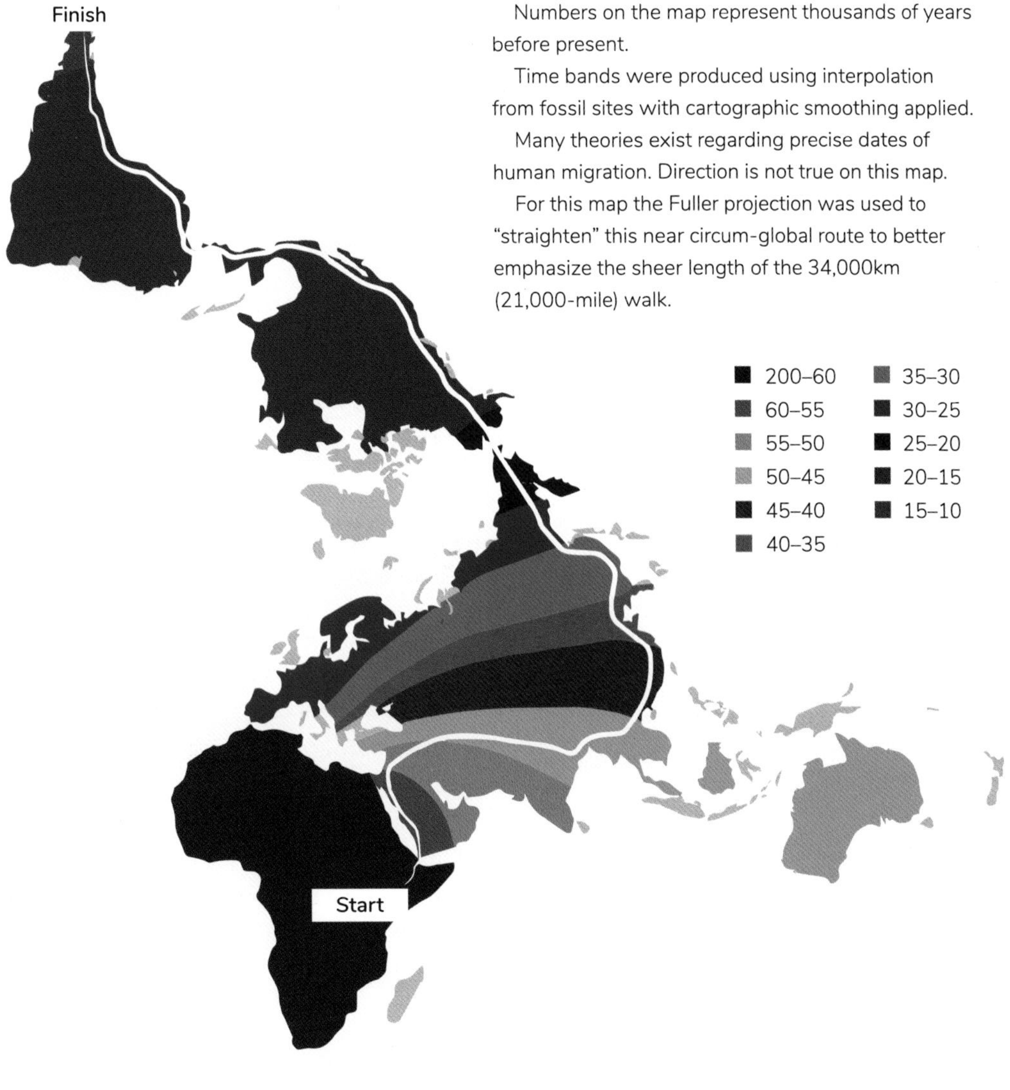

Finish

Start

■ 200–60	■ 35–30
■ 60–55	■ 30–25
■ 55–50	■ 25–20
■ 50–45	■ 20–15
■ 45–40	■ 15–10
■ 40–35	

Thinking upside down

Could it be that we humans would have been better off continuing to wander the earth in small bands and learning how to survive by "living off the land"? At least two reputable scholars have strongly made that case. Yuval Noah Harari suggests that "on the whole foragers seem to have enjoyed a more comfortable life style than most of the peasants, shepherds, labourers and office clerks who followed in their footsteps"[1]. Even living in the most inhospitable environments, surviving hunter-gatherers need about 35–45 hours a week to gather their food, compared with settled populations in the developed world who work 40–45 hours a week, and those settled in the developing world who work nearly double that amount. This argument is extended and documented by James Suzman[2] who has worked among the Khoisan peoples of the Kalahari Basin for nearly 25 years. Their long run is finally coming to an end (as settlement encroaches and the climate changes) but, as Suzman points out, in terms of longevity they are by far the most successful civilization, having enjoyed "primitive abundance" for over 200,000 years. (In that time the Mongol, Chinese, Roman, Achaemenid and Ottoman Empires have crumbled and the sun has set on the British Empire.)

We often imagine civilization as the triumph of the sedentary over the mobile, but human settlements have created enormous problems. With humans bumped up against each other, diseases spread, while many city planners have struggled to provide adequate food, housing, transport, security, education, potable water and sewerage. To feed urban populaces, the countryside has been blighted by commercial agriculture, pesticides and land clearances. As the planet itself has become threatened by pollution, climate change and over-exploitation, perhaps we can learn something from our more ecologically-sensitive migrating ancestors?

A DNA–based map
of early human migration

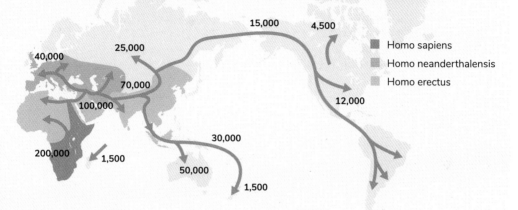

DNA is used principally in medicine, but it can also help in plotting early migration history. As George Busby explains, the DNA of long-expired people and other animals can be recovered from skeletons and fossils. By discovering how old they are and how they combined we can show when (the map shows the number of years ago) humans reached different parts of the world and where they encountered Neanderthals and other early hominids.[3]

Humans did not make a beeline to Cape Horn. There were many diversions and loop backs and along the way *Homo sapiens* met other species. With new research evidence from genetic material, we no longer have to rely solely on fossils to trace the movements of our ancestors. Nonetheless, it was somewhat surprising to find from research published in 2017 that contemporary Europeans have between 1.8 and 2.6 per cent of the genomes made up of Neanderthal DNA. Sexual encounters had taken place mainly in the south-west of Europe and the finding contradicted previous assumptions that the superior intelligence of *Homo sapiens*

had allowed them to avoid or overcome the stronger *Homo neanderthalensis*.

Equally surprising is that *Homo sapiens*, who reached Britain 44,000 years ago, retained their dark skin for over 30,000 years. In 2018, using DNA analysis of a skeleton found in Gough's Cave, Cheddar Gorge, Somerset in 1903, scientists recreated "Cheddar Man".

So why did northern Europeans change their colour? This was probably because of admixtures of people from the Russian and Ukrainian Steppe around 5,000 years ago as well as due to natural evolution. Lighter skins are better at absorbing limited UV light and synthesizing Vitamin D, which is essential to good health.

2
Explorers
Arabic, Chinese and European

For many years, European schoolchildren learned about the rest of the world through a section of their history courses called "The Age of Discovery" – the period between the fifteenth and eighteenth centuries when European explorers and mariners, generally from the Iberian Peninsula, extended European awareness of far-off lands. By circumnavigation, they conclusively demonstrated that the world was indeed round, as had been surmised.

It was a significant period in world history certainly, as it laid the ground for mercantilism, colonialism and missionary activity, all important developments that facilitated migrations, large and small. In another sense, the emphasis on European "discovery" was profoundly misleading. Non-Europeans did not need to be "discovered" as if they were lost objects; they already knew they were there. Neither were the mariners only from Portugal and Spain. Phoenician ships had explored the Mediterranean, Vikings had travelled to modern-day Canada around AD 1000, and dhows had been plying the Arabian and East African coastline for centuries. In terms of recorded long-distance journeys, Islamic and Chinese explorers and navigators long preceded their European counterparts.

Right: Ibn Baṭṭūṭah in Egypt.
Opposite: Islamic astrolabe used for navigation.

Travels of Ibn Baṭṭūṭah

→ 1325–27   → 1330–32   → 1332–46   → 1349–53

Note: Dashed lines indicate routes Ibn Baṭṭūṭah may have followed

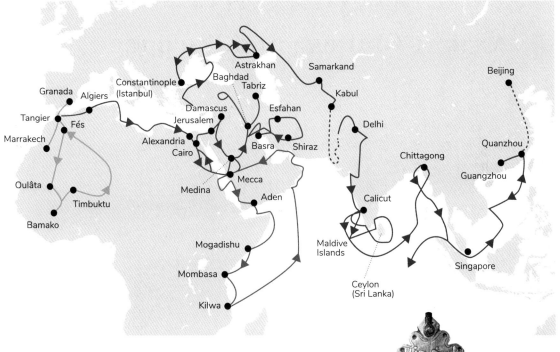

Islamic explorers

Islamic, mainly Arabic, explorers had developed sophisticated instruments and knew about the tides, monsoons, currents and "seas" off Persia, India and the Mediterranean, which, they understood, formed a continuous oceanic space.[1] The most famous Islamic explorer was, without doubt, the Moroccan-born Ibn Baṭṭūṭah (1304–1368/69 or 1377), author of *The Rihlah* (Travels). He described journeys, some of which may have been somewhat embellished, covering 120,000km (74,565 miles), to almost all the Muslim-dominated regions and their adjacent areas.

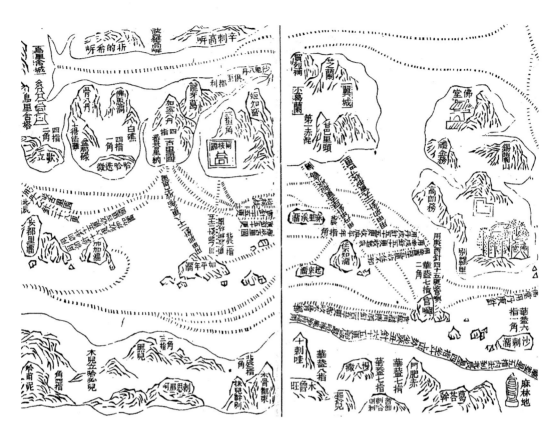

The extent of Zheng He's voyages 1405–33

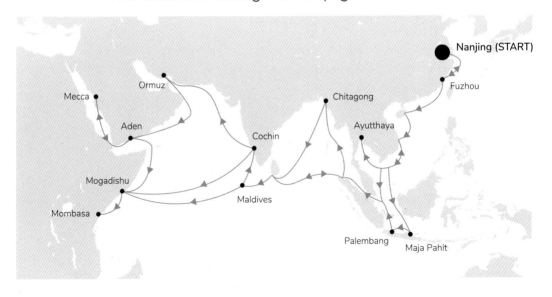

Nanjing (START)

Fuzhou

Ormuz

Mecca

Aden

Chitagong

Ayutthaya

Cochin

Mogadishu

Maldives

Mombasa

Palembang

Maja Pahit

EXPLORERS: ARABIC, CHINESE AND EUROPEAN

The period between the ninth and fourteenth centuries was "the golden age" of Muslim discovery and exploration. As one reputed Dutch scholar of Islam argued, "Europe ought to look upon them [Muslims] as its cultural ancestors in the domain of geographical knowledge, of discovery, and of world trade".[2]

Chinese explorers

Where the Arabs led, the Chinese explorers followed. The most notable by far was Zheng He (1371–1433/35), who was an admiral of the fleet during the early Ming dynasty. Curiously, he was born a Muslim and his father and grandfather had both been on *Hajj* (the religious pilgrimage) to Mecca, perhaps fostering his appetite for travel. By the standard of Arabic and later European mariners, the largest of his ships were enormous, some 127m (416ft 8in), carrying hundreds of sailors on four decks. Sails were unfurled on nine masts. The impressive size of his fleet provided a clue to the main purpose of his voyages, proclaiming the might of the Ming dynasty and promoting trade. His seven expeditions went to Southeast Asia, South Asia, Western Asia, the Red Sea and East Africa from 1405 to 1433.[3] On his fourth voyage he was presented with a giraffe which was taken back to China as a "tribute gift".

As the Mao Kun map opposite demonstrates, Chinese cartography was very different from its European equivalent. Zheng He's voyages are shown in more conventional form below it.

European explorers

Conventional Western history is much more familiar with the explorations of the famous Iberian mariners, though their back stories are more complicated than we commonly assume. Christopher Columbus is the same person as Cristòffa Cómbo (Ligurian), Cristoforo Colombo (Italian) and Cristóbal Colón (Spanish). He certainly did not "land in America" if by that we mean the USA. Rather, his first voyage reached the Bahamas. On his second voyage, he captured 1,500 Taíno on the island of Hispaniola (present-day Haiti and Dominican Republic) and took them to the slave markets of Seville. Under his leadership, the Spanish attacked the Taíno, which, along with the introduction of European diseases (notably smallpox) and forced labour, led to their near extinction within 30 years. Since African slaves were introduced to compensate for this population loss, we can indirectly hold Columbus responsible for the inauguration of the transatlantic slave trade. It is perhaps understandable that Columbus Day, which is widely celebrated in the Americas, has been replaced by Indigenous Peoples' Day or other alternatives in a number of US cities and South American states.

Other major European explorers included Amerigo Vespucci, who gave his name to the Americas and demonstrated that Columbus had not, as he believed, discovered the eastern boundaries of Asia, but a new landmass with

Opposite above: Long after Zheng He's voyages, the Mao Kun map (top) – a rolled-up strip of navigation charts often regarded as a surviving document from the expeditions of Zheng He – was published as a set of navigation charts in the Ming dynasty military treatise Wubei Zhi.

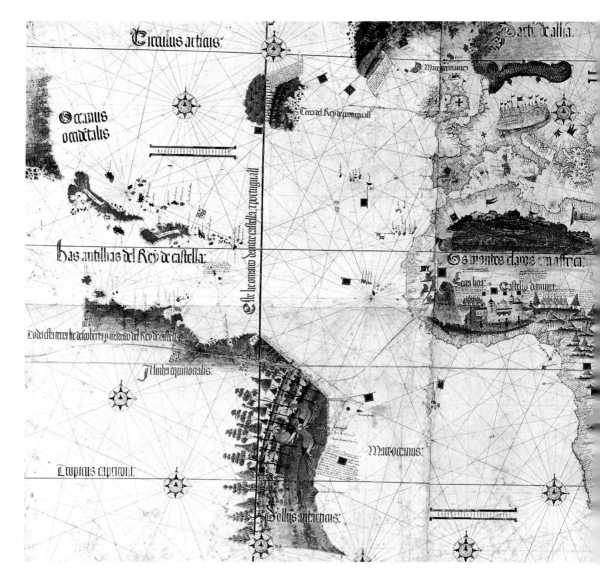

another large ocean, the Pacific, still to traverse. The earlier assumption had given rise to such misnomers as "Red Indians", "Indios" and the "West Indies". Another important milestone was the voyage of Vasco da Gama to India via the Cape route (1497–99), avoiding the Mediterranean and the Middle East, where armed and dangerous intermediaries exacted tariffs on trade. The last leg from Malindi to Calicut was conducted with the aid of a local pilot who knew the way because of established trade routes between East Africa and India.[4]

Elaborate myths and half-truths have sometimes obscured the exact sequence of who got where first. No doubt these will be corrected as global history supersedes

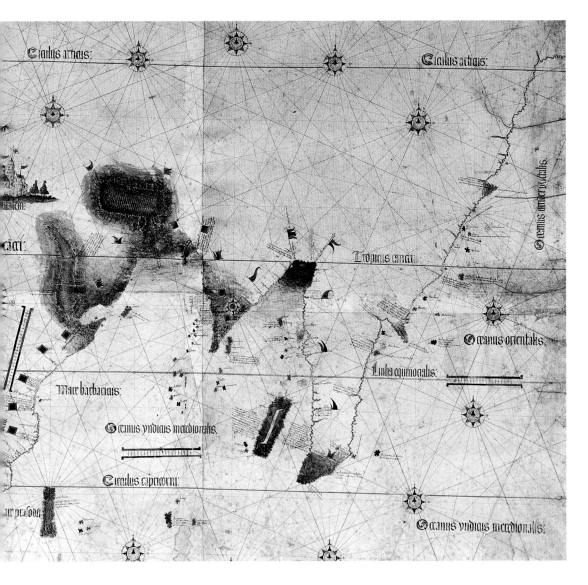

Above: The Cantino planisphere, 1502, is the
earliest surviving chart showing the explorations
of Christopher Columbus to the Americas, Gaspar
Corte-Real to Newfoundland, Vasco da Gama
to India and Pedro Alvares Cabral to Brazil.

nationalist and religious accounts. Connecting
the different parts of the world overland
or across seas was, no doubt, a much more
incremental and democratic process than can
be garnered by focusing solely on the headline
explorers. However, these pioneering journeys
remain important markers in laying the
ground work for establishing trade, empires,
colonies, religious missions and the lattice
work of communications necessary for large-
scale migration.

3
Early Religions and Migration

While mutual tolerance and ecumenicalism are now more common, at the heart of many early religions was a strong conviction that only one doctrine and one faith was true. That faith had to be spread by missionaries, renewed by pilgrimages and assemblies, and protected by expulsions of those who professed another religion. All three dimensions of religion had deep effects on the matrix of migration.

Missionaries

Saul of Tarsus (to give him his Jewish name) was the first great missionary. Converted on the road to Damascus, the re-named Paul became the most ardent follower of Christ and, perhaps more than anyone else, fashioned Christianity as a world religion. On his journeys to Antioch, modern-day Turkey, Greece and Rome he wrote, preached and, to some degree, codified the Christian gospel. Spreading the word of the Lord ultimately engendered proselytizing missions to every corner of the earth. The Church Missionary Society (now the Church Mission Society) expanded along with colonialism and now works in 40 countries. As they penetrated the South American continent, the Spanish colonizers advanced with guns in one hand and bibles in the other. The heartland of Christian missionary work is now the USA, which accounted for 127,000 of the world's estimated 400,000 overseas missionaries in 2010.[1]

Above: St Paul, the first great missionary.
Opposite: Consecration drawing of Gautama Buddha.

EARLY RELIGIONS AND MIGRATION

EARLY RELIGIONS AND MIGRATION

Other early religions also connect to the story of migration. Muhammad's Hegira (his flight from Mecca to Medina) provides a template for the founding and spread of Islam, while the six-year wanderings of Gautama Buddha (or Shakyamuni Buddha) still evoke the need for movement in the search for Enlightenment. Although there is some controversy as to whether the word "missionary" is too Western to describe the spread of Buddhism, Buddha's 45 years of "clearing the dust from people's eyes" and the devotion of Therevada monks to converting people to a "new viewpoint" are missionary activities in all but name.[2] The spread of Buddhism into India, Ceylon, Burma, Thailand, Laos, Cambodia, Vietnam, Indonesia and China (244 million or 18.2 per cent of its total population are Buddhists) is testimony to the massive reach of the Buddhist monks.

Opposite: Muhammad flees to Medina, AD 622.

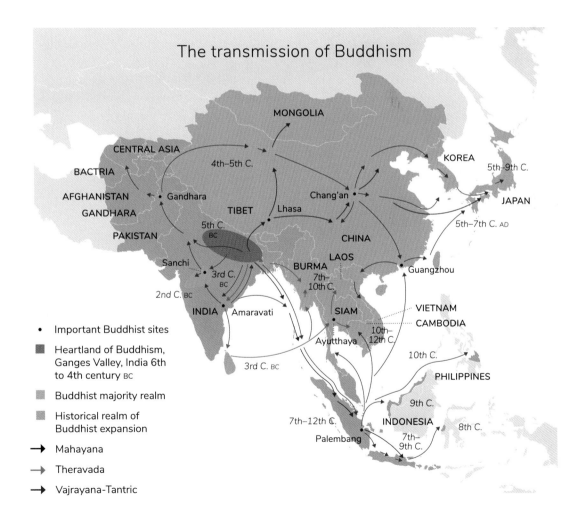

The transmission of Buddhism

MONGOLIA

CENTRAL ASIA

BACTRIA
4th–5th C.

AFGHANISTAN • Gandhara

GANDHARA   TIBET   Lhasa

PAKISTAN   5th C.
                      BC

Sanchi   BURMA
        • 3rd C.   LAOS
          BC
2nd C. BC

INDIA Amaravati

KOREA
5th–9th C.

Chang'an •

CHINA   JAPAN

Guangzhou   5th–7th C. AD

SIAM
Ayutthaya   10th–
             12th C.

VIETNAM
CAMBODIA

10th C.

3rd C. BC

PHILIPPINES

9th C.

7th–12th C.

INDONESIA   8th C.

Palembang   7th–
7th–10th C. 9th C.

- Important Buddhist sites
- ▇ Heartland of Buddhism, Ganges Valley, India 6th to 4th century BC
- ▒ Buddhist majority realm
- ▒ Historical realm of Buddhist expansion
- → Mahayana
- → Theravada
- → Vajrayana-Tantric

Pilgrimages and councils

A separate discussion of the Muslim *hajj* is provided elsewhere in this book, but here we focus on what Dirk Hoerder describes as the "golden age" of pilgrimage in Latin Christendom, namely the period from the eleventh to the fourteenth centuries.[3] The pilgrims criss-crossed the Middle East and Europe, opening up new routes and tracks for carts, horses and pedestrians and trading in small items such as jewels, icons and perfumes. Jerusalem, Rome and Santiago de Compostela (Spain) were particularly favoured destinations. Shrines were visited or newly created, especially where holy relics (some clearly fake) were held. Jesus's shroud, sudarium, crown of thorns, segments of the cross on which he was nailed, the nails themselves, not to mention the veils, bones and remains of the various saints, all attracted large numbers of pilgrims. "Rome-faring" was so popular that in its abbreviated form "roaming" entered the English language (from Old English and Proto-Germanic). Another powerful attraction was the Cathedral of Santiago de Compostela, consecrated in 1211, where St James is said to be buried. Though not all pilgrims defer to this traditional belief, millions have visited the site. In 2017 some 300,000 walked or cycled along "the Way" with various motivations, not always religious, though many were seeking a spiritual experience of some sort.

In addition to pilgrimages, large assemblies of Christian notables periodically took place. One example is the Lateran Council of 1215, which involved 400 bishops and 800 abbots, each of whom required a retinue of about 10 servants and clerics.

The Ways of St James

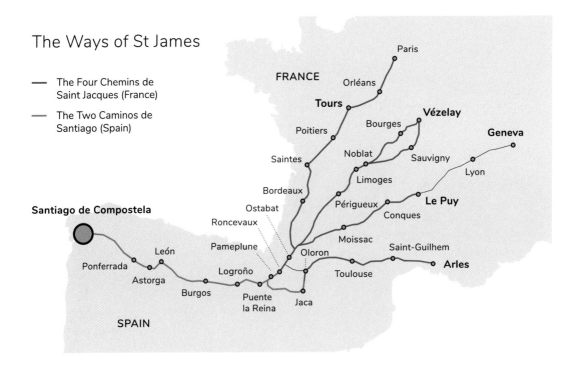

— The Four Chemins de Saint Jacques (France)

— The Two Caminos de Santiago (Spain)

Santiago de Compostela

Ponferrada · León · Astorga · Burgos · Puente la Reina · Jaca · Logroño · Pameplune · Roncevaux · Ostabat · Oloron · Moissac · Toulouse · Saint-Guilhem · Arles · Conques · Le Puy · Périgueux · Bordeaux · Limoges · Noblat · Saintes · Poitiers · Sauvigny · Lyon · Geneva · Vézelay · Bourges · Tours · Orléans · Paris

FRANCE

SPAIN

Expulsion of Jews 1100–1600

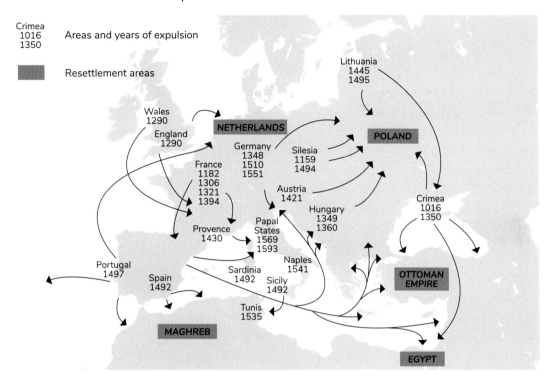

Crimea
1016
1350
Areas and years of expulsion

Resettlement areas

Lithuania
1445
1495

Wales
1290

England
1290

NETHERLANDS

Germany
1348
1510
1551

Silesia
1159
1494

POLAND

France
1182
1306
1321
1394

Austria
1421

Crimea
1016
1350

Papal
States
1569
1593

Hungary
1349
1360

Provence
1430

Naples
1541

Portugal
1497

Spain
1492

Sardinia
1492

Sicily
1492

OTTOMAN
EMPIRE

Tunis
1535

MAGHREB

EGYPT

Expulsions

Belief in the exclusive validity of one religion led to mass expulsions – in medieval and early modern Europe it was the Jews and Muslims who were the common targets. Jews were expelled from England in 1290 and from many other European countries, but the largest and most sustained expulsions were from Spain (in 1492) and Portugal five years later.

The expulsion was ordered by the Alhambra decree of 1492, which particularly targeted *conversos* (converts) who were thought to be secretly practising Judaism. It was perhaps not surprising that Muslims and Jews found it easier to convert rather than face the wrath of those like the Grand Inquisitor, Tomás de Torquemada

(1420–98), who ordered the execution of anyone who would not submit. Because of the suspicion that some *conversos* were crypto-Jews, not true converts, some 200,000 Jews were expelled. The Sephardi (Hebrew for "Spanish") Jews, often speaking the distinctive Ladino language, dispersed to many parts of the world.

Again in 1492 the Emirate of Granada, the last remaining Muslim territory in al-Andalus, fell to the Catholic monarchs Ferdinand II of Aragón and Isabella I of Castile. Although Moriscos (converted Muslims) were able to maintain a precarious existence in Spain for another century, in 1609 Philip of Spain expelled all Moriscos. As in the case of the Jewish *conversos*, many were suspected of secretly retaining their Islamic faith.

4

Nomads

From Acephalous Societies to Empires

For most of human history, migration consisted of small bands of hunter-gatherers moving in response to seasonal changes, searching for fresh water and following the migratory movements of the animals they hunted for survival. While many peoples opted for permanent settlements, raising crops and tending domesticated animals, a nomadic lifestyle never entirely disappeared.

—

Now confined mainly to semi-deserts, jungles, remote islands, or Arctic areas, the old ways of living by moving are under threat. Most hunter-gatherer societies are acephalous; that is they do not have strong leadership structures or anything approximating a state. However, it is erroneous to think that nomadism was always confined to small groups as, in some cases, bands and clans successfully came together under charismatic leaders to dominate large territories, or even create vast empires. In this chapter we consider the surviving small groups, the people known as "Plains Indians", and the Mongol Empire. (In the next chapter we discuss the Romani, often called Gypsies, and Travellers.)

The survivors

While on a broad definition there could be as many as 30–40 million nomads,[1] the small communities of hunter-gatherers are struggling to survive, as remote areas are penetrated by tourism, logging, mining and plantations. Many indigenous groups in the Amazonian forest and elsewhere are threatened by land clearance for palm oil plantations (the oil is used in cosmetics, fuel and food), which have expanded massively over the last decade and now cover 27 million hectares (66 million acres) of land worldwide, the size of New Zealand. There is no escape from the extractive industries, even in the Arctic zone, where oil companies threaten indigenous peoples' ways of life.

Despite the threats to their livelihoods, small nomadic groups nonetheless survive in Amazonia, in central and northern Australia, the Kalahari, the central African forests, India, southern Latin America, and in Canada, Alaska and Greenland. Perhaps surprisingly there are also some remaining "uncontacted groups", which occasionally gain public attention. In November 2018, the Sentinelese in the Andaman Islands killed a missionary with arrows as he sought to "declare Jesus" to "Satan's last stronghold".[2]

Native Alaskans and the *Exxon Valdez* oil spill

One of the most notorious episodes of pollution in the oil industry's history was when the oil tanker *Exxon Valdez* ran aground off the coast of Alaska in 1989 spilling between 257,000 and 750,000 barrels of crude oil. The livelihood of Native Alaskans (this label subsumes 227 tribes) in the area was immediately compromised. One of the Native Alaskans in a village called Tatilek summed up their plight in this way: "There are no stores in Tatilek. If a person is hungry, he goes out and hunts seal or deer, catches salmon or digs for shellfish ... villagers are worried that they may starve looking for food that has not been affected." Another Tatilek resident said, "sad is too sad a word for the village's loss".[3] The village chief of Port Graham, Alaska, Walter Meganack, was equally poignant. Calling his prepared speech "The Day the Water Died", he contended that "the Native story is a different story from the white man's story because our lives are different. What we value is different, how we see the water and the land, the plants and the animals is different. What the white man does for sport and recreation and money, we do for life, for the life of our bodies, for the life of our spirit, for the life of our ancient culture. Fishing and hunting and gathering are the rhythms of our tradition, regular daily lifetime, not vacation time, not employment time."[4]

People of the Great Plains

There are a number of names describing the nomads who inhabited the Canadian Prairies and the Great Plains of the USA long before these countries were discovered by Europeans. In Canada, they called themselves Blackfoot or Saulteaux, while further south, the groups that Hollywood movies made familiar include the Apache, Cheyenne, Comanche, Cree and Crow. Canadians now refer to such peoples as "First Nations", while in the USA the nomenclature "Native American" is more common. While out of favour, the old designation of "Plains Indians" has the virtue of indicating that the groups living in the Great Plains developed distinctive cultural, social and economic practices, particularly in the eighteenth and first half of the nineteenth centuries.

Though some were semi-sedentary, the majority of Plains Indians lived by hunting the vast herds of bison roaming these prairies, herding and killing the animals from horseback. There could have been as many as 60 million bison at the end of the eighteenth century. Despite being formidable animals, the bison could not survive the guns of the incoming white settlers. In one of the most brutal massacres of another species ever recorded, between 1850 and 1895 white hunters turned the Plains into an outdoor slaughterhouse, with numbers of bison reduced to 1,000. For the Plains Indians, the result was calamitous. They made a few brave stands against the incursions of the settlers, after which their nomadic culture collapsed and their descendants are now permanently settled on small reservations.

Map showing the territories (in orange) occupied by the Plains Indian tribes during the middle of the nineteenth century

The Mongol Empire

From 1206 to 1259, the Mongol Empire under Genghis Khan became "the largest empire in world history" stretching from Southeast Asia to Eastern Europe, with an estimated population of over 100 million people.[5] (The world's population was about 360 million at the time.) The Empire combined three elements – military mobility, pastoralism and trade. Conquest and defence of the Empire depended on letting off multiple arrows while mounted on fast-moving horses. A simple invention, the metal stirrup, permitted this – with a stable "seat", mounted cavalry could advance, run alongside the enemy and flee, taking minimal casualties and inflicting considerable damage.

The Mongol Empire expanded not only through military conquest, but also by raising, in order of their respective importance, horses, sheep, camels, cattle and goats. Just as livestock was moved for pasture (a system of transhumance) some settled agriculture was also practised. The military dominance of the Mongol emperors also produced the safe conditions under which long-distance trade could flourish. Although we know it as the "Silk Road" because the trade in Chinese silk was so lucrative, many other products were traded from Constantinople to Hangzhou, with ongoing sea connections.

Opposite: The gifted painter, George Catlin, recorded the heroic struggles of the Plains Indians to maintain their way of life.

Below: The Silk Road (marked in red), a misnomer as many other commodities were traded.

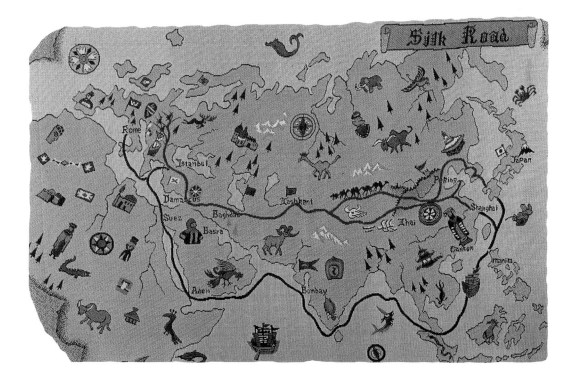

5

The Romani and Travellers

Nomads are usefully classified as hunter-gatherers, pastoralists and "service nomads" – migrants who have a close relationship with sedentary societies, even while retaining their nomadic ways. As the last category is particularly malleable, it is difficult to find an agreed total count of nomads – one encyclopaedic entry suggests 30–40 million people.[1]

The Romani as "service nomads"

In Europe, the best-known service nomads are the Romani or Roma, more popularly known by the exonym Gypsies. The term Gypsy is thought to have derived from a misapprehension that "Gypcians" (in Middle English) were wandering Egyptians. In fact, there is now strong genetic, linguistic and cultural evidence to suggest that the group originated in north-west India, though English, Welsh and Swedish sub-populations show genetic drift and much more admixture from their European neighbours.[2]

A contemporary estimate is that there are five or six million Romani living in Europe, concentrated in Romania, Bulgaria and Hungary, with a quarter of a million in Russia, Spain, Serbia and Slovakia.[3]

The Romani are service nomads in that they work in seasonal agriculture, buy and sell metal scrap and used cars, furniture, antiques and bric-à-brac. They also work in fairgrounds, markets and circuses. Romani women often hawk trinkets, flowers and posies and, not infrequently, offer to tell someone's fortune, aided by crystal balls or tarot cards. In contrast to the squalor of poor sedentary workers, the Romani way of life has often been romanticized, as in Vincent van Gogh's painting.

Unlike the sentimental depictions overleaf of their way of life, the Romani have often been the targets of open discrimination and accused of being child-snatchers, sorcerers, plague carriers, spies and thieves. One British report, commissioned by an NGO and Romani organization, claimed that nine out of ten Romani and Traveller children had suffered "racial abuse" and many were too frightened to go to school. Infant mortality rates are high,

Opposite: The wheel: flag of the Romani people, adopted by the 1971 World Romani Congress.

Romani migrations 900–1720

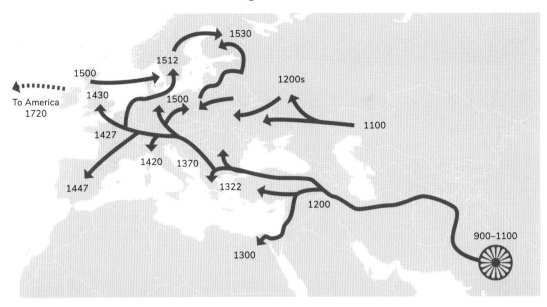

while life expectancy is twelve years lower than that of the general population.[4] Partly in response to the discrimination directed against them, the Romani have become more politically active, having organized nine World Romani Congresses since 1971 to discuss how best to press for rights and representation.

With the rise of nationalism in many European countries, the traditional cross-border mobility of the Romani has either been severely constrained or channelled into new practices.

One study of Romani in France shows how they have adapted to new immigration laws. In 2001–02, when Schengen visa requirements were waived for Romania and Bulgaria, the way was open for a three-month tourist stay, but this meant increased circularity as Romani from those countries were forced to return to "clean" their passports, as they described it.[5]

Above: *The Caravans, Gypsy Encampment near Arles*, 1888, by Vincent van Gogh.

Opposite: A Tinker at work.

Travellers, Tinkers and other nomads

There are other nomadic groups with no genetic connection to the Romani, including circus performers and entertainers in Korea, Swedish Tattare, Norwegian Tatere, Finnish Zigenare and the Bedouins of Israel and nearby territories. While the Bedouins have been nomads historically, other groups, notably the Travellers and Tinkers in the British Isles, have been forced into nomadism by land consolidation, evictions, poverty and famine.[6] The term "tinker" referred to itinerant tinsmiths who went from house to house mending household utensils, notably pots and kettles. In Ireland, the number forced into nomadism was, at first, astonishing. In 1834, the Royal Commission on the Poor Laws estimated that 2,385,000 beggars and their dependants were on the roads of Ireland for at least some of the year. Because they were excluded from the mainstream of social life, Irish Travellers became largely endogamous (married among themselves) and gradually formed an officially recognized ethnic group, a distinct indigenous minority. The 2011 Irish census recorded around 29,500 Irish Travellers.

Glomads, or global nomads

In a strange twist of fate, nomadism re-emerged as a chosen or enviable lifestyle towards the end of the twentieth century. Referring to backpackers, those who accompanied their parents on foreign postings or, more recently, those simply working in locations separated from traditional workplaces ("digital nomads"), this new nomadic lifestyle is commended by life coaches and futurologists. Perhaps the more cynical among us might note that global nomadism of this type may be sustained by a national passport, indulgent parents, an independent income, an iPhone and a laptop. However, to be more empathetic, glomads do represent an implied critique of a sedentary, suburban lifestyle, which perhaps has been oversold and traps many people in one place, in an unfulfilling job with an onerous mortgage and limited cultural choices.

6

Liquid Continent
Pacific Islanders

The unusual expression "liquid continent" signifies that we landlubbers – the writer and the majority of readers of this book – have to alter our "land-centric" outlook to understand the Pacific. As one writer points out, "about 80 per cent of the world's islands lie within a triangle formed by Tokyo, Jakarta and Pitcairn".[1] The people who have found their way to this liquid continent have learned to live with their overwhelmingly marine environment.

———

They are sensitive to the tides, currents and winds, live alongside dugongs, seals and sharks, and have developed affinities with dolphins. As they traverse the ocean, they learn the paths of seabirds, the smell of invisible vegetation and when to head for an island for fresh water and supplies. In short, they have developed a sea culture.

Precisely when the people of the Pacific explored their liquid continent has been a matter of evolving argument and new scientific data. At first, it was assumed that they needed outrigger and dugout canoes for long-distance travel. These watercraft are familiar to many cultures, but may have dated after the migrations that are now assumed to have occurred. It is a reasonable speculation, therefore, that simpler craft, probably rafts made from bamboo, were used to move between the islands.[2]

Were the seafarers driven from island to island by population pressures or shortages of food? Or, were they perhaps brave adventurers and voyagers? The answer is probably more prosaic and can be compared with contemporary motorists setting out along a highway or motorway, who would have a reasonable expectation of coming across a service station where they could fill up with petrol, buy food and drink. Likewise, the early people of the Pacific, with their developed sea culture, could assume that they would soon find a landfall on one of the many islands in their oceanic space.

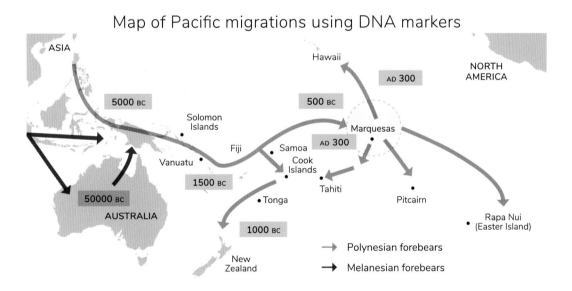

Conventional map of Pacific migrations

ASIA

4000 BC

• Guam

• Palau

Marshall Islands

Caroline Islands

Bismarck Arch

Papua

1200–1000 BC

1500 BC

Vanuatu

Fiji

Samoa

• Cook Islands

• Tonga

New Caledonia

Tubuai

1250–1300

New Zealand

AUSTRALIA

200–0 BC

Marquesas

Tuamotu

Tahiti

Pitcairn

Hawaii

AD 600

NORTH AMERICA

AD 700

Rapa Nui (Easter Island)

Map of Pacific migrations using DNA markers

ASIA

5000 BC

Solomon Islands

500 BC

Hawaii

AD 300

NORTH AMERICA

Vanuatu

Fiji

Samoa

Cook Islands

AD 300

Marquesas

1500 BC

Tonga

Tahiti

Pitcairn

Rapa Nui (Easter Island)

50000 BC

AUSTRALIA

1000 BC

New Zealand

→ Polynesian forebears

→ Melanesian forebears

The differences between accepted and present-day calculations of early migratory flows in the Pacific can be seen in the two maps above. The top one, based on an authoritative history of New Zealand in 1966, relied on palaeontological, archaeological and linguistic evidence. The map below it, based on genetic information, shows similar directions of flow, but a significantly different timescale. Genetic markers, like DNA haplotypes, allow researchers to determine the genetic ancestry of long-established and incomer populations,

Opposite: Traditional outrigger canoes.

The Arrival of
the Maoris in New Zealand

Charles Frederick Goldie (1870–1947) remains one of New Zealand's foremost painters. Trained partly in France, he is celebrated for his probing and sympathetic portraits of Maoris. But he was not merely an ethnographic portraitist. His most famous and ambitious painting, with his colleague and teacher Louis John Steele, depicted the arrival of the Maoris in New Zealand. The painting was partly a homage to Théodore Géricault's *The Raft of the Medusa* (depicting the survivors of a French frigate that was sunk off the coast of Mauritania). Though magnificently executed, the representation of exhausted, emaciated Polynesians just about making it to shore was historically inaccurate. While the painting was intended as a recognition of heroism, it resonated more with the white colonists who saw themselves as risk-takers who had embarked on a hazardous journey in search of a new life in a far-off country. The Maoris understood their own exploration and colonization of New Zealand in more tranquil terms. Despite Goldie's good intentions, many Maoris were upset or angry at the painting, as it seemed to question their legitimacy as the original settlers of the islands, having arrived with somewhat less drama between 1250 and 1300, or earlier if genetic markers are used to make the calculation. Though not a perfect compromise, New Zealanders seem to have worked out some degree of mutual recognition of the claims of the two founding settler communities through the ideas of "bi-nationalism" or "bi-culturalism", though the terms remain contested.

thus opening new ways of understanding the direction, timing and extent of migratory flows.

Migration and social space

The "liquidity" of their continent has led Pacific Islanders to conceive of migration as a culturally informed social space, akin to the Samoan idea of *vā*. As a Samoan researcher explains, *malaga* (migration) is seen as multiple movements back and forth, which can take place for many socially and culturally determined reasons, for instance seeking betrothal, celebrating a legally-sanctioned marriage, announcing a baby's birth, attending a birth or funeral, bestowing a title, opening a guesthouse, dedicating a school or church, receiving or dedicating a tattoo, ordaining the minister or attending a graduation ceremony.

Migration for the purposes of education, health or economic opportunity is often integrated into the notions of *vā* and *malaga*, thus leading to a loose idea of necessary mobility, approved by social custom.[3]

Traditional ideas of mobility for social reasons have now been challenged by the need to move in the face of rising sea levels. At least eight reef islands in the Solomon Islands have been completely lost, while coastal erosion has severely affected others. Sadly, the customary seafarers of old will be some of the climate refugees of the future.

Opposite: *The Raft of the Medusa,* 1818–19, by Théodore Géricault.

Below: A sketch for *The Coming of the Maori,* 1901, by Louis John Steele. In the final painting the Maoris look more desperate and emaciated.

7
Atlantic Slavery

There are many kinds of slavery, a social practice that is simply defined as appropriating the labour of other people while exercising control over their freedom of movement. Domestic slavery of this general sort appeared in many societies and is well documented in Islamic cultures and in ancient Greece and Rome.

———

That domestic slavery also existed in Africa before European contact is undeniable, but the demand for slave labour in the Americas massively transformed the scale and character of West African slavery. The formal ownership of slaves as property and their organization for outdoor work in gangs under constant, often brutal, supervision replaced the menial work characteristic of domestic slavery. As slaves were now commodities, they (and their offspring) could be bought, sold, bequeathed and inherited. And when, finally, slavery was legally abolished, slave-owners successfully demanded compensation for the loss of their property.

Within Africa, emergent empires – notably the Ghanaian, Malian and Songhai empires – consolidated their power around the supply of slaves for the Atlantic market. On the coast, trading posts formerly used for the trade in wood, gold and ivory became dedicated "slave castles"; some 40 of them were built or converted along the Gold Coast of West Africa.

The dungeons at Cape Coast Castle held up to 1,000 slaves awaiting shipment.

Goods that European traders brought to Africa comprised the first side of what came to be called "the triangular trade"; the second side, or "middle passage", was the transhipment of slaves across to the Americas and, finally, the third side was the return of tropical commodities such as cotton, cocoa and sugar to Europe. The cruelty of the "middle passage"

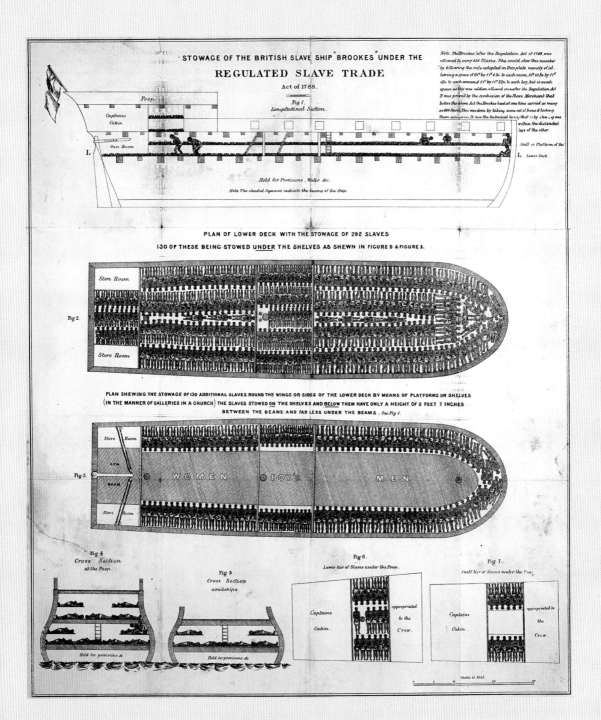

STOWAGE OF THE BRITISH SLAVE SHIP "BROOKES" UNDER THE

REGULATED SLAVE TRADE

Act of 1788.

Fig 1.
Longitudinal Section.

Captains
Cabin

Poop

Gun Room

L

Hold for Provisions, Water &c.

Note. The shaded Squares indicate the beams of the Ship.

Note. The Brookes' after the Regulation Act of 1788, was
allowed to carry 454 Slaves. She could stow this number
by following the rule adopted in this plate: namely of allowing a space of 6ft by 1ft 4in. to each man, 5ft 10 in by 1ft
4in. to each woman 5ft by 1ft 2in. to each boy, but so much
space as this was seldom allowed or met after the Regulation Act
B was proved by the confession of the Slave Merchant that
before the above Act the Brookes had at one time carried as many
as 609 Slaves. This was done by taking some out of Irons & locking
them spoonwise (to use the technical term) that is by stowing one
within the distended
legs of the other.

Shelf or Platform of the
L Lower Deck

PLAN OF LOWER DECK WITH THE STOWAGE OF 292 SLAVES

130 OF THESE BEING STOWED UNDER THE SHELVES AS SHEWN IN FIGURE D & FIGURE S.

Fig 2.

Store Room

Store Room

PLAN SHEWING THE STOWAGE OF 130 ADDITIONAL SLAVES ROUND THE WINGS OR SIDES OF THE LOWER DECK BY MEANS OF PLATFORMS OR SHELVES

(IN THE MANNER OF GALLERIES IN A CHURCH) THE SLAVES STOWED ON THE SHELVES AND BELOW THEM HAVE ONLY A HEIGHT OF 2 FEET 7 INCHES

BETWEEN THE BEAMS: AND FAR LESS UNDER THE BEAMS. See Fig 1.

Fig 3.

Store Room

GUN
ROOM

Store Room

W O M E N   B O Y'S   M E N

Fig 4.
Cross Section
at the Poop.

Fig 5.
Cross Section
amidships

Hold for provisions &c

Hold for provisions &c

Fig 6.
Lower tier of Slaves under the Poop.

Captains
Cabin

appropriated
to the
Crew.

Fig 7.
Shelf tier of Slaves under the Poop.

Captains
Cabin

appropriated to
the
Crew.

Scale of Feet.

Opposite: Slave fort, Cape Coast, Ghana.

Above: Stowage plans for a British slave ship.

has often been the subject of commentary. Eric Williams, Trinidad's former prime minister and a historian of the connection between capitalism and slavery, argued that the abolitionists exaggerated the "horrors" of the middle passage to build public support for their cause.[1] It was not that much of an exaggeration. Slaves were allocated a space of just under 1.68m x 41cm (5ft 6in x 1ft 4in), less room than a body in a coffin. This lack of space and periodic epidemics, rather than any systematic brutality, explain the loss of life. Slaves were, after all, valuable commodities and their owners wanted as many as possible to be landed in good condition at the Caribbean and American ports. Because the shipping records covering these "commodities" were so detailed, Philip Curtin was able to provide the first comprehensively researched count, estimating that 9,566,000 African slaves were landed alive in the Americas.[2] There were undoubtedly grave losses along the way, during captivity, in the slave castles and on board – perhaps about 1.5 million people – but the numbers remain disputed.

Atlantic slave trade, 1701–1810

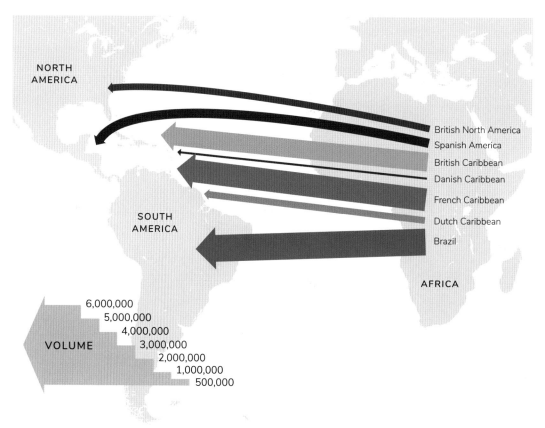

NORTH AMERICA

British North America
Spanish America
British Caribbean
Danish Caribbean
French Caribbean
Dutch Caribbean
Brazil

SOUTH AMERICA

AFRICA

6,000,000
5,000,000
4,000,000
VOLUME
3,000,000
2,000,000
1,000,000
500,000

The aftermath of transatlantic slavery

The Atlantic slave trade, which many European countries and companies undertook, had numerous ramifying consequences. African and Afrocentric commentators and researchers frequently argue that the deleterious effects of having lost so many young, fit adults from the continent were permanent and cumulative. That Africa's relative underdevelopment can be accounted for by the slave trade alone stretches the argument, but the emotional and economic wounds remain deep and a worldwide movement for reparations, which started in the 1990s, remains active and persistent.

The protests of humanitarians and abolitionists partially offset the profound moral wrong of Atlantic slavery for the descendants of those who had participated in the trade and exploitation of slave labour. The first prominent consumer boycotts at the turn of the eighteenth and nineteenth centuries, which women notably led, helped to turn the tide of public opinion against slavery. In England, the Peckham Ladies' African and Anti-Slavery Association published a poetic answer to the question "Do you take sugar in your tea?"

No dear lady, none for me!
Though squeamish some may think it,
West Indian sugar spoils my tea:
I cannot, dare not drink it.[3]

In the Americas, the descendants of the slave populations provided the dominant populations in most of the Caribbean islands. With the notable exception of Haiti, where a bloody and debilitating slave revolt expelled the French, the archipelago was marked by a largely peaceful transition to statehood in the twentieth century. The progeny of slaves also provided large minority populations in north-east Brazil, where syncretized African religions thrive, and in the USA, where non-Hispanic blacks comprise 12.3 per cent of the population. African American struggles for equality and dignity are the subject of thousands of popular stories and movies, while the determined fight for civil rights that Martin Luther King led was an inspiration to oppressed people in many countries. In 2018, 37.7 per cent of the prison population was African American, while a disproportionate number were shot dead by police. This suggests that African Americans still have a long way to go to achieve equality.

Below: Teapot with an anti-slavery message.

8

Indian Indentured Workers

When slavery ended in most British colonies in 1834, plantation owners looked for compensation for their forfeited "property", then scoured the world for replacement labour. Though indentured labourers were recruited in Japan, China and elsewhere, most came from the Indian sub-continent.

—

The overwhelming number of recruits were destined for sugar plantations in Natal, British Guyana, Fiji, Trinidad, Ceylon, Malaya, Burma and Mauritius, but workers were also deployed to build ports and railways, including the Kenya–Uganda Railway.

Indenture is a form of bonded labour whereby workers are locked into an exclusive contract with a single employer and are subject to many restrictions. Indian indentured workers characteristically signed on for five years and in return were given a free passage, medical attention, housing and a modest wage. In many cases a free or subsidized passage back to India was guaranteed after 10 years. The period of indentured labour lasted from 1834 to 1917 and, though figures are inexact, estimates of about a million-and-a-half workers are common.

Indentured labourers from India, 1830s–1917

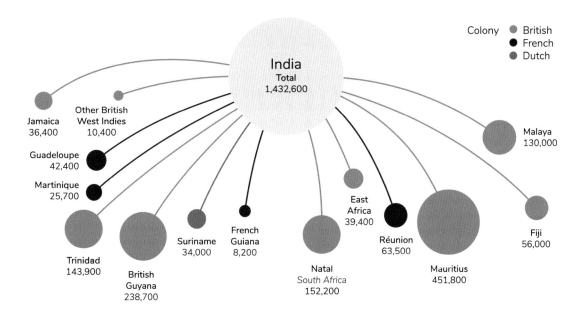

Colony ● British
● French
● Dutch

India
Total
1,432,600

Jamaica
36,400

Other British
West Indies
10,400

Guadeloupe
42,400

Martinique
25,700

Trinidad
143,900

British
Guyana
238,700

Suriname
34,000

French
Guiana
8,200

East
Africa
39,400

Natal
South Africa
152,200

Réunion
63,500

Mauritius
451,800

Malaya
130,000

Fiji
56,000

Hugh Tinker's carefully documented account of the history of Indian labourers abroad is a stunning indictment of what, quoting British Prime Minister Lord John Russell, he considers was a "new system of slavery". Though all the workers went through a formality of signing (or marking) a consensual contract, many were simply rounded up by agents and frogmarched to the ports of embarkation at Madras and Karaikal. They frequently only had the vaguest idea of their destinations. Medical inspections to determine whether recruits were fit for the arduous journeys and work conditions they faced were cursory. What made this system close to slavery were the mortality rates on the ships (which, for example, averaged more than 17 per cent on ships to the West Indies in 1856), the poor housing and health conditions, the miserable wages and, above all, the extensive use of penal sanctions.[1]

The British colonial authorities appointed "Protectors" at the ports of disembarkation, but they were generally ineffective. In one year (1892), over 40 per cent of the adult indentured population was convicted under the penal labour laws of Fiji. By contrast, in the same year only one conviction of an employer was obtained on a charge brought by his employees. Even when indentured workers took advantage of their right to a return passage, they could end up in a condition of distress. The "humble petition" of one Thakur Gajadhar to the Protector of Emigrants in Calcutta after 15 years

Opposite: Construction of the Uganda Railway in British East Africa at the beginning of the twentieth century.

Above: From 1834 to 1917, when the system was ended, the British transported nearly 1.5 million indentured workers to the colonies, mainly to work on sugar plantations.

INDIAN INDENTURED WORKERS

in Suriname has survived. He lamented that he was "void of money, refused and driven, without help ... do me such favour as I get to my native place, Banda, by railway, as I have none here to help me with a copper".[2] It is unclear whether his petition was heard with favour.

Most indentured labourers did not return to India and many of their descendants made remarkable leaps in social mobility. To take two examples, the great-grandmother of Sir Shridath Ramphal, Secretary-General of the Commonwealth and formerly Foreign Minister of Guyana, was an indentured labourer who moved from Calcutta to Georgetown in 1881. The grandparents of Sir Vidiadhar Surajprasad Naipaul, who won the Nobel Prize for literature for his bleak novels on colonial life, were indentured labourers shipped to Trinidad.

Indentured labourers were far removed in class and occupational terms from later generations of Indian professionals who migrated abroad, but their dispersal to 19 different colonies had laid the basis for contemporary India's considerable global cultural and economic reach.

Above: Photograph of newly arrived indentured workers in Trinidad.

Below: The author Vidiadhar Surajprasad Naipaul.

The creation of plural societies

The arrival of so many Indian immigrants to colonial societies had profound effects on inter-group relations in their countries of settlement.

- In Trinidad and Guyana, ethnic tension was common, but the populations descended from African and Indian forebears were more or less equal in number, which helped to avoid the worst forms of group violence.
- In Fiji, Indo-Fijians remain a significant minority of the population, but their situation is more precarious. The indigenous Fijians, who are of Melanesian origin, frequently challenge their right to belong and to own freehold land. Inter-ethnic conflict, particularly accusations that they were behind several political coups, have led to the emigration of Indo-Fijians. From being the majority of the population from 1956 through the late 1980s, the Indo-Fijian share of the total population of 885,000 dropped to 37.5 per cent by 2017.
- In South Africa, the indentured workers on the Natal sugar plantations were augmented by so-called "free Indians", merchants and businessmen who soon established niches in the emerging colonial economy. After the election of the apartheid government in 1948, Indian-South Africans found their rights further eroded and often sought a political alliance with the oppressed African majority.
- Of all the overseas Indian populations, Indo-Mauritians are the most politically and numerically dominant, usually forming the government and occupying key positions in the administrative, business and professional elites. As the island had no indigenous population before colonization, there was a much greater blending of the imported groups, including Chinese, French, African and Malagasy immigrants into a creolized population. More recently, with the island's reconnection to "Mother India", an assertive Indian ethnic identity has become more common.

Above: Mahendra Chaudhry became Fiji's first Indo-Fijian Prime Minister on 19 May 1999, but was taken hostage in the coup of 2000 and then sacked by the President. He was able to resume a political career after another coup in 2007.

9

Empires
Their Labour and Military Regimes

Emperors loved great public works. Some were useful, like the Roman aqueducts bringing fresh water to citizens, but many were vanity projects designed to assuage the gods, massage the egos of powerful rulers, impress their subjects and intimidate their enemies.

———

The Great Pyramid at Giza, Egypt, was built, one source suggests, by two gangs of 100,000 men, each organized into five units of 20,000.[1] The Cholula pyramid in Mexico was twice the size of Giza. Blocks of stone had to be quarried, cut and put in place. Ropes and pulleys helped, but hordes of workers still had to be dragooned from far-off places and coerced by gangmasters.

Empires also needed soldiers, a standing army like the Roman citizen legionaries, but also auxiliaries drawn from the provinces. In addition to the legions and auxilia, "numeri" were recruited from "barbarians" on the edge of the empire. The famous leader of a slave revolt, Spartacus, was described as a Thracian of nomadic background. At its height in AD 211, the Roman army comprised 450,000 men. Roman troops could be posted anywhere in the Empire – for example there are isotopic analyses of teeth and bones and contemporary accounts to support the idea that African troops were stationed at Hadrian's Wall, separating the Roman province of Britannia from the Picts and other northern Ancient Britons.

Left: A detail of Trajan's column, Rome, showing a marching column of citizen soldiers.

Opposite: An engraving (1996) by Theodoor de Bry depicting the hellish condition in the Potosí mines.

European colonial empires

Subsequent empires, including those formed in the modern period in the Spanish, Belgian and French colonies, were also crucially dependent on forced labour and military recruits. In the case of Spanish rule in the Americas, an *encomendero* was awarded land and labour in perpetuity. Between 30 and 300 "Indians" had to fulfil work tasks allocated to them and deliver a share of their produce in exchange for the *encomendero* providing their material (housing, clothing, food) and spiritual (Catholicism) needs. Though it authorized

agricultural estates, the Spanish crown was interested, above all, in extracting gold and silver. The mining town of Potosí in Bolivia was founded in 1546, and over the next 200 years more than 40,000 tons of silver were extracted. Thousands of the indigenous people were forced to work at the mines, as were 30,000 imported African slaves. Many died of mercury poisoning (mercury was used to extract the silver) and as a result of brutal treatment.[2]

Though it seems barely possible to exceed the horrors of Potosí, the Belgian King, Leopold,

succeeded in doing that in the Congo. He ran the area as his private fiefdom where Congolese were compelled to collect rubber. Any resistance proffered was met by violence, with many being killed. As one contemporary French journalist commented of the Congo at the time: "We are tree fellers in a forest of human beings".[3] Campaigners such as the liberal reformer E. D. Morel railed against "Red Rubber", metaphorically bloodied by the cruelty of Leopold's private gendarmerie, the *Force Publique*. The campaigners were eventually successful in forcing the King to relinquish control to the Belgian government.

Though the Spanish and Belgian examples were notable, the French empire-builders also, at first, relied on forced labour. When they occupied Madagascar in 1896, the French governor freed 500,000 slaves, but in December of that year proclaimed a legal obligation to work. An outcry in France about the death rate of compulsory labour and military projects led to the repeal of compulsory labour and the setting aside of penal sanctions on contract labourers. Yet it was only in 1946 in their other colonies that the French finally abolished conscript military labour and *prestation*, a labour "tax" that permitted the

administration to compel adult males to work on public projects for a number of days each year.[4]

The French greatly relied on troops recruited in their colonies to police their empire. Berbers and "Harkis" (from Muslim Arab backgrounds) fought for the French in Algeria, though they were often seen as "traitors". But the most famous battalions, some 42 of which served

in France, comprised Senegalese Tirailleurs. The African troops were notably disciplined, holding their nerve despite the cold trenches and heavy losses they sustained. At the 90th anniversary commemoration of the Battle of Verdun, President Chirac paid tribute to the 70,000 colonial combatants killed during the First World War.[5]

Opposite: King Leopold's private army of 16,000 mercenaries coerced the population into meeting forced labour quotas by killing, mutilation, village burning, starvation and hostage-taking. This photograph was taken by the missionaries Alice Seeley Harris and her husband John Harris to campaign against the brutalities in the Congo.

Above: Soldiers of the Senegalese Tirailleurs. Men in these battalions were recruited from the various African colonies of the French Empire during the nineteenth and twentieth centuries.

10

The *Hajj*
The Fifth Pillar of Islam

One of the five pillars of Islam to which every good Muslim must commit is the *hajj* –
a pilgrimage to Mecca (Makkah), the place to which a triumphant Muhammad returned
after his long exile in Medina. Though there are exclusions on the grounds of, inter alia,
youth, health and the ability to pay, making the journey at least once in one's lifetime
is "obligatory" (Fard). Provided you have a "pure mind", the *hajj* will expiate any sins.

———

Second or additional pilgrimages (*Umrah*)
are also common. As there are about a billion
Muslim adults worldwide (2018), the potential
number of pilgrims is vast. Over 2 million people
fulfilled their religious obligation in 2018.

The spread of Islam from Indonesia in the
east to the western edge of the Sahel long
preceded the development of railways and
aircraft, so most Muslims outside the Arabian
Peninsula had little chance of going on *hajj*.
After the 1950s, the number of pilgrims
rocketed, culminating in 3.16 million arriving
in 2012, after which restrictions on numbers
were put in place by authorities. The major
countries sending pilgrims are shown in
the map opposite.

Number of pilgrims 1920–2017

YEAR	TOTAL	YEAR	TOTAL	YEAR	TOTAL	YEAR	TOTAL
1920	58584	1990	827200	2000	1913263	2010	2789399
1921	57255	1991	720100	2001	1944760	2011	2927717
1922	56319	1992	1015700	2002	2041429	2012	3161573
1941	24000	1993	992800	2003	2012074	2013	1980249
1950	100000	1994	997400	2004	2164479	2014	2085238
1950s	150000	1995	1046307	2005	2258050	2015	1952817
1960s	300000	1996	1865234	2006	2378636	2016	1862909
1970s	700000	1997	1942851	2007	2454325	2017	2352122
1980s	900000	1998	1832114	2008	2408849	2018	2371675
1989	774600	1999	1839154	2009	2313278		

Note: Figures ending in 000 are approximations.

Top 10 countries with highest numbers of *hajj* pilgrims 2017

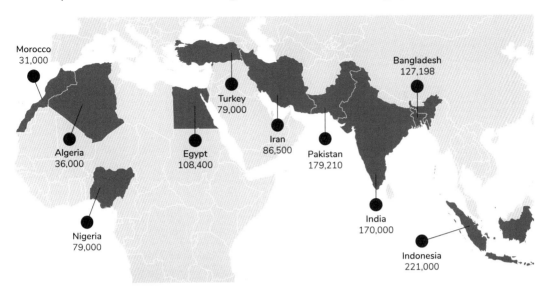

Morocco
31,000

Algeria
36,000

Turkey
79,000

Egypt
108,400

Iran
86,500

Pakistan
179,210

Bangladesh
127,198

India
170,000

Nigeria
79,000

Indonesia
221,000

Above: Thousands of tents in Mina near Mecca, during the *hajj*.

The *hajj* journey

Al Jumuah magazine presents a colourful look at Hajj al-Tumattu and its rites in an easy to follow step-by-step chart. May you all have a Hajj Mabroor.

1. IHRAM
Bathe yourself (Ghusl). Put on Ihram garments. Make intention for Umrah. Recite Talbiyah. Avoid forbidden acts during Ihram.

2. UMRAH
Make Tawaf around the Ka'bah. Pray two rak'ah behind Maqam Ibrahim Make Sa'i between Safa and Marwah. Trim hair and remove Ihram garments.

3. GOING TO MINA
Noon, the 8th: Put on Ihram garments again. Make intention for Hajj. Remain in Mina during the Tarwyah Day (the 8th of Thul Hijjah) and perform the five prayers starting from Dhuhr prayer and ending with the Fajr prayer on the Day of Arafat.

4. GOING TO ARAFAT
Morning, 9th: Leave for Arafat on the morning of the 9th of Thul-Hijjah and stay until sunset. Stay in any part of Arafat. Glorify Allah, repeat supplication, repent to Allah and ask for forgiveness. Combine Dhuhr and Asr.

5. GOING TO MUZDALIFAH
After sunset, 9th: Leave for Muzdalifah soon after sunset of the 9th day of Thul Hijjah. Perform Maghrib and the Isha salah combined (Isha is shortened to two rak'ah). Stay overnight and perform the Fajr salah.

6. RETURN TO MINA
Sunrise, 10th: Shortly before sunrise, leave Muzdalifah for Mina. Go to Jamarat Al-Aqabah and stone it with seven pebbles. Slaughter your sacrifice. Shave your head or trim your hair. Take off Ihram garments. All Ihram's restrictions are lifted except sexual intercourse.

7. TAWAF AL-IFADHA
On the 10th or after: Make Tawaf Al-Ifadha. Make Sa'i between Safa and Marwah. After Tawaf Al-Ifadha, all restrictions of Ihram are lifted.

8. RETURN TO MINA
The 10th, 11th, 12th and 13th: Spend the Tashreeq days in Mina. After Dhuhr of each day, stone the three jamarat starting from the small and ending with Al-Aqabah. You may leave on the 12th after stoning the Jamarat.

9. FARWELL TAWAF
After the 12th: Go to Makkah and make Tawaf. Perform two rak'ah of Tawaf. Let the Tawaf be the last thing you do in Makkah.

10. GOING HOME
One is encouraged to visit the Prophet's masjid in Madinah, but it is not a part of Hajj.

Periodic outbreaks of disease, stampedes resulting in fatalities, fires and disorder have sorely tested the capacity of the Saudi authorities to organize the *hajj*. This is not through want of trying. The Saudi Arabian government has invested about US$20 million per year since 2000 on renovating religious sites and on airports, roadworks, safety barriers and crowd control measures. They have also built a city of 100,000 air-conditioned tents in Mina, 8km (5 miles) to the east of Mecca. Organizers and guides have compared overseeing the *hajj* with hosting the Olympics every year[1].

Travel agents who are in tune with the aims of the *hajj* have prepared handy guides to the *hajj* journey, illustrating a benign mixture of practicality and spirituality.

Unfortunately, in a sad reflection of human nature, unscrupulous travel agents take advantage of the zeal of intending pilgrims and many cases of fraud are reported each year. Khalid Pervez, general-secretary of the Association of British Hujjaj (Pilgrims) UK, said his organization received 3,000 complaints in 2013 – far more than the previous year: "We call it a rip-off ... The *hajj* companies tell [pilgrims] they're getting a 5-star hotel, but they get there and it's a 2-star place. They con people, give them the wrong impression. And there are cases when they sell packages and don't deliver the service at all".[2] The Association of British Travel Agents has now issued an advert warning about potential fraud.

Most pilgrims do not, of course, expect to be cosseted for their stay and many make the journey in difficult circumstances. This can be illustrated by the story of Senad Hadzic, a 47-year-old Muslim from Bosnia-Herzegovina, who set out on foot in December 2011 "invited to Mecca by God". He walked 5,697km (3,540 miles) across Bosnia, Serbia, Bulgaria, Turkey, Syria, Jordan and Saudi Arabia, reaching Mecca in October 2012, in time to perform *hajj*. Along the way he slept in mosques, parks and streets and deployed his Koran as a passport when crossing war-torn territories. "I'm really very happy and this is the most beautiful place in the world," he told a reporter from the British newspaper *The Independent*.[3]

The specular nature of the annual *hajj* and its central significance in the spiritual life of Islam have led to the neglect of other Islamic journeys, including "visits to sacred shrines of holy men, the graves of saints and imams, and the tombs of martyrs of the faith". Such journeys are called *ziarat* and involve "millions of people".[4] If we think of mobility in general rather than more narrowly defined definitions of migration, pilgrimages and other forms of religious circulation are under-researched. Buddhists, Taoists, Christians and Hindus all venerate religious pilgrimages and sometimes the numbers involved are staggering. The Kumbh Mela, a Hindu pilgrimage to Allahabad, takes place every 12 years. On the last occasion in 2013 about 120 million people visited the confluence of the Ganges, Yamuna and "invisible" Saraswati rivers over a two-month period.

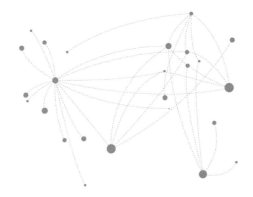

PART TWO

Migration in
Recent History

11

Irish Emigration and the "Famine Exodus"

One of the two great progenitors of the Communist Movement, the German Friedrich Engels, managed a Manchester cotton mill, partly owned by his father. His job did not prevent him from co-authoring the 1848 *Communist Manifesto* with his more famous comrade, Karl Marx. Three years earlier, Engels had published (in German) his powerful account of *The Condition of the Working Class in England*, based mainly on his observations in Manchester.

———

How, one might ask, did a foreign factory manager know so much about the working class in England? The answer is that his insights were derived, at least in part, from his lover and housekeeper of nearly two decades, Mary Burns.

Though born in England, Mary's parents were Irish, and they were part of the migrant Irish community living in slum conditions in "Little Ireland" – Manchester. Mary was the "real thing", a working-class Irish woman who had started

The "Great Famine" emigration (1845–51)

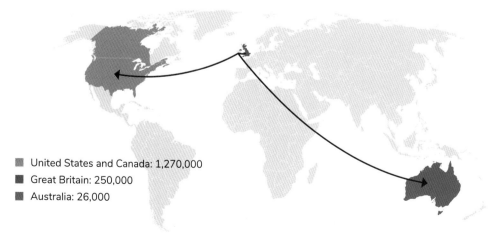

■ United States and Canada: 1,270,000
■ Great Britain: 250,000
■ Australia: 26,000

Right: A public sculpture of despairing men and women trudging towards their boat in the quay at Dublin, Ireland, by Rowan Gillespie, unveiled in 1997.

work at around the age of 9 as a "scavenger" (picking up the fluff and fabric scraps in cotton factories), then as a domestic servant, and perhaps later as a prostitute. It seems that Engels learned about Irish migrant workers by living with one of their number.[1]

The movement of Irish workers to England during the Industrial Revolution was the key historical experience informing the Marxist theory of migration, a theory that still generates a challenging alternative to conventional ideas. Marx started by observing that, although it was widely believed that "population pressed on capital", the true relationship was inverted – "capital pressed on population". The purpose was to release enough labourers to staff the emerging factories while depressing the cost of labour, but without destroying the peasant economy. That had to be sufficiently preserved to ensure that the cost of reproducing workers (covering pre-natal feeding, birth, child-

raising, education and old-age care) fell not on the capitalist, but on the source country or zone. Migrant workers could thus be recruited when needed and ejected when not, while simultaneously reducing the bargaining capacity of indigenous workers.

It is an elegant theory and there is enough in it to be plausible, but the implied rational balancing of countervailing forces was too conspiratorial and mechanical. In the mid-nineteenth century no cunning capitalist plan was able to preserve the Irish peasant economy, which was at a fragile tipping point. At nearly the same time that Marx and Engels were publishing their momentous *Manifesto*, a potato blight struck Ireland and the Great Famine (1845–50) commenced. About 1.5 million Irish people left the country, mainly to North America, but also to the rest of the United Kingdom and Australia.

There were antecedents to this dramatic misfortune. The "Scots Irish" of Ulster and other

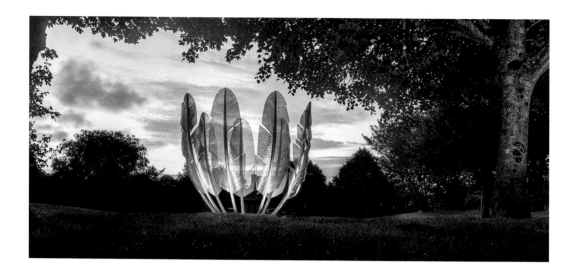

impoverished peasants were already dislodged from their land and found it increasingly difficult to continue as crofters or landless labourers. Nonetheless, the scale and speed of the famine exodus was unprecedented, and the character of the emigrants shifted. The pre-famine migrants were predominantly from Protestant families. However, this social profile changed, with many more single, younger, Catholics leaving from poorer provinces such as Connaught and Munster.[2]

The famine exodus left permanent psychological and cultural scars on Ireland. The sight of penniless, starving emigrants was etched forever into the collective psyche. The conditions on the ships, known as "coffin ships", resembled the slave ships of the Atlantic trade. Perhaps as many as 30 per cent died en route, often from existing medical conditions. These experiences are movingly memorialized in the Famine Memorial sculpture on the Dublin quay.

The Irish in Britain and the USA were often subjected to discrimination and name-calling, with people mocking their traumatic experiences. "Pot-Lickers" was one English epithet, referring to Irish famine victims having to lick their pots clean to get every last morsel of food. The Irish in US cities were often compared with impoverished and enslaved African Americans. One author suggested that the Irish in America only "became white" by embracing the discriminatory practices of the established white population.[3]

Fortunately, other reactions to the famine show a more agreeable side of human nature. Perhaps most affecting was the gift of the Native American people, the Choctaws, who donated US$170 (equivalent to US$4,700 today) to help the Irish famine sufferers. They had themselves been displaced by Andrew Jackson's government in a forced movement known as the "Trail of Tears".

Above: A sculpture in Cork, Ireland, depicts eagle feathers in the shape of a food bowl. It commemorates the donations given by the Choctaw nation at the time of the Irish famine.

Opposite: President Reagan on his trip to Ballyporeen in 1984. "Today I come back to you as a descendant of people who were buried here in paupers' graves."

The transnational practices arising from Irish migration

Social, cultural and political practices on both sides of the Atlantic have been profoundly affected by Irish migration.

In the USA

- Catholicism, from being regarded with disfavour by the early Puritan and Protestant settlers, has become a firmly established Christian denomination.
- Irish immigrants used the Tammany Society (known as "Tammany Hall") to penetrate the Democratic Party political machine in order to control nominations and patronage.
- Despite the collapse of the Tammany Hall system in the 1960s, powerful Irish Catholic families were able to use their wealth to propel their children into commanding positions. Joseph P. Kennedy Sr., whose son, John, became the first Catholic president of the USA, was a notable example.

- St Patrick's Day parades, to celebrate Irish culture and heritage, are widely supported in cities across the USA.

In Ireland

- It has become common in Ireland to convene an "American wake", which mourns the death of an American relative.
- US citizens, generally of Irish heritage, participate in transatlantic matchmaking festivals.
- American politicians with (sometimes remote) Irish ancestry looking for Irish-American votes make a habit of visiting "the Emerald Isle".
- When she served as Irish president (1990–97), Mary Robinson placed a candle in the window of her official residence, saying "there will always be a light on for our exiles and our emigrants."

12

Workers in South Africa's Mines

When diamonds were discovered in Kimberley, in the northern Cape, in 1867 and gold on the Witwatersrand, Transvaal, some 19 years later, a "gold fever" ensued, followed by an immediate demand for labourers. By the end of the century almost 100,000 workers were employed in the gold mines. Local Africans were reluctant to undertake the dangerous and debilitating work in the mines, especially as the white gold-rush settlers had created a sudden demand for meat and vegetables, stimulating local African agriculture.

The Anglo–Boer War (1899–1902) disrupted the labour market just as 300 new companies were set up. At the end of the war, the mine owners demanded that the new British High Commissioner, Lord Milner, solve the labour shortage.

He reluctantly complied. Though "dead against Asian settlers and traders", Milner thought "the indentured Asian would prove controllable".[1] Some 64,000 so-called coolies were therefore recruited from China between 1904 and 1907. The British government, however, under pressure from humanitarians protesting against the conditions of their contracts, brought this system to an end. Nearly all the Chinese were sent back.

The seams of gold near the surface were soon exhausted, and deeper mines proved far more costly. Rather than seek relatively expensive local African labourers, the mine owners widened their zone of recruitment, first to the "native reserves" and then to other African regions. Portuguese East Africa (present-day Mozambique) was the prime target. Predatory labour contractors were already at work, rounding up gangs of workers and bribing African chiefs and officials to facilitate their trade. In exasperation at having to deal with these greedy and unpredictable suppliers, the

Opposite: A group of miners with safety lamps in a gold mine on the Witwatersrand, South Africa.

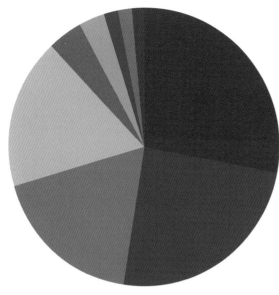

Origins of mineworkers, 1970

- Mozambique (28.2%)
- Tropical countries (mainly Malawi) (24.5%)
- Cape Province (17.9%)
- Lesotho (17.7%)
- Botswana (4.1%)
- Transvaal (3.1%)
- Orange Free State (1.7%)
- Natal and Zululand (1.5%)
- Swaziland (1.3%)

WORKERS IN SOUTH AFRICA'S MINES

Collection points and migration routes

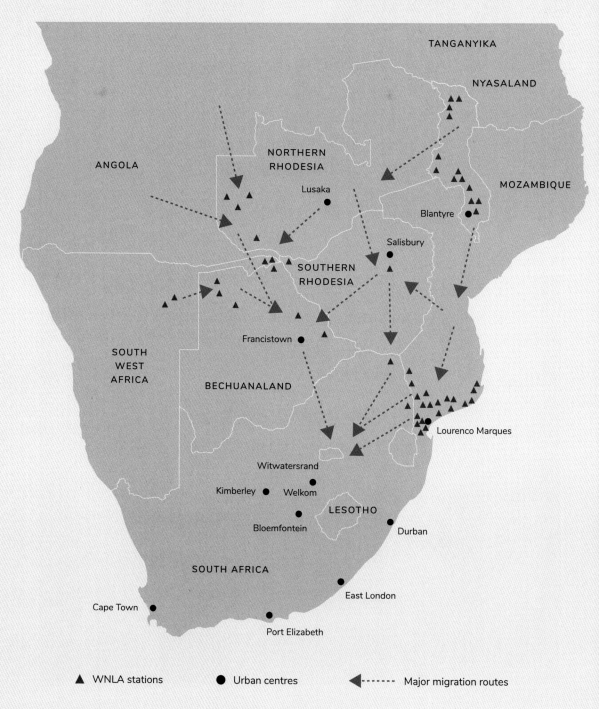

TANGANYIKA

NYASALAND

ANGOLA

NORTHERN
RHODESIA

MOZAMBIQUE

Lusaka

Blantyre

Salisbury

SOUTHERN
RHODESIA

SOUTH
WEST
AFRICA

Francistown

BECHUANALAND

Lourenco Marques

Witwatersrand

Kimberley   Welkom

LESOTHO

Bloemfontein

Durban

SOUTH AFRICA

East London

Cape Town

Port Elizabeth

▲ WNLA stations   ● Urban centres   ◀----- Major migration routes

Chamber of Mines decided to take on the job itself. It set up the Witwatersrand Native Labour Association (WNLA), which was to turn into the biggest labour recruiting organization in the world, contracting hundreds of thousands of workers to work at the Witwatersrand, the mining seams around Johannesburg.

The WNLA built roads into the interior, commissioned trains, and eventually acquired fleets of trucks and aircraft to bring workers to the mines and to repatriate them when their contracts ended. Several of the surrounding countries came to rely on remittances sent home by miners and additional payments made by the mining companies to the local administrations.

Life in the mines was brutal and dangerous: two years was all that most Africans were prepared to endure. The recruiting agents found a steady supply of young men ready to take the opportunity to earn a wage for a fixed period, but the human cost proved enormous. Between 1945 and 1984 more than 50,000 workers died in the mines. The damp conditions underground wreaked particular havoc on the so-called "Tropicals" – workers from north of the 22nd Parallel – who suffered from pneumonia and tuberculosis.

The contract system in the mines was part of a wider system. After 1948, when the apartheid regime was instituted, the system was extended to cover all African labour recruitment. Although many Africans were already living in the "white areas", redundant labour and "black spots" were removed and many areas re-zoned in an attempt to try to create racially homogeneous spaces. The regime designated areas as "Bantustans", four of which (Ciskei, Transkei, Venda and Bophuthatswana) attained the status of "independent homelands". Here, Africans were assigned residence, citizenship and civic rights, downgrading their status in South Africa to that of "temporary foreign workers". Long hours of daily commuting across internal frontiers became a way of life for hundreds of thousands of workers forced to live in these "homelands".

With the election of Nelson Mandela as president in 1994 conditions changed for the better. The Bantustans were abolished and black South Africans acquired citizenship and the right to move around the country without "passes", which had restricted their movement in the apartheid era. Conditions also improved on the mines. In 1993, 615 miners had died underground. By 2009, the number had dropped to 167 and kept falling, reaching a record low of 73 in 2016. In February 2018, Cyril Ramaphosa, a former general-secretary of the National Union of Mineworkers in the 1980s, became president of South Africa.

Opposite: WNLA's recruitment stretched deep into the surrounding African countries, 1970s.

13

From Convicts to "Ten Pound Poms"

British Migration to Australia

There were several official phases of organized British migration to Australia, starting with colonial settlers, then moving on to convict labour, child migration and, finally, sponsored family migration. In 1770, the Royal Navy captain James Cook claimed possession of the east coast of Australia on behalf of the British crown, ignoring the claims of the Aboriginal people. Just eight years later, the first fleet of 11 ships loaded with convicts formed the first penal settlement at Sydney.

Penal colonies were also established in Tasmania (1803) and Swan River, Western Australia (1850). Other parts of Australia were designated for "free settlers", though some received convict labour until 1868, when the last convict ship dropped anchor. The significant proportion of convicts in the early colonial history of Australia is shown in this graph.

British settler population in New South Wales

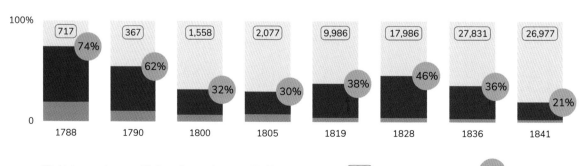

717	367	1,558	2,077	9,986	17,986	27,831	26,977
74%	62%	32%	30%	38%	46%	36%	21%
1788	1790	1800	1805	1819	1828	1836	1841

■ Male convicts   ■ Female convicts   Free settlers   [100] Total no. convicts   % % of total population

Many present-day Australians of British descent are defiantly proud of their convict origins. At the same time, Australian historians are clearly deeply preoccupied with discussing why Australians should not feel diminished by the so-called "convict stain". In all, 24,906 female convicts and 132,308 male convicts were transported to Australia from the British Isles.[1] "Transportation" was a common penalty for many who had committed petty crimes or who were, simply, landless labourers and "vagrants" pushed off the land and struggling to survive in the grim industrial towns. Others were sailors and soldiers discharged at the end of the Napoleonic Wars. Successive Vagrancy Acts criminalized their plight and transportation was seen as a necessary and practical alternative to imprisonment.

Nineteenth-century commentators were particularly harsh on female convicts transported to Australia, often dismissing them *tout court* as "prostitutes". This was both a gross exaggeration and an assumption based on notions of immorality that we would nowadays consider inappropriate. In particular, despite this practice being common in the British working class, co-habitation without marriage was conflated with promiscuity.[2] Ideas of female depravity reflected the judgemental Christianity of the time rather than the harsh realities facing poorer women in Great Britain.

Child migrants

Just as transportation to the colonies was an easy fix for the judiciary, rather than improving provisions at home, British welfare agencies used emigration as a means of coping with abandoned or delinquent children. No fewer than 14 societies were implicated (including the Child Emigration Society, Dr Barnardo's Homes, the Church Army and the Church of England's

Below: Child migrants from Britain playing football at Fairbridge Farm School at Pinjarra, Western Australia in 1933. They emigrated there through the Child Emigration Society.

FROM CONVICTS TO "TEN POUND POMS": BRITISH MIGRATION TO AUSTRALIA

Waifs and Strays Society). Special schemes, often endorsed by royalty and subsidized by the British and Dominion governments, proliferated. One notable example was the Big Brother Scheme to Australia. Started in 1924, the idea was that well-established Australian citizens would agree to act as a big brother to a little brother from the homeland.[3]

In all, between 6,000 and 7,000 child migrants arrived from 1912 to the early 1970s, when the schemes were finally abandoned. Initially represented as a means of giving unfortunate children a chance to rebuild their lives in a sunny, healthy climate, as the migrant children grew up and were able to speak for themselves, the narrative changed. While many spoke of resilience and survival, others recounted bitter experiences at the hands of exploitative farmers and unsympathetic families. But the harshest words were reserved for the orphanages and farms, often run by Christian orders, where some of the child migrants were subjected to sustained sexual abuse.

Ten Pound Poms

Welcoming child migrants shipped to Australia in 1938, the Archbishop of Perth declared that "when empty cradles are contributing woefully to empty spaces, it is necessary to look for external sources of supply. And if we do not supply from our own stock, we are leaving ourselves all the more exposed to the menace of the teeming millions of our neighbouring Asiatic races."[4] This push to encourage white British immigration took a new form after the Second World War, when the Australian government introduced an Assisted Passage Migration Scheme. Because the prospective migrant was

responsible only for £10 in processing fees for the chartered ships and aircraft the expression "Ten Pound Poms" became a common colloquialism to describe the sponsored British citizens who migrated to Australia after 1945.

The number of British migrants who left under this scheme was substantial – more than 1.25 million migrants between 1945 and 1972, one of the largest planned migrations ever. Unlike the earlier schemes, this one was pitched to families with young children and those with skills and aspirations. Faced with rationing at

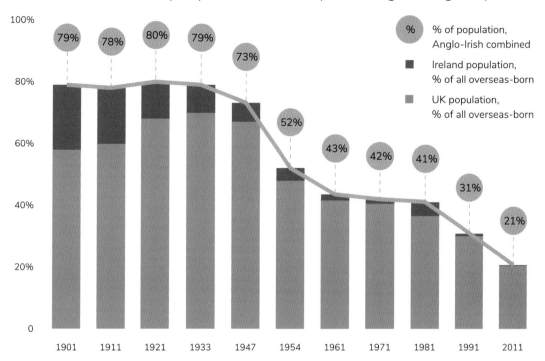

UK/Irish born people in Australia (excluding Aborigines)

Legend:
- % — % of population, Anglo-Irish combined
- Ireland population, % of all overseas-born
- UK population, % of all overseas-born

Percentages: 79% (1901), 78% (1911), 80% (1921), 79% (1933), 73% (1947), 52% (1954), 43% (1961), 42% (1971), 41% (1981), 31% (1991), 21% (2011)

home, the allure of a subsidized passage, and the promise of housing and a job to follow, seemed too good to be true. Nearly 400,000 people applied in the first year alone. One of the most famous Ten Pound Poms was Julia Gillard who left her modest home in Wales as a child and, in due course, served as Australia's first female prime minister (2010–13). Interviewed at their retirement village in Adelaide, Gillard's father commented: "We came here with modest aspirations, to work hard and educate my daughters." Reflecting their Welsh Labour Party affiliations, Mrs Gillard added that her daughter would be "the best [prime minister] there is, so long as she doesn't turn into Maggie Thatcher."[5]

Although the Assisted Passage Scheme was a great success, it was fatally marred by its overt discrimination against anyone who was not from "the old country". There is no doubt that the scheme was intended to improve and augment "British stock", a racial description echoing Australia's interest in the breeding of sheep and cows. By the 1970s such a notion looked more and more out of step with the times. Ultimately, a "white Australia" policy was comprehensively rejected, and immigration policy changed to reflect Australia's economic needs and skills shortages. The UK- and Irish-born share of the population declined, opening a gateway for Asian and other non-British migrants.

Opposite: Australian-born actor Vincent Ball chats to two children who are about to emigrate to Sydney with their parents under the Ten Pound Poms scheme, at Olympia, London, 1956.

FROM CONVICTS TO "TEN POUND POMS": BRITISH MIGRATION TO AUSTRALIA

14

The "Great Atlantic Migration" to the USA

The largest ever free movement of migrants occurred over the period between 1836 and 1914, when 30 million European immigrants crossed the Atlantic to the USA. Generally, they were escaping harsh conditions in their country of origin, while the USA was hungry for industrial labour. Some 12 million immigrants arrived at a small island in the Upper New York Bay where a gigantic Statue of Liberty, erected in 1886, greeted them. Displayed on the pedestal of the statue was Emma Lazarus's famous welcoming poem:

—

Migration from Europe to the USA, 1815–1914

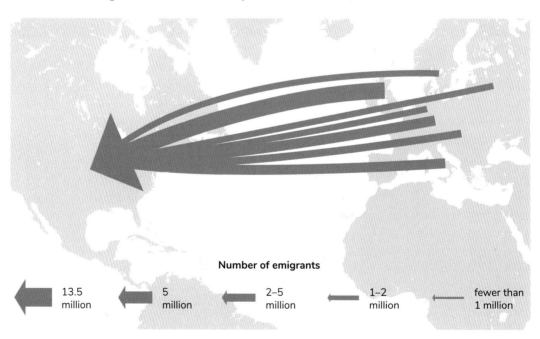

Number of emigrants

13.5 million | 5 million | 2–5 million | 1–2 million | fewer than 1 million

Give me your tired, your poor
Your huddled masses yearning to breathe free;
The wretched refuse of your teeming shore;
Send these, the homeless, tempest-toss'd, to me;
I lift my lamp beside the golden door.

The stories of the Ellis Island migrants have become the stuff of legend. Hundreds of tons of wood pulp and thousands of metres of film have been used to dramatize their reminiscences. The immigration museum on the island currently receives 2 million visitors a year. The expressions "land of the free", "from rags to riches" and "the golden door", originate from Ellis Island. So, too, does the idea of a "melting

Above: Aerial view of Ellis Island, 1955, the gateway to the USA for millions of immigrants.

Right: Original programme cover for Israel Zangwill's play, *The Melting Pot*.

pot" of people. Some of the "huddled masses" would have been sufficiently in pocket to buy tickets for Israel Zangwill's 1908 Broadway hit play, *The Melting Pot*, in which the pogrom-orphan protagonist declared in his powerful monologue that divine intervention, "the fires of God", would incinerate prior immigrant identities. "German and Frenchmen, Irishmen and Englishmen, Jews and Russians" would be thrown into the crucible. "God", he declaimed, "is making the American".

In this narrative, migrants were on a one-way ticket, abandoning their impoverished pasts and their old ways for a land of opportunity and freedom. Even before they were officially admitted to the USA, the children of the immigrants took part in flag-waving parades at Ellis Island, where they were screened for entry to New York.

THE "GREAT ATLANTIC MIGRATION" TO THE USA

They were expected to learn English, embrace their new identities with patriotic zeal and help to build their new country. Cautious historians warn us that it was not quite like that in practice. Old ways persisted, while some migrants returned to their homelands, particularly during the Depression of the 1930s. For Eastern Europeans, who faced poverty and discrimination, there was not much to go back to, but nearly one-quarter of Scandinavians and over half the immigrants from south Italy returned home.[1] Nor was cultural adaptation complete. As many commentators have pointed out, the expected direction of assimilation was along a path marked WASP (White, Anglo-Saxon, Protestant), a preference that ignored the African American population and marginalized an increasing proportion of the new admissions who were Catholics from Ireland, southern Europe or Eastern European Jews. In the end, a hyphenated identity – Italian-American, Polish-American and many more – became a way of reconciling ethnic origins and national loyalties.

The Naturalization Act of 1790, which offered citizenship to "free White persons of good character", was gradually replaced by more complex classifications. The lengthy 1911 Dillingham Commission on Immigration at first plumped for a five-fold racial classification – Caucasian, Mongolian, Ethiopian, Malay and American. By volume 9 of this report,

Opposite: Immigrant children being examined by a New York City health officer on Ellis Island.

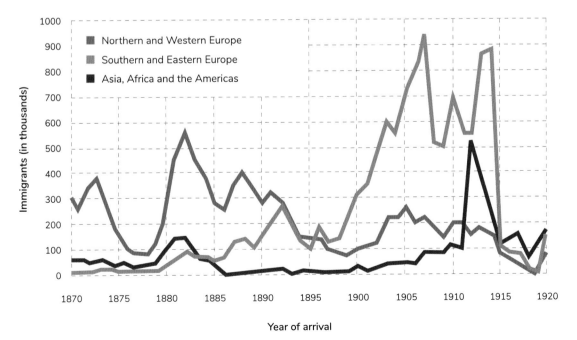

European immigration to the USA, 1870–1920

- Northern and Western Europe
- Southern and Eastern Europe
- Asia, Africa and the Americas

Immigrants (in thousands)

Year of arrival

THE "GREAT ATLANTIC MIGRATION" TO THE USA

however, 45 "races or peoples" were identified among immigrants to the USA, 36 of which "are indigenous to Europe". To offset the flow of southern Europeans, who were seen as genetically inferior, quotas by national origins and other restrictions confirmed the bias towards northern Europeans. In any case, the outbreak of the First World War when German U-boats threatened commercial shipping, had dramatically reduced the volume of cross-Atlantic migration.

Although Atlantic migration never ceased, it gradually diminished in importance compared with trans-Pacific crossings and inward migration from the rest of the American continent.

Opposite: Poster for the Red Star Line, one of the most important shipping companies travelling from Europe to the USA.

Steamships and the emigration ports: Antwerp

The advent of inter-continental mass migration was made possible by the replacement of sail by steamships. The journey time was cut from five to six weeks to under two weeks. Steamships were safer, more comfortable and much larger. Iron hulls and screw technology meant that ocean crossings became much more popular. By 1870, more than 90 per cent of immigrants to America arrived by steamship. Although ocean crossings became less of an ordeal for everyone, there were massive class differences on board. Luxury meals, games and extravagant accommodation was provided for the few, but tough, crowded conditions met those who were travelling "steerage". Just a few decks separated them.

There were many ports of embarkation (including Liverpool, Le Havre, Bremen, Hamburg and Glasgow), but the best preserved is in Antwerp where the Red Star Line museum has been created in the very buildings from which more than 2 million emigrants departed. Poorer passengers were groomed for the journey. Lice-ridden clothes were boiled in large vats and showers were provided. Medical inspections were carried out. Simple puzzles and tests, which mirrored the ones administered on Ellis Island, were given to passengers who appeared mentally challenged. Filtering the emigrants in this way proved effective: the companies had to carry back at their own expense only 2 per cent of the 12 million who landed at Ellis Island.

One of the poorer passengers was a 5-year-old boy, Israel Isidore Baline, who travelled with his family from Belarus and embarked on the Red Star Line's *Rijnland*. After changing his name to Irving Berlin, he became a prolific songwriter who, perhaps more than any other, evoked and crystalized the American dream, penning such iconic songs as "White Christmas" and "God Bless America". One can sense that he meant it when he wrote "God bless America, land that I love / Stand beside her and guide her / Through the night with the light from above."

THE "GREAT ATLANTIC MIGRATION" TO THE USA

THE "GREAT ATLANTIC MIGRATION" TO THE USA

15

Jewish Refugees from Nazi Rule

Between Adolf Hitler's rise to power in 1933 and the Nazi invasion of western Europe in 1940, more than 450,000 Jews fled the Nazi campaign of terror in Germany, Austria and Czechoslovakia to find safety abroad. Several thousand more managed to trickle out during the war. The majority of the friends and family they left behind died in the Holocaust. By 1945, nearly 6 million out of Europe's prewar population of 8 million Jews had been murdered.

Famous figures who escaped Nazism

Albert Einstein
theoretical physicist

Max Born
mathematician
and physicist

Henry Kissinger
diplomat and
political scientist

Hannah Arendt
Philosopher and
political theorist

Billy Wilder
Hollywood writer
and director

Sigmund Freud
psychoanalyst

In 1933, the year that Hitler became Chancellor of Germany, there were approximately 500,000 Jews living in the country – less than 1 per cent of the total population. For the most part they were fully integrated into German society, participating in most areas of national life. The Jewish contribution to law, medicine, the arts and music, science, scholarship and politics was outstanding. More than 100,000 German Jews had died for their country in the First World War.

Many people, however, held that Jews could not be "real" Germans as their first loyalty would always be given to their fellow Jews, in whatever country they lived, rather than to Germany. In the early years of the twentieth century, there were widespread quasi-scientific theories about genetic heredity that held that some races were superior to others, not only in Germany but in many other European countries and in the USA. From these the myth developed of a pure white "Aryan" race threatened by an international conspiracy of "Semites" (Jews). For extreme German nationalists, the Volk – the German-speaking peoples of Germany, Austria and eastern Europe – represented the highest form of racial type.

Making a new life

The refugees from Nazism who settled in the USA included such famous figures as the physicist Albert Einstein, who became a US citizen in 1940. Many were able to carry on with careers as musicians, scholars and scientists after leaving Germany.

Although large numbers of refugees held professional qualifications, such positions were among the most difficult to find

Children in flight

Within days of Kristallnacht on 9–10 November 1938 (a night of violence directed at Jewish synagogues, businesses and homes across Germany) the British government authorized the Jewish Refugee Committee to arrange for the safe passage of Jewish children from Germany. The scheme became known as Kindertransport (child transport). Over the next nine months, until the outbreak of war in September 1939, 10,000 German, Austrian, Czech and Polish Jewish children, aged 2 to 18, were brought out in this way.

The Kindertransports began on 2 December 1938. Each child was allowed two bags of belongings. They were sent by train through Germany to the Netherlands, and then made the short sea voyage to Britain. Here they were placed in a transit camp before being sent to join the families who had volunteered to take them in.

The children were puzzled and confused by many aspects of their new life in Britain. "Why do the English eat this wet meat?" asked Beate Siegel on being given a plate of Irish stew. Around 80 per cent of these children never saw their parents or other family members again.

Jewish emigration from Germany, 1933–1940

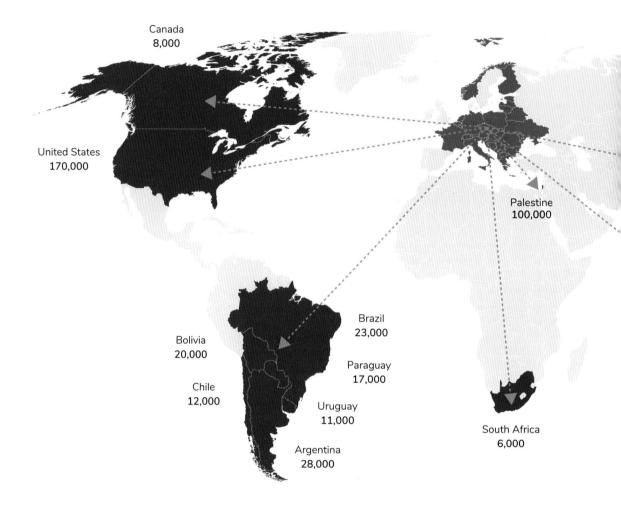

Canada
8,000

United States
170,000

Palestine
100,000

Brazil
23,000

Bolivia
20,000

Paraguay
17,000

Chile
12,000

Uruguay
11,000

South Africa
6,000

Argentina
28,000

during the Depression years of the 1930s and language difficulties meant that many immigrants could only find menial jobs. When Britain found itself at war with Germany in September 1939, Jewish immigrants were considered potential security risks and placed in internment camps – despite being the recent victims of Nazi oppression.

Jews who didn't get away

For those who did escape, by far the most distressing aspect of their lives was not knowing the fate of family and friends left behind after the war in Europe closed all exits from 1940. Some Jews failed to get out because they did not recognize the imminent danger. Some had been unable to find a country willing

China
20,000

Australia
9,000

Jewish populations of Germany, Poland, Hungary, Czechoslovakia and Austria before and after the Second World War

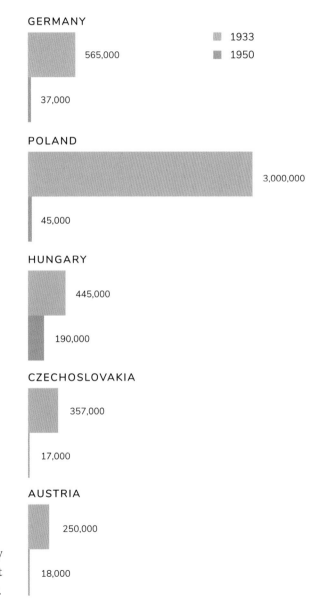

GERMANY

- 1933
- 1950

565,000

37,000

POLAND

3,000,000

45,000

HUNGARY

445,000

190,000

CZECHOSLOVAKIA

357,000

17,000

AUSTRIA

250,000

18,000

to accept them, or could not get together enough money for the fare.

Some 117,000 German and Austrian Jews had migrated to other European countries such as Poland, France and the Netherlands. When these countries were invaded and occupied by Germany in 1939 and 1940, foreign-born Jews were the least likely to escape the death camps of the Holocaust.

16

Palestine
Jewish Immigration and the Displacement of the Palestinians

Who are the Palestinians? In 1969, the former prime minister of Israel, Golda Meir, declared "There were no such thing as Palestinians. When was there an independent Palestinian people with a Palestinian state? It was either southern Syria before the First World War, and then it was a Palestine including Jordan. It was not as though there was a Palestinian people in Palestine considering itself as a Palestinian people and we came and threw them out and took their country away from them. They did not exist."[1]

This statement dramatizes the denial of one people by an important representative of another. The response of the Palestinian leadership has been divided. Whereas Mahmoud Abbas of the Palestinian Authority, based in the West Bank, has recognized the legitimacy of the Israeli state, the leaders of Hamas, based in Gaza, see Jews as unwanted occupiers and colonialists of Palestine. Thomas Friedman summarizes the outcome well. "For 100 years, through violence and delegitimization, Israelis and Palestinians have made sure that the other was never allowed to really feel at home in Israel."[2]

From the point of view of the Palestinians, the harshest blow was the displacement of 726,000 Palestinians who fled or were expelled during the 1948 war that accompanied independence. Several million Palestinians and their descendants now live in the states and territories surrounding Israel. Palestinians describe these events as the *Nakba* ("catastrophe" or "cataclysm").

Migration and politics

It is difficult to reach a balanced view on Palestinian history because anger, half-truths and prejudice overlay an already complex situation. With respect to migration matters, the best place to start is with the League of Nations Mandate of 1923–48 (in practice it started in 1920), which allowed Britain to administer "Palestine". Although the wider area was part of the old Ottoman Empire, the territory was split into two main units, Palestine and Trans-Jordan. Jewish settlement was permitted in the first and prohibited in the second. During the Mandate period, 350,000 Jews migrated to Palestine legally while an additional 50,000 entered illegally.

While Golda Meir's taunt was true – there was never an independent Palestinian nation-state – a sense of a separate Palestinian identity began to grow as the number of Jewish settlers increased. The British tried, with varying degrees of success, to limit Jewish immigration in the hope of placating Palestinian opinion but, as Nazism spread in Europe, it became politically difficult to restrict Jewish settlement. After the Second World War, as the concentration camps emptied, and the remnants of European Jewry languished in displaced persons camps, the dilemma became more acute for the British authorities.

The sailing of the SS *Exodus* to Palestine in July 1947 with 4,515 Jewish survivors of the Holocaust on board symbolized the drama of Jewish immigration. Although the British navy intercepted the ship and returned the

The British mandate

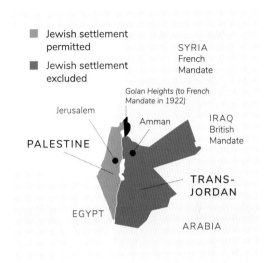

Below: The arrival of the SS Exodus occasioned an intense propaganda battle about the legitimacy of Jewish immigration to Palestine.

PALESTINE: JEWISH IMMIGRATION AND THE DISPLACEMENT OF THE PALESTINIANS

passengers to Cyprus and Germany, the voyage was a moral victory for those who demanded unrestricted Jewish immigration to Palestine. After a desultory plan to partition Palestine into Arab, Jewish and British segments, and faced with an armed revolt by the Jewish Irgun, the British cut and ran, leaving the Palestinians to their fate. By January 1949, after Britain's recognition of the Israeli state, all the passengers of the SS *Exodus* were sent to Israel.

Before 1948, Palestinian land held by Arabs was gradually acquired by purchase on the principle of "willing buyer, willing seller", but what was to happen to the land and property that Palestinians held following their expulsion or flight? The Israeli armed forces damaged or demolished some 615 Arab villages in 1948, leading to mass displacement. Palestinian militias offered little resistance, though Arab armies from outside Palestine destroyed 26 Jewish settlements.

Apparently concerned with the legal niceties, the acquisition of Arab land and property after 1948 proceeded in a four-stage process over the following 12 years. Stage one involved the temporary legal appropriation and reallocation of land seized during the war. In stage two, the temporary basis became permanent, the legislation allowed the Israeli state unhindered use of the land. The third stage addressed the normalization of land that had not yet been appropriated, while the final phase integrated this stock of land into "Israel Lands", a new legal category.[3]

According to Al Husseini, of the 726,000 refugees who fled Israel, the biggest group (280,000) went to the "West Bank" (a territory west of the River Jordan, later incorporated into the Kingdom of Jordan). Others ended up in the Gaza Strip (200,000), Syria (75,000), Lebanon

The displacement of the Palestinians, 1948

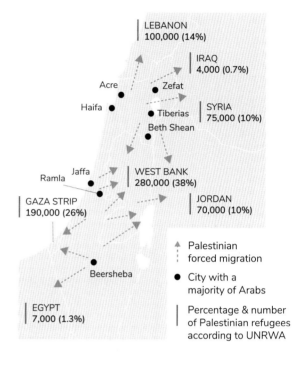

LEBANON
100,000 (14%)

IRAQ
4,000 (0.7%)

Acre   Zefat

Haifa   Tiberias

SYRIA
75,000 (10%)

Beth Shean

Jaffa   WEST BANK
Ramla   280,000 (38%)

GAZA STRIP
190,000 (26%)

JORDAN
70,000 (10%)

Beersheba

▲   Palestinian
forced migration

●   City with a
majority of Arabs

| Percentage & number
of Palestinian refugees
according to UNRWA

EGYPT
7,000 (1.3%)

(97,000) and Iraq (4,000).[4] Some of the displaced Palestinians gradually became absorbed into their countries of settlement (Gaza was, of course, not a country), but a remarkable number remained in refugee camps and zones, their grievances still nurtured by their bitter historical experience and the expansion of Israeli settlements into the West Bank. In 1950, faced with an almost impossible situation, the UN established a special agency, the United Nations Relief and Works Agency for Palestine Refugees (UNRWA), to accord recognition, protection and shelter to Palestinian refugees. Sadly, nearly 70 years later, the agency's work still continues, though with increasing difficulty after the US contribution to UNWRA's main budget was cut in 2018.

UNWRA refugee camps, 2010

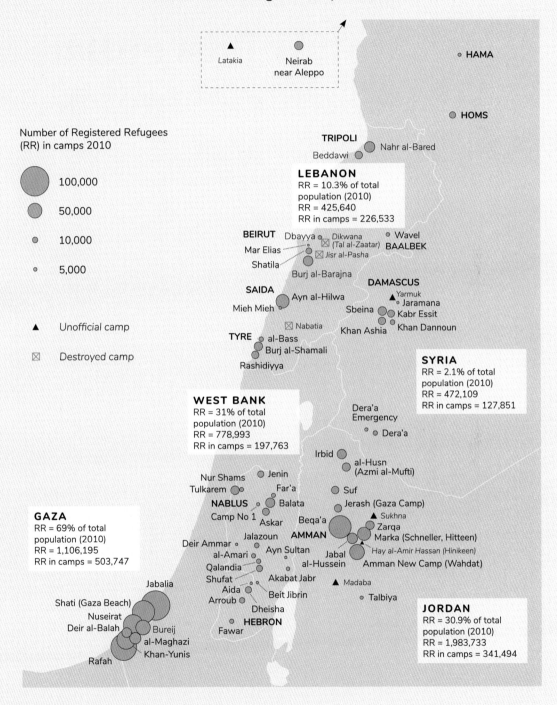

Latakia ▲   Neirab ● near Aleppo

○ HAMA

○ HOMS

Number of Registered Refugees (RR) in camps 2010

● 100,000

● 50,000

○ 10,000

○ 5,000

▲ Unofficial camp

⊠ Destroyed camp

TRIPOLI
Beddawi ● Nahr al-Bared

LEBANON
RR = 10.3% of total
population (2010)
RR = 425,640
RR in camps = 226,533

BEIRUT   Dbayya ○   ⊠ Dikwana   ○ Wavel
    (Tal al-Zaatar) **BAALBEK**
Mar Elias ●   ⊠ Jisr al-Pasha
Shatila ●
    Burj al-Barajna ●   **DAMASCUS**

SAIDA   Ayn al-Hilwa ●   ▲ Yarmuk
Mieh Mieh ●   ● Jaramana
    Sbeina ●   ● Kabr Essit
    ⊠ Nabatia   Khan Dannoun ●
TYRE   al-Bass ●   Khan Ashia ●
    Burj al-Shamali ●
Rashidiyya ●

SYRIA
RR = 2.1% of total
population (2010)
RR = 472,109
RR in camps = 127,851

WEST BANK
RR = 31% of total
population (2010)
RR = 778,993
RR in camps = 197,763

Dera'a ○
Emergency
    ○ Dera'a

Irbid ●
    al-Husn ●
    (Azmi al-Mufti)

Nur Shams ○ Jenin ●
Tulkarem ○○   Far'a ○   Suf ●
NABLUS ○   Balata ●   Jerash (Gaza Camp) ●
Camp No 1 ○   Askar ○   ▲ Sukhna
    Beqa'a ●   Zarqa ●
Jalazoun ○   **AMMAN**   Marka (Schneller, Hitteen) ●
Deir Ammar ○   Ayn Sultan ○   Hay al-Amir Hassan (Hinikeen)
al-Amari ●   Jabal   Amman New Camp (Wahdat) ●
Qalandia ○   al-Hussein ●
Shufat ○   Akabat Jabr ○
Aida ○   ▲ Madaba
Arroub ○   Beit Jibrin ○
    Dheisha ●   ○ Talbiya
    ● **HEBRON**
Fawar ○

GAZA
RR = 69% of total
population (2010)
RR = 1,106,195
RR in camps = 503,747

Jabalia ●
Shati (Gaza Beach) ●
Nuseirat ●
Deir al-Balah ●   Bureij ●
    al-Maghazi ●
Rafah ●   Khan-Yunis ●

JORDAN
RR = 30.9% of total
population (2010)
RR = 1,983,733
RR in camps = 341,494

PALESTINE: JEWISH IMMIGRATION AND THE DISPLACEMENT OF THE PALESTINIANS

17

"New Commonwealth" Migration to the UK

Although there is a long history of non-European settlement in the UK, it was only after the Second World War that the government authorized the systematic recruitment of labour from the colonies.

———

Faced with an acute labour shortage estimated at 1,346,000 in 1946, a young Labour Party politician, James Callaghan (later to be prime minister), argued in the House of Commons that:

In a few years' time we in this country will be faced with a shortage of labour, and not with a shortage of jobs. ... It may be revolutionary to suggest that we ought now to become a country where immigrants are welcome, but that is really the logical development of our present position in the world. ... Who is going to pay for the old age pensions and social services we are rightly distributing now, unless we have an addition to our population, which only immigrants will provide in the days to come?

Although the subsequent release of Public Record Office papers has revealed that politicians and civil servants were worried, as one put it, that "there could be no authority for deporting coloured British subjects if they felt they wished to stay", the countervailing arguments prevailed. Commonwealth workers were versed in British ways, spoke English and were easier to recruit than foreigners, precisely because they were British subjects.

Take, for example, the case of the British textile industry, which cheaper Asian imports were seriously threatening. Short of a huge investment in new machinery, which the textile industry was in no position to finance, competition with Asian imports depended on the ability to use existing machinery to the fullest capacity. What was needed therefore was an assured, steady, low-cost supply of labourers, including those who were prepared to work a relay system and endure staggered rotas. Migrant labourers filled this gap. In the 1960s, one-third of black workers in Britain worked shifts, which was more than twice the percentage of white workers. Migrant labourers were also strongly in demand in other areas of manufacturing: 47 per cent of migrants, compared with 33 per cent of indigenous workers, were employed in the British

Above top: Less than a year after the race riots of 1958, black residents in Notting Hill try to calm the waters after a black carpenter, Kelso Cochrane, was murdered. It is now believed that the police knew who the white murderer was but decided not to risk another riot if they sought to convict him.

Above: It sometimes worked out fine. Two bus conductors, Jamaican Eric Cox (left) and his co-worker Charlie Pinder, share a cigarette in Nottingham, 1960s.

"NEW COMMONWEALTH" MIGRATION TO THE UK

manufacturing industry in 1971, while Ford's largest car plant in Britain (at Dagenham, East London) was 60 per cent black.[1]

At first, the British West Indies (now referred to as the Caribbean) was the source of many of the new workers, British residents of Caribbean birth soaring from 15,000 in 1951 to 172,000 a decade later, when the British government decided to slam the brakes on. This was in direct response to the race riots in Notting Hill, London, in 1958, and the general growth of white racist sentiments.

The invention of the "New Commonwealth"

Alarmed by the growth of racial tension, politicians and civil servants sought to restrict non-white Commonwealth migration by legislation and linguistic inventions of gymnastic proportions. UK citizens were asked to ponder the difference between the New Commonwealth and the Old Commonwealth, defined not by when a territory became a British colony (1627 in the case of Barbados), but when it had become, or was set to become, independent. The 1962 Commonwealth Immigrants Act avoided the expression "New Commonwealth" but, as was readily understood at the time, was clearly intended to restrict migration from the non-white Commonwealth. The 1971 Immigration Act spelled it out: only those who had a parent or grandparent who was *born* in the UK would be allowed a "permanent right of abode" (residence). To sustain this idea a Home Office official had invented the unfortunately gendered concept of "patriality", not hitherto in any dictionary. Again, the racial sub-text was easily decoded.

The law of unintended consequences is an adage elaborated by the US sociologist, Robert K. Merton. It perfectly describes the outcome of immigration restrictions to the UK. Widely discussed for at least 18 months, a bill was introduced to the British parliament at the end of 1961, was made law early in 1962 and finally implemented on 1 July of that year. This long gestation sent an unmissable signal to the Caribbean and elsewhere in the New Commonwealth. The rush was on "to beat the ban" and many more migrants arrived than would have been the case. Previously, the pattern of migration closely mirrored employment vacancies in the UK – why go unless you had a job waiting for you?[2] In the 18 months before enforcement, the net inflow was similar to the flow for the previous five years combined.[3]

Asians join the immigrant population

Whereas the Caribbean population declined after 1961 – there were few new arrivals and many ultimately retired to the islands – a significant migration from India, Pakistan and Bangladesh (after a violent civil war, Bangladesh split from Pakistan in December 1971) soon followed. In the case of India, the Indian population of the UK almost doubled between 1961 and 1971, while in 2011 Indians became the largest foreign-born population in the UK. As in the Indian case, the Pakistani-born population grew fastest between 1961 and 1971, to 136,000. Bangladeshi immigration followed, much of it to London. By the turn of the century, migration from the New Commonwealth had peaked and the source countries changed from the Commonwealth to Europe.

Ethnic groups in the UK, 1991 (per 100,000s)

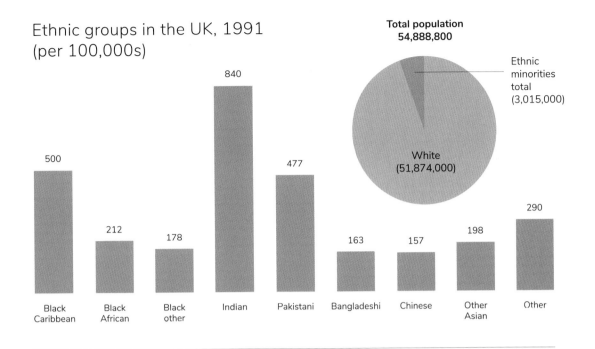

Total population 54,888,800

Ethnic minorities total (3,015,000)

White (51,874,000)

Black Caribbean	Black African	Black other	Indian	Pakistani	Bangladeshi	Chinese	Other Asian	Other
500	212	178	840	477	163	157	198	290

The changing ethnic and national mix of migration to the UK

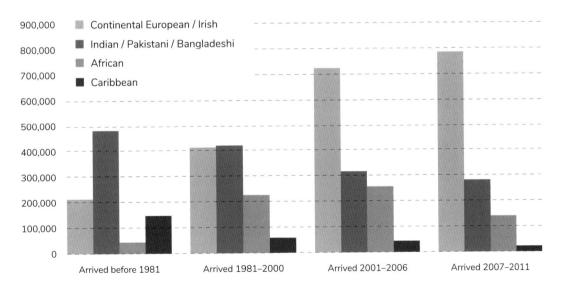

- Continental European / Irish
- Indian / Pakistani / Bangladeshi
- African
- Caribbean

Arrived before 1981   Arrived 1981–2000   Arrived 2001–2006   Arrived 2007–2011

Above: Post-war migration flows into the UK used to be mainly from the "New Commonwealth" (the Caribbean, Pakistan, Bangladesh and India), but since 2001 they have been overwhelmingly from Eastern Europe and the Irish Republic.

18
Turkish Migration to West Germany

The chaotic conditions in Germany following the Nazi defeat in the Second World War resulted in massive population movements. About 12 million people – displaced persons, returning prisoners of war, repatriates and among them 2.5 million children – "wandered across a scarred landscape of ruins of rubble".[1] It is a testimony to the "economic miracle" of its recovery that, by the mid-1950s, West Germany was experiencing a labour shortage. The steady trickle of migrants from East Germany was cut off by the communist regime. In some desperation, the West German government sought labourers from other countries, mainly from Italy and then, when the supply proved inadequate, from Turkey.

Turkish migration to West Germany can be divided into three phases: (a) the *Gastarbeiter* (guest worker) period, 1961–73; (b) the period of family reunification and the "putting down of roots", 1974–2005; and (c) the period of transnational migration from 2006 until the present.[2] Obviously, this threefold division is very schematic and the phases merged into one another.

Guest workers

Throughout the 1950s and 60s it was commonplace for West German politicians to proclaim that, "Germany is not an immigration country", by which the country's leaders meant that they had no intention of allowing permanent settlement – they wanted workers, not settlers.

The turn to Turkey, which had a large labour surplus, dramatized the dilemma. Turkey was not a member of the European Economic Community and, despite the secularism of the Ataturk period, many Turks were Muslims and were seen to be unassimilable. The means deployed to resolve this conundrum was to adopt the idea of guest workers, assumed to be males coming for a limited period, without families, with no rights to either permanent settlement or citizenship, and who were expected to return to Turkey after they were no longer needed in the workplace.

The German-speaking Swiss writer, Max Frisch, spotted the obvious contradiction: "we asked for workers, but in the end human beings came."[3] Employers complained that the initial two-year contracts were too short: it did not

make economic sense constantly to recruit and train new cohorts of workers. The West German government yielded, allowing extended contracts and family reunification, thus

changing the system in practice, even if they continued to proclaim it in theory.

Above: Turkish men wait outside the German consulate in Istanbul to get their visas, 1973.

Family unification and the fight for citizenship

The global recession of the early 1970s, triggered by the oil crisis when the price of oil quadrupled, brought the first phase of Turkish immigration to an abrupt halt. In 1973, the West German government stopped hiring foreign workers and about one-third of those who had been recruited returned to Turkey. For those who remained, a normal family life gradually became possible. As the chart (right) reveals, the number of Turkish women and children joining their male counterparts or being born in West Germany gradually normalized, at least in demographic terms.

By 2005, there were about 3.5 million people of Turkish descent in the reunified Germany. However, issues of integration and acceptance were never far from the surface. One Turkish scholar argued that in the 1980s latent anti-Turkism was rife, with Turks being shown "as ludicrously different" and pointing also to the Heidelberg Declaration signed by 16 university professors calling for the expulsion of Turks to preserve the "Christian Occidental values of Europe".[4]

Turkish children born in Germany attended German schools, but some struggled with fluency in language and issues of social identity and acceptance. Citizenship was only conferred after long residence, while those not from the EU and Switzerland were normally required to renounce their prior citizenships, which many Turks were reluctant to do. Legal reforms to the nationality laws in 1990 and 1999 did, however, enhance rights for permanent residents.

Turkish citizens living in West Germany according to age and sex, 1991

AGE GROUP	WOMEN	MEN	TOTAL
0–5	84,150	94,235	178,385
6–10	65,957	75,458	141,415
11–15	75,092	93,573	168,665
16–20	98,628	117,639	216,267
21–25	102,479	111,158	213,637
26–30	84,498	126,785	211,283
31–35	46,761	63,114	109,875
36–40	50,953	45,338	96,291
41–45	63,537	48,490	112,027
46–50	53,962	75,429	129,391
51–55	36,828	73,670	110,498
56–60	18,842	40,579	59,421
61–65	8,329	13,732	22,061
66 & over	4,945	5,425	10,370
TOTAL	**794,961**	**984,679**	**1,779,640**

Transnational migration, 2006–present

Migration flows from Turkey to the reunified Germany and vice versa had been declining quite rapidly since the 1990s, but finally, in 2006, they became negative, with exits from Germany exceeding entries (see graph below). It is difficult to put this down to a single reason. Restrictive entry requirements, social discrimination and financial incentives to return given by the German government all played their part, but better economic opportunities in Turkey were also vitally important in explaining Turkish return migration.

There is still a significant movement between the two countries, but this reflects a switch in the form of migration from the first phase of guest-worker migration, and the second phase of securing permanent residence (even if not full citizenship), to the current period, which involves more complex movements for social as well as economic reasons. Turks in Germany may choose to retire in Turkey or engage in oscillating migration between the two countries for an education or for family and lifestyle reasons. In so doing they develop both opposing and complementary loyalties. The football star Mesut Özil ended the 2014 FIFA World Cup qualification campaign as Germany's top scorer with eight goals. However, Turkish fans wrapped in their national flag denounced his decision to play for Germany not Turkey. That he was still firmly attached to his Turkish roots was indicated by Özil posing for photographs with Turkish president Recep Tayyip Erdoğan in May 2018, with a Turkish general election on the horizon. This time young German Turks criticized Özil for his support for so conservative a leader.

Opposite: Turkish women in a German park, signifying that a normal sex ratio was gradually emerging in the 1970s and 80s.

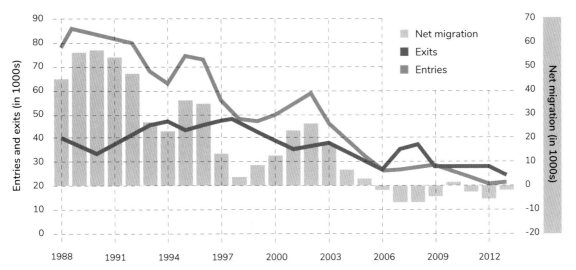

Entries, exits and net migration of Turks to and from Germany (1988–2014)

19

The Vietnamese Boat People

A large-scale exodus of Vietnamese migrants followed the collapse of the US-backed government of South Vietnam and the military victory of the communist forces in April 1975. Within the Vietnamese population, many ethnic Chinese were particularly targeted as complicit in the discredited capitalist regime, with their businesses being closed and their properties confiscated. Faced with the choice of their "removal" as labourers to rural economic zones, many bought permission to leave the country from their new rulers, who demanded an exit fee.[1]

In the 20-year period between 1975 and 1995 about two million people left, around 800,000 of whom were "boat people". Although making up fewer than half the emigrants, the boat people became the centre of public attention because of the dangers they faced, often in overcrowded, unseaworthy boats.

The boat people fled first to Asian countries (Hong Kong, Indonesia, Malaysia, the Philippines, Taiwan, Singapore and Thailand) where they were held in camps and detention centres. Some stayed, but many were permanently resettled in the UK, the USA, France and Australia, among other countries. Towards the end of the period, with the Vietnamese state turning away from state socialism towards a market economy, some tens of thousands voluntarily returned to Vietnam.

Countries of first asylum in Southeast Asia, 1975–95

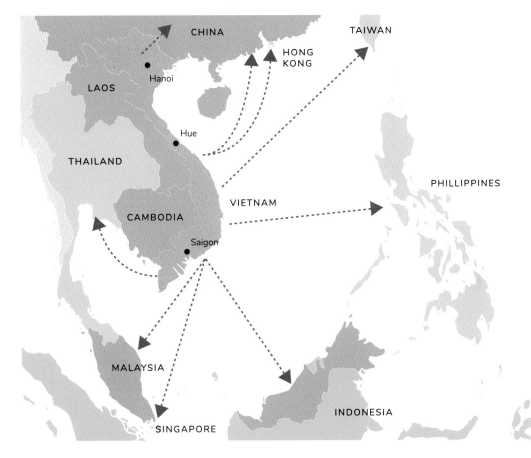

Hong Kong

People's motives for receiving, processing and supporting the Vietnamese boat people varied. Since the early migrants were ethnic Chinese, there was public sympathy for their plight in Taiwan, Hong Kong and Singapore. Again, many of this group were anti-communist, which resonated particularly in Hong Kong, which was still a British colony (but in 1997 was retroceded to the People's Republic of China). As Kwok Bun points out, despite the colony being very densely populated, over the period 1975–95 the Hong Kong government spent HK$6,638 million on the care and maintenance of the boat people, compared with the UK government's HK$849 million and the United Nations High Commission for Refugees' HK$1,253 million.[2]

Opposite: Thirty-five Vietnamese boat people await rescue from their small fishing boat after spending eight days at sea.

Following pages: The last freighter loaded with panicked refugees flees from Da Nang harbour two days before the city's fall in 1975.

France

For their part, three of the countries of final settlement had a complex entanglement with the region, which created at least some moral responsibility for accepting Vietnamese boat people. The French had been the colonial governors of French Indo-China (Vietnam and Cambodia) before being driven out by communist insurgents in 1954. Some of the 300,000 Vietnamese in France arrived after the end of colonialism, but the fall of Saigon in 1975 rapidly accelerated the numbers joining kith and kin. The wonderful Vietnamese restaurants in many parts of France are a visible reminder of the arrival of the Vietnamese.

Below: The famous dish pho is a combination of Vietnamese rice noodles and French beef slices, together with broth made from knuckle bones and oxtail.

USA

The resettlement of Vietnamese in the USA arose from the traumatic involvement of the country in trying to suppress the rise of communism in Asia. Some 58,220 military personnel lost their lives in the Vietnam War and the political turmoil and emotional scars that followed had long-term effects; accepting Vietnamese boat people was one way of assuaging them. Although the motives behind accepting the Vietnamese were primarily political, one study suggests that, in the long run, marked economic advantages accrued to the USA.

In general, immigrants are useful in facilitating trade with their home countries. They know the language, the formal and informal "rules of the game" and are able to use trusted networks to lower the costs and

The intercontinental resettlement of the Vietnamese boat people

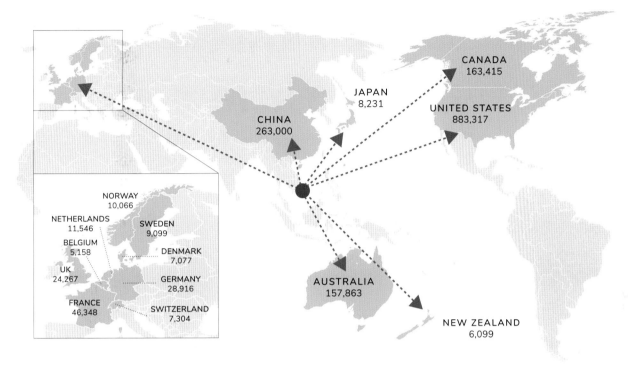

CANADA
163,415

JAPAN
8,231

UNITED STATES
883,317

CHINA
263,000

NORWAY
10,066

NETHERLANDS
11,546

SWEDEN
9,099

BELGIUM
5,158

DENMARK
7,077

UK
24,267

GERMANY
28,916

FRANCE
46,348

SWITZERLAND
7,304

AUSTRALIA
157,863

NEW ZEALAND
6,099

improve the gains of contracts. Christopher Parsons and Pierre-Louis Vézina drew on these general observations and used the distribution of Vietnamese boat people and their descendants in the USA as a "natural experiment" to examine trade after sanctions were lifted in 1995. They found that for every 10 per cent increase in the Vietnamese network, exports to Vietnam from the USA rose by between 4.5 and 14 per cent, while a doubling of the Vietnamese population enhanced exports by between 45 per cent and 138 per cent.[3]

UK

As well as their positive contribution to the US economy, the children of the Vietnamese boat people have achieved marked educational success, consistently outperforming other ethnic groups and local populations in a number of settlement countries. This is also true of the UK, which took in Vietnamese people from its colony, Hong Kong. For example, a study in Southwark, London, conducted in 2002, found that around 47 per cent of the Vietnamese pupils achieved five A*–C grades in their school examinations compared with 34 per cent of their white British counterparts. However, this general educational success was marked by significant gender differences. Vietnamese girls did spectacularly better than Vietnamese boys, who seemed to be held back by fears that they were seen as "boffins" and insufficiently "one of the lads".[4]

20
Post-Soviet Migration

At its height, after the Second World War, the Soviet Union comprised 15 Soviet Socialist Republics. It was always a ramshackle affair, containing over 100 nationalities scattered over a vast area with 11 time zones. Moreover, a number of Eastern European countries had been politically and somewhat reluctantly bolted on to the Soviet Union following the Warsaw Pact in 1955. By 1991, communism had collapsed and the edges of the empire rapidly split from what was left, the Russian Federation. A swirl of populations followed. Co-ethnic groups sought to return to their ethnic heartlands, while Russian soldiers and Russian minorities were drawn back from the peripheral countries into the centre.[1]

Co-ethnic returnees from the Soviet Union

We consider here just four of the returnee ethnic groups – Jews, Germans, Greeks and Poles. Jewish emigration from the Soviet Union had already been significant prior to 1991; it accelerated after that date when visas were largely unrestricted. As the "law of return" allowed Jews automatic entry to Israel, by early 1991 about 500,000 people had entered the country claiming Jewish origin (though the definition was stretched in many cases). Soviet Jews also left for Austria and Germany, at first in small numbers despite the Jewish-German Council welcoming the new migrants as a means of rebuilding a community nearly totally obliterated by the Holocaust. By 2014, the Jewish population of Germany, including arrivals from countries other than the Soviet Union, had stabilized at 118,000.

Germans

A second group of returnees comprised ethnic Germans (*Russlanddeutsche*), including 2.5 million Volga-Germans – descendants of people forcibly relocated by Stalin to Kazakhstan and Siberia. Thinking they might link up with the Nazis, Stalin had deported the Volga-Germans in 1941. Many were forced to work in labour camps and were stripped of their citizenship, which was not restored until after Stalin's death. Between 1992 and 2007, a total of

1,797,084 ethnic Germans from the former USSR emigrated to Germany.[2]

Greeks

A third co-ethnic group that sought return to its motherland was the Greeks, some 500,000–1 million of whom were Greek Pontians – descendants of eighth-century Greek immigrants who in the Second World War, like the ethnic Germans, were forcibly relocated by Stalin to Kazakhstan. As the Soviet Union collapsed, many Pontian Greeks, together with Greeks from Georgia, returned to Greece, a country that has always been open to Greek diaspora returnees. With the breakdown of the Greek economy following the global recession of 2008, there has been a significant re-migration of ethnic Greeks to their homelands in the former Soviet Union.

Polish

The complex, intertwined history of Polish-Soviet relations followed the various partitions of the country in the nineteenth century by Russia, Austria and Germany. Poland was also at the heart of the Nazi *Generalplan Ost* (General Plan for the East). Many ethnic Poles, Jews and Romani lost their lives, emigrated or were forcibly deported. After the implosion of the USSR, perhaps as many as two-thirds (half a million) of the Soviet citizens of Polish origin returned to Poland, though many had been separated from Poland by several generations.

Migration flows to and from the Russian Federation and the former Soviet Union

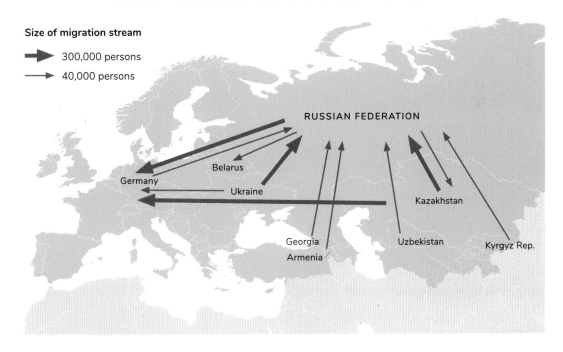

Russians in Baltic States (Estonia, Latvia and Lithuania)

After the Second World War the USSR made determined efforts to settle ethnic Russians in the Baltic States for strategic reasons. For example, ethnic Estonians comprised 88 per cent of the population before 1939, but by 1970 the figure had dropped to 60 per cent. These Russian settlers were augmented by around 150,000 Russian troops. The Kalingrad enclave is still fully Russian and the Russian troops elsewhere in the Baltic were only gradually withdrawn, the last leaving in October 1999.

While many Russian troops, administrators and their families were repatriated to the Russian Federation, the sizeable Russian and Russian-speaking minorities in the Soviet successor states remain as harbingers of possible

Ethnic Russians in the former Soviet republics, 2015

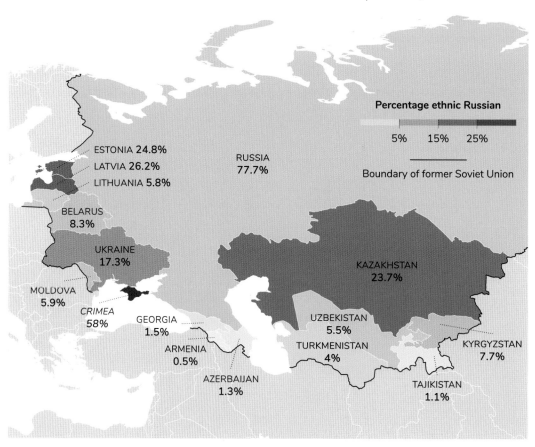

Russian speakers in Ukraine, 2008

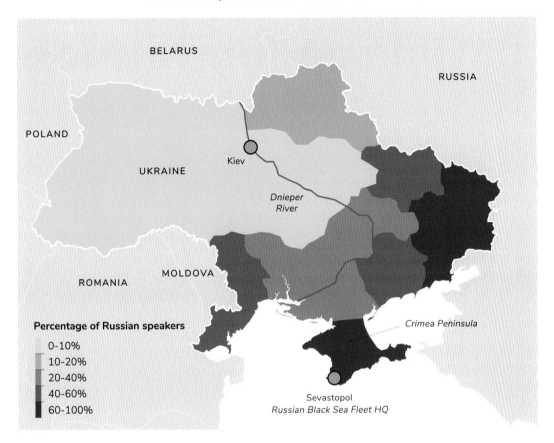

BELARUS

RUSSIA

POLAND

UKRAINE

Kiev

Dnieper
River

ROMANIA

MOLDOVA

Crimea Peninsula

Percentage of Russian speakers

0-10%
10-20%
20-40%
40-60%
60-100%

Sevastopol
Russian Black Sea Fleet HQ

emerging conflicts. This was observed in the Russo–Georgian War of August 2008 (Europe's first war of the twenty-first century) and continuing tensions over "citizenship issues" in Latvia, Estonia and Kyrgyzstan.[3] These tensions burst into a major conflict starting in February 2014 when Russian troops, without insignia, invaded Crimea, part of Ukraine. As there were so many Russian-speakers on the peninsula, it was not surprising that they voted, in an illegal referendum, to join the Russian Federation.

Continuing conflicts in the eastern part of Crimea have been fomented by separatist and pro-Russian forces, particularly in the self-declared Donetsk and Luhansk People's Republics. The Ukrainian government and NATO forces have remained largely impotent in containing this threat to Ukraine's sovereignty.

21
Caribbean Migrations

There is no perfect definition of "the Caribbean", but in discussing migration to and from the region we allude here to the archipelago of islands in the Caribbean Sea, together with "the Guyanas" – Guiana, Guyana and Suriname. Most of the inhabitants of the Caribbean encountered by European seafarers (Columbus stepped ashore in the Bahamas in 1492) were Taíno, with a subgroup known as Caribs, thus the region's name. They originated in South America, with a much more remote migration history as Mongols who had gradually crossed the Bering Strait. The considerable genetic divergences between Native American and Mongolian populations suggests that they were stuck along the way for long periods [1] and developed distinctive genetic profiles.

The local populations collapsed as the European mercantile powers – Britain, Spain, the Netherlands, France and Denmark – jostled for possession, then struggled to establish tropical plantations of tobacco, sugar and coffee. Some Taíno made heroic last stands against the Europeans' muskets; many succumbed to unfamiliar diseases and, in a few dramatic cases, Caribs leapt to their death, rather than yield to European rule or an overseer's whip.

If the plantations were to succeed labourers would have to be imported, lots of them. At first English and Irish indentured servants were transhipped, many to Barbados. In 1840, the total white population of Barbados was 12,000, two-thirds of whom were indentured, often indigent, "poor whites". One contemporary observer remarked, "this Illand is the Dunghill

whareone England doth cast forth its rubidg."[2]

Rubbish or not, clearly European migration would not suffice, so the planters turned to African slaves. If we take the marker year of 1807 (when the British abolished the slave trade) there were 1,150,000 slaves in the Caribbean, two-thirds of them in the British Caribbean.[3]

Though the trade was abolished, slavery itself continued until 1834, when the abolitionists finally had their victory. Or did they? For about four years former slaves were tied to the plantations as apprentices, a period that neatly segued into the recruitment of indentured labour, mainly from India (see Chapter 8). Over the period from 1838 to 1917, 538,642 Indians arrived in the Caribbean, most to British Guyana and Trinidad, with a significant number also shipped to the French territories.

Emigration to the Americas and Europe

As the price of sugar collapsed after 1865, Caribbean populations had to seek work elsewhere. Some 150,000 Caribbean people of African descent were recruited to work on digging out the Panama Canal. The death toll was horrendous. More than 22,000 workers died from malaria, snake bites, swamp fever, industrial accidents and poor conditions.[4]

The majority of twentieth-century migrants went to the USA. Temporary contract workers cut cane in Florida; Haitians often arrived as illegals; and now many middle-class and professional Caribbean emigrants occupy important roles in medicine, teaching and retail services. The Caribbean community monopolizes the laundries, travel agents and hairdressing shops in several New York districts. Moreover, Caribbean people have played a prominent role in political movements – in the Back-to-Africa Garveyite movement, the civil rights struggles and the Black Power Movement, the last led by a Trinidadian.

In contrast to the USA, the fortunes of the Caribbean migrants in Europe have been less happy. The explanations for this may be complex: different groups may have gone to Europe, the opportunities on offer may have varied, while some migration (to the UK and the Netherlands) was "panic" migration – with the

Above: Popular art depicting the mass suicide of Caribs north of the town of Sauteurs ("Leapers"), Grenada in 1651. Grenada's last remaining Caribs hurled themselves over the cliff face to the sea 30m (100ft) below, preferring suicide to domination by the French.

CARIBBEAN MIGRATIONS

networks of friends, relations and openings in business and education not fully prefigured or prepared. Many Caribbean migrants, particularly in Britain, insist that the high levels of racial discrimination and disadvantage present in that country have also worked seriously to jeopardize their chances of success.

The number of Caribbean immigrants going to the Netherlands is about half that of those coming to the UK – about 250,000 compared with Britain's 500,000. The numbers are, however, much more significant when considered as a proportion of the Dutch population and of the Caribbean source population. So large was the departure that about half the population of Suriname was depleted.

Caribbean migration to France arises in a different form from the cases just considered. The major source areas are the territories of Martinique and Guadeloupe. Because of the juridical status of these territories, as organic parts of France, migration to the continent is officially considered internal migration – simply as if one French citizen moved from one *département* to another. The numbers involved are thought to be about 200,000; urban centres, particularly Paris, being the main destinations.

The Caribbean has moved decisively from being a region of immigration to a region of emigration, generating large diasporic populations. Among the more dramatic examples are Guyana, Saint Vincent and Suriname, with emigrant populations of 58.2 per cent, 55.6 per cent and 49.2 per cent respectively of their home populations. One telling way of expressing this is that the region has created diasporas of its diasporas.

Opposite above: Jamaicans building the Panama Canal.

Opposite below: The annual Notting Hill Carnival in London was started in 1966 by Caribbean migrants.

Immigrant and emigrant populations in selected Caribbean countries

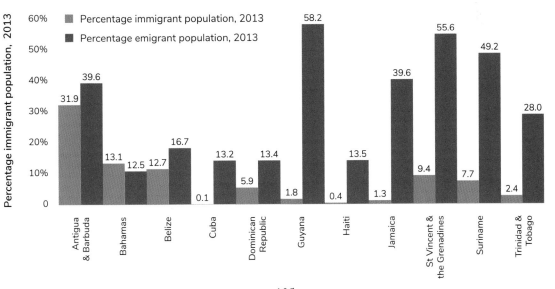

105

22

The Overseas Chinese

The expression "Overseas Chinese" is commonly used to describe those who moved as free or indentured labourers in the nineteenth century, the merchants and business people who preceded and followed them and the contemporary migrants who work on Chinese construction contracts abroad or are entrepreneurs in retail, real estate and importing.

There are about 50 million such Overseas Chinese (2012 estimates) spread over 151 countries, but the count excludes those in Macau, Hong Kong and the Republic of China (Taiwan), some 29 million more. Here we only consider early Chinese emigration patterns, before moving to China's mercantile expansion into Southeast Asia, the nineteenth-century indentured labourers and the foundation of Chinatowns in many countries.

Early emigration and the opening out to Southeast Asia

The expansion of China's population was both land-based and overseas. One of the most successful periods of enlargement of China's territory was during the Han dynasty (206 BC–AD 220) when agricultural colonies protected by military expeditions consolidated the western regions. However, there is evidence too of overseas farming colonies or exploratory parties being sent to Japan (210 BC), and much later to the Philippines (seventh century) and Sumatra (tenth century).

China's trading empire notably accelerated during the Tang dynasty (AD 618–907) with Chinese traders being found in Persia, Mesopotamia, Arabia, Egypt, Aksum (Ethiopia)

Above: The Chinese quarter in Medan, North Sumatra, 1925.

Chinese in Southeast Asia, 1600s to 1980s

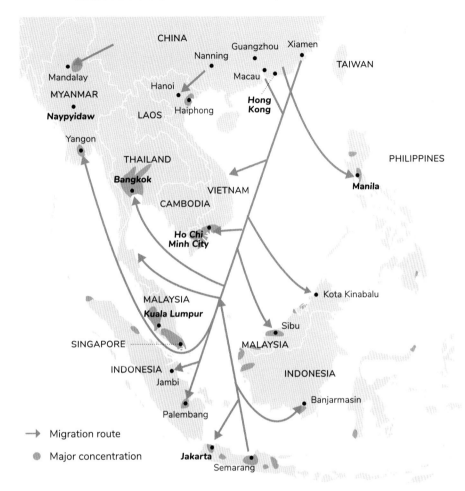

→ Migration route

● Major concentration

and Somalia. An Arab merchant called Shulama observed Chinese traders and their families located at the mouth of the Tigris and Euphrates rivers and also noted that Chinese ships carried as many as 600–700 passengers. While the Chinese mercantile empire fanned out towards Southeast Asia and Africa, foreign traders arriving in cities such as Guangzhou included "Persians, Arabs, Hindu Indians, Malays, Bengalis, Sinhalese, Khmers, Chams, Jews and Nestorian Christians of the Near East, and many others".[1]

As the trade in Chinese goods increased from around the thirteenth century onwards, ports in Java, Sumatra and elsewhere housed larger and larger concentrations of Chinese merchants, together with their Chinese and local children.

Chinese settlement was welcomed by the colonial authorities as a means of building up their colonies and connecting them to the global circuit of trade. For example, heading off competition with the Dutch and Portuguese, the Spanish officials enticed Chinese to Manila with various inducements. Within 30 years, the Chinese population had reached 10,000 and a thriving trade in silks, tools, textiles, food, furniture and porcelain commenced.[2] Thailand now has the largest Chinese population in Southeast Asia, 6–9 million people (depending on how mixed-heritage Thai Chinese are counted). Although there are significant Chinese populations in all of Southeast Asia, only in Singapore are Chinese a majority population.

Chinese indentured workers

There is some dispute about the etymology of the word "coolie", which was widely applied to Chinese indentured labour in the nineteenth century, but there is no doubt that it was derogatory referring, as it did, to workers sometimes recruited by force or guile ("shanghaied") and working in demeaning conditions. Inflation, population pressures and political turmoil weakened China just as labour recruiters scoured the Far East for indentured workers to develop ports, railways and roads in the expanding economies of the Americas, and to replace slave labourers in the cotton and sugar plantations of the tropical world.

Though numbers are far from exact, one scholar suggests that between 1847 and 1874 about 500,000 Chinese indentured workers were recruited.[3] At a later period, particularly controversial examples are the recruitment of 140,000 men to the Chinese Labour Corps to relieve British and French troops during the First World War, and the deployment of 63,000 Chinese workers to the South African gold mines

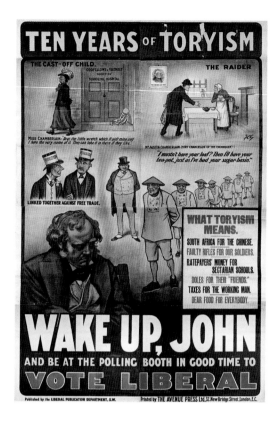

(1904–07). Opposition to recruiting Chinese to South Africa featured large in bringing the Liberals to power in the UK in 1906.

Though Chinese scholars tend to avoid the discussion of indentured Chinese, Jin Hui Ong breaks new ground by taking a much more positive view of the achievement of the indentured labourers.[4] He praises their endurance in the face of backbreaking work and their frugality in making lives for themselves and their descendants. Moreover, those who decided to stay after their indenture formed the nucleus of the Chinatowns that are now so evident in many large cities.

Above: Liberal Party poster, UK 1906 Election.

Opposite: Chinatown, San Francisco, late nineteenth century.

Chinatowns

Like many ethnic enclaves, Chinatowns were concentrations of working-class immigrants in the poorer districts of cites. However, unlike many ethnic enclaves, Chinatowns became a way of straddling cultural difference, being in, but not necessarily of, the societies in which Chinese settled. The clans, triads (crime syndicates) and hometown associations often ran the show, keeping order within the community on the one hand and providing a protective shield against integration and control by outsiders on the other. There are about 35 significant Chinatowns worldwide, in Africa, the Americas, Asia, Australia and Europe.

Chinatowns are changing as global and local tourists seek out what TripAdvisor and the guidebooks call "authentic", but what are often new socially constructed versions of supposedly traditional Chinese practices. Tourist buses, herbalists, acupuncturists, kitchenware shops, sages, dim sum parlours, fluffy pineapple buns, masseurs and restaurants proliferate as the Chinese learn to offer yet another commodity to the global marketplace – their ethnic quaintness.[5] The *Huffington Post*'s rather breathless guide to Binondo, Manila (the oldest Chinatown in the world, founded in 1594), suggests that visitors "Start in Umbrella Alley, where you'll choose from oodles of savoury street food carts. They're a mere warm-up for the infamous Café Mezzanine, home of the infamously slimy bull testicle soup."[6]

Beyond the tourist gazes and the bubble worlds of the Chinatowns, the descendants of Chinese settlers, as well as those joining them more recently from Mainland China, Hong Kong and Taiwan, are entering into professional and business life in significant numbers. Typically, incomes and educational attainments of Chinese settler populations are higher than those of the native populations; however, reflecting their endogamous past, participation in public life and politics is still modest. (After 200 years of settlement, the first UK Member of Parliament of Chinese descent was elected only in 2015.)

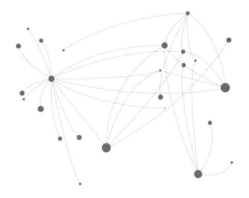

PART THREE

Contemporary Migration

23

Hukou and Internal Migration in China

We think of passports as a means of regulating the movement of people across national frontiers, but there are a number of examples of similar documents being used to control movement *within* countries.

One example is the regulation of the movement of all people travelling to Paris by the leaders of the French Revolution who were alarmed by evidence of counter-revolutionary plots. In 1932, Stalin reintroduced an internal passport (one had existed in tsarist times) to prevent impoverished peasants flowing into the over-crowded cities. The British colonial authorities introduced a *kipande* certificate in Kenya for much the same purpose. And, notoriously, during the apartheid years, the South African state excluded unwanted African migrants from cities through the use of "passes".

Though the South African and Soviet restrictions on mobility were conducted on a large scale with many ramifying social and political consequences, the *hukou* system in China, which developed from the 1950s, exceeded even these precedents in scale and significance.[1] The core idea was to head off any possible unrest from the urban population by placating it with subsidized housing, welfare

Above: A Chinese woman lays out the array of identity documents she has accumulated during her periods of registration in Beijing, China.

Opposite: Large numbers of rural migrants worked on communal farms in the 1950s during the Great Leap Forward.

benefits and increased wages. However, these advantages could not conceivably be extended to China's vast population. This meant distinguishing between urban and rural Chinese by creating a "household registration system", which recorded the birth, death, residence, education and occupation of every member of every household. Introduced first in Shanghai, the *hukou* system soon went national and, linked to the census, became the principal means not only of regulating labour supply to the cities and industries but also, in the absence of a fully developed market, of providing a way of rationing food, particularly the distribution of grain. With successive legal provisions passed in the course of a decade, Chinese people were effectively denied freedom of movement without a "migration certificate".

Despite the legal crackdown on rural–urban movement, the Chinese urban population expanded by 30 million over the 1957–60 period. As John Torpey explains, Mao Zedong responded by reinforcing the status distinction between peasant and worker, allowing only a limited permeable membrane between the two. Service in the army or the party, outstanding educational achievements or, for women, marriage to an urbanite allowed upward mobility to the ranks of an urban resident.[2] As the *hukou* system was introduced alongside the compulsory

collectivization of agriculture, more and more peasants were forced to move to bureaucratically defined collectives, resulting in many deaths. This period, known as the Great Leap Forward (1958–60), was effectively a war on the peasantry by the state and triggered an appalling famine, the worst in human history. Some estimates suggest that between 15 and 30 million rural people perished. The very vagueness of these figures is itself an indictment of the regime and of outside scholars who have failed properly to document this dreadful set of events.

By the mid-1980s, an identity card that all Chinese people, rural and urban, carried replaced the *hukou* documents that mainly rural dwellers had carried. These cards are targeted at individuals, not households, and are simpler to carry around. However, they continued to be used as a way of distinguishing between those who have limited access to benefits in urban

areas and those whom the urban authorities recognize as legitimate residents, entitled to a superior education, housing, health and welfare benefits. The expressions "rural" or "agricultural *hukou*" continue to indicate that rights are held in the countryside. China's urbanization has continued apace, though only 36 per cent of its total population are urban *hukou* holders. As the graph below indicates, China's urban population is projected to peak, then flatten out at 1 billion by the year 2040.

The massive growth of the Chinese urban population (by 2018 China had 160 cities with populations of more than a million) has been accomplished without the ribbon of informal shacks and slums seen in countries such as Brazil, Mexico and Nigeria. This is an impressive achievement, but it has come at a considerable cost. A "floating population", namely one that is caught between town and country, is

China's urban population

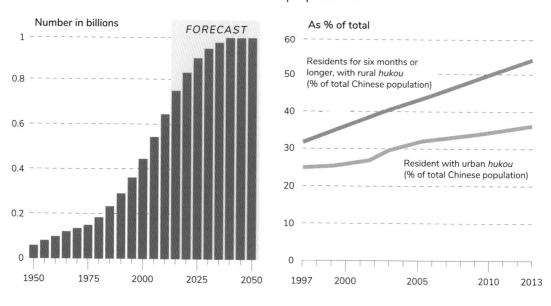

precariously housed; in fact, it is not uncommon to find migrant workers being temporarily housed in factory dormitories.

Demands to improve the conditions of those holding a rural *hukou* are growing. Take, for instance, farmer Dong Helong and his wife Chen Ying who sort materials for recycling – cardboard, plastic and cloth. They make about US$400 a month, many times more than the income from their soybean and potato farm. "I want to have a Shanghai *hukou*, so we can be treated the same as the Shanghainese", he said. "We've been in Shanghai for 15 years. We kind of fit into this city already."[3]

The government has responded by promoting a "people-centred" urban plan, announcing that it wants 60 per cent of China's people to live in cities by 2020, 45 per cent of whom will be granted a full urban *hukou*. Seen in a long historical perspective, this will be an unprecedented shift, trebling the proportion of urban residents in a matter of 40 years. Despite this shift to urban dwelling, there are still expected to be more than 250 million migrant workers in the floating population by the same year.[4]

Above: Street scene in the west side of Beijing, 2015. Although housing for migrants is often modest, the authorities have largely avoided the growth of slums and shacks.

24

Population Transfer and the Partition of India

The end of British colonial rule of India in 1947 was accompanied by one of the most tragic events in migration history, partition. Despite the desperate pleas of Mahatma Gandhi for peace between Muslims, Hindus and Sikhs, the three principal ethnic groups involved, through acts of miscalculation, fear and desperation, people in the Indian sub-continent found themselves propelled into a nightmare.

Instead of a unified decolonized India, the country was split in two, Pakistan and India both coming into existence at midnight on 14–15 August 1947. Population transfers on a mass scale took place, as Muslims fled for Pakistan and Hindus left for India. Ultimately, 14 million people were displaced while half-a-million people lost their lives in the accompanying violence.

The background to these momentous events was complex. As Yasmin Khan points out, "partition emerged from a cauldron of social disorder".[1] She explains that during the Second World War India had mobilized the largest volunteer force in history – two-and-a-half million soldiers had signed up to defend the Allied cause. Tens of thousands had died or

were injured and there was considerable unrest among the demobbed soldiers. Meanwhile, mass protests against the continuation of the British Raj were raging. Only a fortnight after the marching bands paraded around Delhi during Victory Week, the British delegation arrived to negotiate the path to independence.

In March 1946, shortly after the end of the war, Clement Attlee, the Prime Minister of Great Britain, had noted in a speech to the House of Commons that:

India is today in a state of great tension. ... Is it any wonder that today she claims – as a nation of 400,000,000 people that has twice sent her sons to die for freedom – that she should herself have freedom to decide

Partition of India, 1947, and subsequent boundary changes

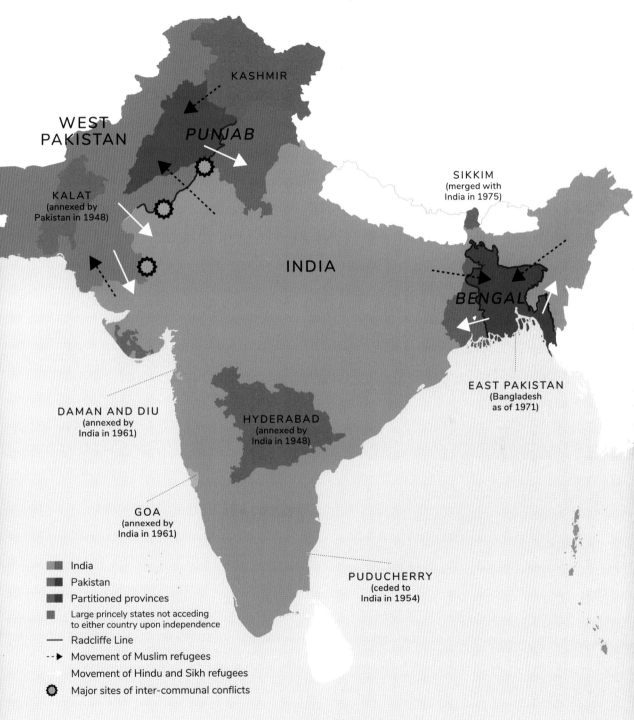

KASHMIR

WEST
PAKISTAN

PUNJAB

SIKKIM
(merged with
India in 1975)

KALAT
(annexed by
Pakistan in 1948)

INDIA

BENGAL

DAMAN AND DIU
(annexed by
India in 1961)

HYDERABAD
(annexed by
India in 1948)

EAST PAKISTAN
(Bangladesh
as of 1971)

GOA
(annexed by
India in 1961)

PUDUCHERRY
(ceded to
India in 1954)

- India
- Pakistan
- Partitioned provinces
- Large princely states not acceding
  to either country upon independence
- — Radcliffe Line
- --▶ Movement of Muslim refugees
- Movement of Hindu and Sikh refugees
- ✹ Major sites of inter-communal conflicts

POPULATION TRANSFER AND THE PARTITION OF INDIA

The personal account of Arghwani Begum, recorded 31 August 2015

Arghwani Begum was born to a Muslim family on 2 January 1922 in Uttar Pradesh. Residents of the villages were mainly Muslim, Hindu and Christian families and most of them were farmers, she recalls. ... By 1947, Arghwani Begum was pregnant with her third child. She was 25 years old when Partition was announced. She was in her eighth or ninth month of pregnancy. "I really didn't have any clear understanding of what is going on when our boxes were getting packed with valuables and necessities. My family told me that we are moving out of the haveli and nothing else."

She gave birth to her third child, a son, at the Old Fort migrant camp at Delhi, a day after Partition. They stayed at the Old Fort for two days and carried on to the Nizamuddin Railway Station in Delhi in the army jeeps that were expected to pick them up. "At the station, while everyone was worried about having something to eat before the train departed, I wanted to get on the train immediately. I hadn't eaten for nearly three days but had no hunger for food. I just wanted the journey to end," she says.

During her journey to Lahore from Delhi that started on 17 August 1947, her train made stops at various stations. She witnessed the massacre of Sikh passengers in a train passing by theirs in the opposite direction. "There were men climbing and entering that train with swords and knives. I saw the sudden commotion and heard their screams and cries of panic. I also witnessed men jumping off that train with their women and girls. It was horrifying."

Her train finally made it to the Wagah border on 20 August, but it was not the end of the ordeal as her train had come under attack too. "It was so sudden. We immediately sealed shut the windows of our train with whatever we could get our hands on. My baby almost fainted due to lack of oxygen in our berth. One of the male helpers in the train helped my baby get some air through the train's main entrance while the killing spree [continued]. ... A lot of people, especially children, from many berths of that train had been killed. I saw their bloodied bodies when we finally got out of the train."

In 1980, she visited her birthplace in India with two of her daughters. Her daughter says, "She had practically started shaking and crying as we approached her house. It was very intense for her".[2]

Opposite: The Old Fort in Delhi, 1947, where an estimated 20,000 Muslim displacees were temporarily housed.

her own destiny? My colleagues are going to India with the intention of using their utmost endeavours to help her to attain that freedom as speedily and fully as possible.

Unfortunately, the task was Herculean, and the people assigned to undertake it were not up to the job. Viceroy Mountbatten recklessly forced the pace of independence. He established a Boundary Commission under the chairmanship of Cyril Radcliffe, a British judge, who was accurately described by the Indian historian, Joya Chatterji, as a "confident amateur". Radcliffe was given five weeks to complete the demarcation and, given that he had never been to India, it was not surprising that his attempt to divide the country on religious lines produced some startling anomalies.

The Radcliffe Line went down the middle of Punjab province leaving a large minority (29 per cent) of Muslims in West Bengal and a similar percentage of Hindus in East Bengal. Sikh demands were sidelined while Kashmir was left free to accede to either India or Pakistan. Confusion and despair set in as large swathes of the population rushed to get to the right side of the line. Most people could not get access to the printed version of the line and rumours abounded that they would wake up to find that it had changed from one day to the next.

The New York Times.

Copyright, 1947, by The New York Times Company.

LATE CITY EDITION
Hot and humid with scattered showers today. Cooler tomorrow.
Temperature Range Today—Max., 90; Min., 72
Temperature Yesterday—Max., 85.8; Min., 72
Full U. S. Weather Bureau Report, Page 36

VOL. XCVI..No. 32,710.

NEW YORK, FRIDAY, AUGUST 15, 1947.

THREE CENTS NEW YORK CITY

LAWS ON GAMBLING BREED CORRUPTION, O'DWYER DECLARES

Mayor Says, However, He Will Enforce Them and Keep the Police Department Clean

ASKS INQUIRIES BY JURIES

Praises Wallander for the Job He Is Doing — Inspector Kennedy Raids Dice Game

By MEYER BERGER

Existing gambling laws, Mayor O'Dwyer said at City Hall yesterday, tend to breed corruption. He said he would, as long as his administration lasts, like to see a grand jury in each county in the city inquire into gambling and its attendant evils.

"The Police Department," the Mayor said, "has a responsibility for enforcing a law which applies outside the forces of a racetrack, but not inside—a law for which a considerable portion of the public has shown very little respect.

There is a danger of corruption in this picture. One investigation after another during my thirty-seven years in this city has politically charged corruption in the enforcement of these laws. It is something with which every honest administration of the city's business is deeply concerned. This administration is no exception. We need and will need all the help we can get from law agencies to prevent corruption.

Praises Queens Jury

Mr. O'Dwyer praised the Queens County grand jury inquiring into alleged police grafting on book-makers, which on Wednesday advocated that the state legalize off-the-track betting because existing laws are unenforceable and breed rackets.

Mr. O'Dwyer was asked what he intends to do about the current situation.

"I am going to enforce the law as best I can and keep the Police Department as clean as I can," he said. "That is why I am so happy to have the aid of grand juries—to do both, enforce the law and prevent corruption."

Someone wanted to know if Police Commissioner Arthur W. Wallander, who has shaken up his reforms in an anti-gambling crusade, is "fighting for his job."

"The city," the Mayor warmly, "could stand 100 Wallanders. That's based not only on his record since he became Commissioner but on the thirty-one years I have known him intimately. He can be Commissioner as long as I want him; as far as I am Mayor, if he wants it. A man who works as long and as intelligently as he does deserve the job."

Inspector James R. Kennedy, in charge of the Eighth Uniformed Division, Manhattan East, led a raid last night on a four-story vacant building at 203 East 101st Street. The police arrested nineteen men, whom they said were playing dice in a room on the ground floor.

Seventeen of the men were booked at the East 104th Street station for disorderly conduct and two for violation of Section 970 of the Penal Code. The two were Ralph M. Once, 37 years old, of 1354 Second Avenue, accused of being the "cutter" in the game, and Joseph Benfari, 22, of 219 East 101st Street, charged with being the "steerer."

Inspector Kennedy, who was accompanied by Lieut. George Oest and six plainclothes men, was the only one of twenty-three inspectors who was not transferred in the recent shake-up.

3 Booked for Perjury

Three witnesses who had appeared before the Queens grand jury and who were named by that body on Wednesday in perjury informations, surrendered yesterday in District Attorney Charles P. Sullivan's office in Long Island City. Each was booked on a perjury charge and held for hearing on Nov. 18.

The three are Eugene Condillo, 42 years old, of 41-38 Seventy-seventh Street in Jackson Heights; William (Willie The Ice) Perillo, 42, of 21-12 Twenty-eighth Street, Astoria, and William (Willie Shepherd) Mazza, 44, of 235 of Thirty-third Street, Astoria, all of Queens. They were accused, among other alleged perjurious statements before the grand jury, of denying they are, or were, bookmakers.

The charges against Perillo and he testified that he had quit book-making ten months before he appeared as a "cases and had returned to the to the business," when

Continued on Page 4, Column 2

Truman Backs Price Inquiry As Possibly Showing Gouge

He Says Clark's Investigation May Reveal Who Is Causing High Cost Levels—Plea for Labor-Farm-Industry Talk Is Rejected

By LOUIS STARK
Special to The New York Times.

WASHINGTON, Aug. 14—President Truman expressed approval today of Attorney General Tom C. Clark's investigation to determine who might be responsible for continuing to increase prices of food, clothing and housing.

Reporters asked whether the President felt that the Federal inquiry would check the rise in prices or indicate the rise had profited beyond normal margins.

While Mr. Truman believed that the latter result would be the outcome of Mr. Clark's efforts, he said that as far as a possible check on prices the newsmen wanted to the wait and see.

In giving his endorsement to the Attorney General's investigation, the President indicated that he held high hopes for the inquiry. The President was asked whether the corn crop which has been affected by great food damage. He said that a Cabinet food committee was looking into the entire

The Chief Executive indicated that he had no plan for calling together spokesmen for labor, industry and agriculture to consider the problem of prices, as suggested several days ago by Emil Rieve, administrative chairman of the Congress of Industrial Organizations.

Recalling that he had convened a labor-management conference in November, 1945, and that it had not been successful, the President turned down Mr. Rieve's proposal.

The question on crops addressed to the President was intended to ascertain if he had been considering some possible limitation on exports in view of the reduced crop outlook in some commodities. He felt, he said, that the Cabinet committee would determine whatever steps might be necessary in the recovery.

Continued on Page 14, Column 7

RELIEF FROM HEAT LIKELY TOMORROW

Continued High Temperatures Today Expected to Be Ended by Thunder Showers

Relief from the heat wave has been forecast for tomorrow by the Weather Bureau last night. The forecast followed a high temperature of 91.6 degrees at 4:15 P. M. yesterday, the second successive day when the mercury touched 91.

Collars, shirts and dresses are expected to wilt again today as the spokesman for the bureau said it would be hot and humid with the highest thermometer reading near 90. Afternoon or evening thunder showers probably will precede the cool air mass pushing in from the West that, it is hoped, will end the hot spell on the Eastern seaboard.

Meanwhile, in the Midwest, according to The Associated Press, scattered showers cooled that area after a two-day heat wave had reduced harvest prospects, especially for corn.

Locally, the lowest temperature for the twenty-four-hour period yesterday was 73, registered at 6 A. M. The mercury mounted steadily during the early morning, generally recording a point or two higher each hour than for a corresponding hour Wednesday.

By noon the thermometer registered 85, two degrees below the rating at noon Wednesday, but the humidity stood at 72 per cent, 1 higher than at the same time the preceding day.

After that hour the mercury rose and the humidity decreased, the humidity standing at 60 per cent when the high temperature for the day was reached. The highest humidity of the day was 95 per cent at 6 A. M.

[A table of prevailing temperatures is on Page 36.]

Although many persons felt as if they were perspiring more because of accumulated heat, the temperature dropped steadily during the early evening. Thermometer readings for 5, 6 and

Continued on Page 36, Column 2

U.S. RENT CURB HERE IS BADLY SNARLED

Many Tenants Tell of Futile Attempts to Get Relief— ORC Soon to Cut Staff

By CHARLES GRUTZNER

A bad snarl in the administration of Federal rent controls in New York came to light yesterday, with the backlog of tenant complaints increasing in area rent offices.

At the same time, the Office of Rent Control announced it would drop "about 150" employes in this city on Sept. 15 in line with a 20 per cent nation-wide reduction in staff. The Federal agency will also close its area offices at St. George, S. I., and Mineola, L. I. The Brooklyn office will take over Staten Island cases, and the Queens office is to absorb the Nassau and Suffolk work loads.

Tenants, attorneys and representatives of veterans and civic organizations told yesterday of repeated and futile attempts to obtain action on cases where excess rents allegedly have been charged for several months and in a few cases for a full year. Their descriptions of local rent offices ranged from "overloaded with work" to "completely demoralized."

Not Covered by City Law

Tenants have been coming to the City Rent Commission at 100 Park Avenue with cases involving apartment house rentals and evictions, although the city law covers only hotels and rooming houses. The apartment dwellers have said they went first to the Federal rent offices and were advised to seek advice from the municipal agency.

The expected passage by the City Council of three bills sponsored by Vice Chairman Joseph T. Sharkey will give the City Rent Commission power to prosecute violations of Federal and City rent laws covering apartments and small houses as well as hotels and rooming houses. Although this will take more of the 100 Park staff time,

Continued on Page 15, Column 3

U.S. CANCELS DEBTS OF BILLION BY ITALY IN FINANCIAL PACTS

Frees $60,000,000 in Blocked Properties—Will Return 29 Freight Ships to Rome

WOULD RELIEVE BURDENS

Lovett Expresses Hope Accords Will Reduce the Weight of Peace Treaty Clauses

By WALTER H. WAGGONER
Special to The New York Times.

WASHINGTON, Aug. 14—The United States today crossed off about $1,000,000,000 in debts owed by Italy and, in addition, liberalized the interpretation of some of the financial sections of the Italian peace treaty to aid that country's frail economy.

The State Department, in making the agreement public, said the action would relieve Italy of many "burdensome" financial and economic clauses in the peace pact and "substantially" in her recovery.

Terms of the debt relief were contained in one of three "memoranda of understanding" with which the two Governments concluded three months of negotiations. The other documents provided for protection of private American property in Italy and the disposal of German assets there. France and Great Britain joined in the negotiations on the last point.

Hopes It Will Help Italy

Robert A. Lovett, Acting Secretary of State, said upon signing the documents relating to American claims that he hoped the agreement would ease Italy's "difficult financial situation."

"These understandings, furthermore," he went on, "reflect the recognition given to the fact that the Italians themselves overthrew the Fascist Government, and beginning September, 1943, your people joined the Allies as a co-belligerent against the Nazis.

"The questions which have been settled in these negotiations constitute an additional substantial step in the establishment of good economic and political relations between our two countries."

On behalf of his government, Ivan Matteo Lombardo, chief of the Italian economic and financial delegation and signer of the agreement, declared that the prosperity of Italy "is highly beneficial to the greater prosperity of this country, and in turn corroborate greater

Continued on Page 4, Column 1

TWO INDIAN NATIONS EMERGE ON WORLD SCENE

The New York Times.

Princely states that have not yet adhered to either India or Pakistan are shown without shading. Pakistan has recognized the independence of Kalat, on the Arabian Sea. The boundaries running through Bengal (A) and the Punjab (B) are to be announced by a commission.

WORLD PEACE TIED TO AMERICAS TALKS

Marshall, at Rio de Janeiro, Says Hemisphere Defense Aim Is Within Framework of U.N.

By C. P. TRUSSELL
Special to The New York Times.

RIO DE JANEIRO, Aug. 14—Secretary of State George C. Marshall, landing amid applauding crowds of Brazilians at this city's Santos Dumont Airport today, said the United States desired to the inter-American defense conference had come "for the purpose of helping to consolidate the peace of the world."

In thus going beyond the strictly hemispheric implications of the twenty-nation conference that is to open in the summer capital of Petropolis tomorrow, Secretary Marshall put upon the American republics the obligation of setting an example for all nations.

To the Brazilian and the diplomatic

Continued on Page 7, Column 2

'Crudest' U. S. Interference In Greece Charged by Soviet

By THOMAS J. HAMILTON
Special to The New York Times.

LAKE SUCCESS, N. Y., Aug. 14—Andrei A. Gromyko, Soviet Deputy Foreign Minister, launched a determined attack today on the new United Nations resolution under which the United Nations Security Council would order Yugoslavia, Albania and Bulgaria to "cease and desist from rendering any further assistance or support in any form to the guerrilla fighting against the Greek Government."

Mr. Gromyko's statement was interpreted as giving unmistakable notice that he would veto both the United States resolution and an Australian proposal, which, without attributing responsibility to either side, orders all four nations to stop the fighting. Both resolutions invoke "chapter VII of the Charter, applying to threats to the peace, breaches of the peace, or acts of aggression, under which the Council can order enforcement measures, going as far as a collective declaration of war by the fifty-five member nations.

The Soviet representative said that the "internal affairs of Greece. He added that the Australian resolution was worse than an earlier and milder United States resolution, which he vetoed two weeks ago, and "competes successfully with the second American resolution."

"One cannot solve the Greek question as proposed in the American and in the australian resolutions," said Mr. Gromyko. "They are missing their mark. They may correspond to the interests of one or two countries but not to the interests of the development of good neighborly relations between states and, consequently not to the interests of the United Nations as a whole."

Mr. Gromyko was silent, how-

Continued on Page 5, Column 1

TASS SAYS GREEKS MOLEST RUSSIANS

Charges Workers in Embassy Are Seized and 'Tortured'— Sees Threat to Relations

By The Associated Press.

LONDON, Friday, Aug. 15—The Soviet news agency Tass said today by a dispatch from Athens that Greek authorities had "been arresting and even subjecting to torture persons at work in the Soviet Embassy" in the Greek capital.

The dispatch said the Soviet Chargé d'Affaires in Athens had protested to the Greek Government that such actions were "incompatible with the maintenance of diplomatic relations between Greece and the Soviet Union."

A summarized version of the dispatch was distributed in London by the Soviet Monitor.

The arrests and torture, the dispatch said, extended to members of "other Soviet institutions in Greece" beside the Embassy.

"Persons who have commercial ties with the Soviet Union are subjected to persecutions," it added.

"This dispatch failed to make clear, however, whether the persons affected by the alleged mal-treatment were Soviet citizens, Greeks working for the Soviet Union"

Continued on Page 5, Column 2

INDIA AND PAKISTAN BECOME NATIONS; CLASHES CONTINUE

Ceremonies at New Delhi and Karachi Mark Independence for 400,000,000 Persons

NEHRU ACCLAIMS GANDHI

But He Warns of Trials Ahead —Death Toll in Communal Fighting Reaches 153

By ROBERT TRUMBULL
Special to The New York Times.

NEW DELHI, Friday, Aug. 15—India achieved her long-sought independence today through the transfer of British power to two dominions into which that land was divided, India and Pakistan.

While the ceremonies marking this major historic event were taking place communal strife continued to cast a grim shadow over the new nation.

(Communal clashes, fires and looting continued in Lahore, Punjab, with the rising death toll estimated at 153. The Associated Press reported. In London, King George conferred an earldom on Viscount Mountbatten for his role in solving the Indian problem and the Government made available to the Indian Government £150,000 of India's sterling balance.)

The Dominion of India marked the goal of freedom here at midnight with minimum celebration and a few speeches that stressed the gravity of the tasks ahead of the new nation.

In Karachi, capital of Pakistan, Mohammed Ali Jinnah will take the oath this morning as Governor General of the Moslem dominion which he was the primary figure in creating against the demand for a united India.

Viceroy at Both Ceremonies

It is the Rand Provincial Government House, which is now Mr. Jinnah's official residence, will be the only event marking the transfer of power from British to Indian hands in that dominion.

The Viceroy, Viscount Mountbatten, addressed the Pakistan Constituent Assembly yesterday— his last official act as Viceroy— and then flew back to New Delhi to attend the formal transfer here. No special events were scheduled in Karachi, as they were in New Delhi, to mark the actual moment when the rule of the King-Emperor came to an end at midnight except in so far as both dominions continued to owe formal allegiance to the British crown.

Climax at Midnight

The Constituent Assembly of the Dominion of India declared its sovereign power solemnly in a special session that began at 11 P. M. last night and reached its climax at twelve o'clock. As the hands of the clock in the stately assembly hall of India building appeared for the first time at midnight India's Cabinet assembled here announced the chimes of the hour.

As the last note died an unidentified member blew a conch shell of the kind used in Hindu temples to summon the gods to witness a great event. Instantly a great cheer arose. Gifts of that moment had become a free member had become a free citizen of the British Commonwealth of Nations — free even to leave the commonwealth if she chooses.

The members then stood and repeated after the Assembly President a solemn pledge to work with the people of India, through suffering and sacrifice have secured the Palestine rights in repelling deprivations of roving Arab crowds.

When a small band of Arabs invaded the highly inflammable area about daybreak, there was a fusillade of shots as the area of the British Commonwealth of Nations — free even to leave the

Continued on Page 2, Column 3

World News Summarized

FRIDAY, AUGUST 15, 1947

Today is Independence Day in India. British rule over the vast land, with its population of 400,000,000, ended at midnight and the territory was divided into two independent nations, the dominions of Pakistan and India. Viscount Mountbatten gave up his role of Viceroy and became Governor General of India. [1:8.]

Earlier, he addressed the Pakistan Constituent Assembly and rode to the Government House in a state procession with Mohammed Ali Jinnah, who is to be the new Governor General of Pakistan. [2:3.] In Lahore, the capital of the Punjab Province, which is to be divided between Pakistan and India, 153 persons had been reported killed in two days. [2:8.]

In Palestine, fighting between Arabs and Jews in the Tel Aviv region continued for the fifth day. Jewish underground forces went to the rescue of areas attacked by Arab mobs. [1:6-7.] In Jaffa, the swept the Netherlands Jerusalem Deflex Petroleum Board fought a main dump at the port of Tel-Jungjevisk. Saboteurs were believed to have set the blaze. [3:1.]

The Indonesian Republic, appealing for the first time before the United Nations Security Council, urged the Council to order the Netherlands to evacuate all of her troops from Java, Sumatra and Madura. [3:3.] Andrei A. Gromyko declared that a United States resolution before the Security Council, asking it to order Yugoslavia, Albania and Bulgaria to stop aiding Greek guerrillas, was "the crudest interference" in the internal affairs of Greece. His at-

...tack was taken to foreshadow a Soviet veto. [1:6-7.]

Moscow may sever relations with Athens, it was feared, following charges that Russians who had been tortured by Greeks in Athens. [1:7.]

About $1,000,000,000 of debts owed by Italy were canceled by the United States in an effort to help Italy's difficult economic position. Rome also was relieved of several other "burdensome" clauses of the peace treaty in recognition of Italian help to the Allied cause in the latter part of the war. [1:4.]

The United States has offered to rehabilitate the Bikini coal mines with 600,000 tons of American steel ingots. [4:4.]

In Nuremberg, twenty-one former officials of the I. G. Farben chemical trust pleaded not guilty when arraigned before the war crimes court on charges of having plotted the war for profit. [5:4.]

President Truman marked the second anniversary of V-J Day by expressing disappointment that world peace, whose attainment had seemed so certain two years ago, had yet to be achieved. [5:6-7.] He said he could see no justification for calling a special session of Congress before January. [4:1.]

Secretary of State Marshall and his party of delegates arrived in Rio de Janeiro for the Inter-American Conference, which opens today. He told a steering crowd of Brazilians at the airport that the United States delegation would work "to consolidate the peace of the world." [1:2-3.]

Actors Win an Anti-Bias Contract In Fight on Negro Ban in Capital

The League of New York Theatres, an organization of theatre owners, operators and producers, agreed yesterday to sign a new contract with Actors' Equity Association embodying a clause whereby actors shall not be required to play in Washington unless Negroes are admitted to the audiences.

James F. Reilly, executive director of the league, said the disputed clause would be in the next agreement, becoming effective on Aug. 1, 1948, at which time the nation's capital would face a virtual ban that would keep all actors and stage attractions out of its theatres unless the rule against Negroes was revoked. The present two-year contract between Equity and the League expires on Aug. 31.

Mr. Reilly asserted that the lone element in the controversial clause was included to permit theatres in Washington to effect a change in policy. He said other factors remained to be cleared up before the agreement is accepted by both sides, but that it was his belief

...that a complete agreement may be reached "by early next week."

The league's action was taken at a closed meeting yesterday afternoon at the Astor Hotel. While the league made no detailed statement on its capitulation to Equity's contractual demand, it was reported that forty-six members attended, with twenty-six voting in favor of the Equity condition, seven against and ten abstaining. Attendance by forty-two members constitutes a quorum.

Even as the league acceded to Equity's demand, Hilton Heiman, president of the operating company for the National Theatre in Washington, declared last night that he would not lift the ban on Negroes as prices.

When informed of the league's vote, Mr. Heiman referred to an announcement he made on Tuesday regarding the situation. He reiterated that the National would drop its white-only rule only if: 1. The "crudest interference" in the in-

Continued on Page 10, Column 6

Jews, Arabs Battle Amid Fires; Armed Zionist Troops Aid Police

JERUSALEM, Aug. 14—For the first time Jewish underground defense forces came today to the rescue of Jewish districts menaced by Arab mobs in the scheduled bordering region between Tel Aviv and Jaffa.

Three more Jews and one Arab were slain, a fourth Jew died of stab wounds received yesterday. More than fifty Arabs and Jews were wounded today.

The three wounded Jews were all truck men whose vehicles were stoned and shot at by Arab gangs. One of them, Aharon Hanovici, 27, was an American. He was discharged last year from the United States Army, in which he served as a truck driver in North Africa with the 404th Quartermaster Company.

The inquiry culminated at Attorney General Clark into the high prices of food, clothing and housing was approved by President Truman. He said the investigation might show who was profiteering. [1:2-3.]

The fourth day of the rioting which appeared to be intensifying rather than diminishing despite appeals from Arab and Jewish leaders, brought wholesale destruction of property. Three great fires lighted the sky tonight over the

...silent and deserted no man's land between the twin Arab and Jewish cities, whose border areas have been placed under a dawn-to-dusk curfew. The curfew area was extended eastward today after clashes between Arabs and Jews began to spread.

While counseling Jews to avoid provocation, Haganah, the Zionist secret militia, came into the open with its arms today to reinforce the Palestine police in repelling deprivations of roving Arab crowds.

When a small band of Arabs invaded the highly inflammable area about daybreak, there was a fusillade of shots as the Arab gangs were dispersed on

Continued on Page 5, Column 2

The partition of India led to intermittent hostilities between India and Pakistan, not least about the future status of Kashmir and issues of annexation and division in the princely states of Hyderabad, Junagadh and Jammu. It also led, notably, to the secession of Bangladesh from Pakistan in 1971.

Above: Muslim refugees sit on the roof of an overcrowded train when trying to leave Delhi, 19 September 1947.

Opposite: The front page of the New York Times, 15 August 1947, recording the moment India was partitioned.

Below: By 2001, the religious composition of the three countries had stabilized, but there are still significant minorities of Muslims and Sikhs in India.

Communal compositon after partition: India, Pakistan, Bangladesh, 2001

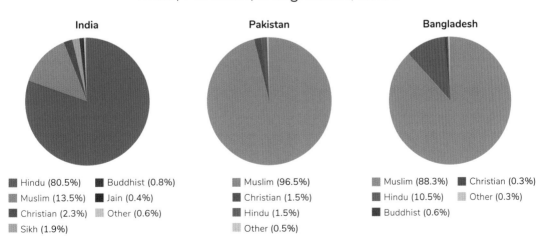

India

- Hindu (80.5%)
- Muslim (13.5%)
- Christian (2.3%)
- Sikh (1.9%)
- Buddhist (0.8%)
- Jain (0.4%)
- Other (0.6%)

Pakistan

- Muslim (96.5%)
- Christian (1.5%)
- Hindu (1.5%)
- Other (0.5%)

Bangladesh

- Muslim (88.3%)
- Hindu (10.5%)
- Buddhist (0.6%)
- Christian (0.3%)
- Other (0.3%)

25

The Export of Workers
The Philippines

The large-scale emigration of Filipinos dated from the end of the Spanish colonial period when, from 1905 to 1935, the USA treated the Philippines as a "ward" – a vague legal category signifying US control. Filipinos were employed as indentured labourers in Hawaii and, by 1930, there were more than 100,000 Filipinos working in the USA.[1]

In the 1930s, the idea of pre-training workers in the Philippines for "export" to the USA was rehearsed in the development of Nursing Education in the Philippines. This laid the ground for the internationalization and enormous expansion of this model from the 1970s onwards.

As the government of the Philippines coordinated its efforts to expand and monitor the overseas employment of Filipino workers, it founded the Philippine Overseas Employment Administration (POEA) in 1982. The POEA engages in what it describes as "labour diplomacy", signing a succession of bilateral labour agreements with many countries. By November 2011, the POEA listed 125 countries in which Filipinos were encouraged to work. The agency issued ID cards to Overseas Filipino Workers (OFWs). At the same time, the POEA banned or decertified 41 countries in which Filipinos could not be legally employed because these countries failed to comply with the

standards the agency set, which covered human rights, safety and working conditions.

Not all Filipinos working or living abroad are sponsored by the POEA. Of the stock of 10 million overseas Filipinos enumerated in December 2013, there were 4.9 million permanent settlers, 1.2 million illegal workers and about 4.2 million issued with OFW identity cards, about one million of whom were in Saudi Arabia.[2] Filipinos are found in many occupations, acting as care workers, domestics, nannies and skilled nurses, among others. About 55 per cent of Filipino workers abroad are women. Male workers predominate among Filipino seafarers, who numbered 460,000 in 2013. This is an astonishing proportion, some 25 per cent, of the total of all seafarers, and by far the biggest single nationality at sea.

Filipino seafarers act in various roles from mates, deckhands, waiters, cabin attendants on cruise liners, to oilers, bosuns and engineers, but the government's policy is to enhance the skills of Filipino seafarers through providing

The annual flow of OFWs over a 40-year period, 1975–2017

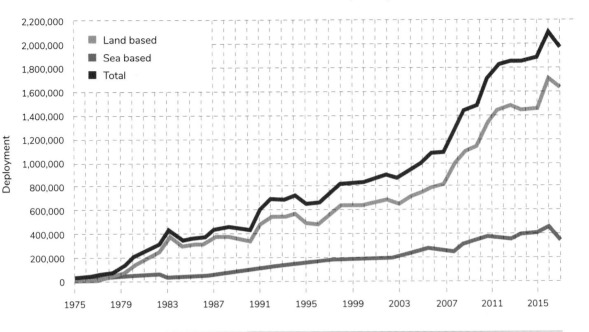

New hires of Filipino nurses overseas, 1998–2016

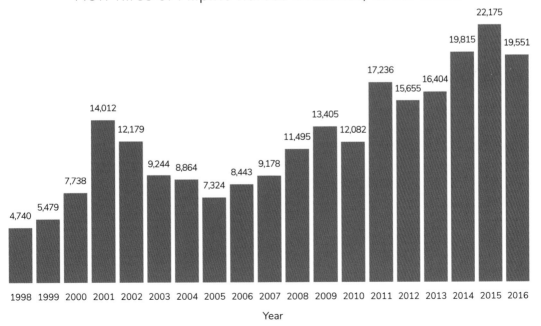

training at some 100 maritime schools that have been established for that purpose.

On the whole, the export of Filipino workers has been a success for the country, although, of course, it sometimes goes horribly wrong (see opposite). Enhancing the skills of intending overseas workers leads to better pay and conditions and increases the level of remittances. This has resulted in significant economic gains – seafarers alone contributed US$5.5 billion to the Philippine economy in remittances in 2016. Rather than being seen as a brain drain, OFWs are seen as a national asset and praised for the sacrifices they are making for their families and country. There are certain tax exemptions available to OFWs and tax-friendly schemes to encourage them to invest in business opportunities in the Philippines as well as supporting their families.

Top: Philippine nurses complete a training course in the Japanese language.

Above: Training Filipinos for domestic work, 2013. All Filipino household workers on official schemes for overseas work have to be accredited.

The case of Flor Contemplacion

Flor Ramos Contemplacion was a 42-year-old Filipina domestic worker executed in Singapore for murder in 1995. Her execution severely strained relations between Singapore and the Philippines, despite the many safeguards built into the labour contracts agreed by the two governments.

The case involved another Filipina domestic worker and a 3-year-old boy in her care who were both found dead. Although there was no direct evidence linking Contemplacion to their deaths, she confessed – perhaps because she was tortured by police or was experiencing a mental breakdown. During the course of the investigation, she had manifested a number of bizarre medical symptoms following a seizure.

As the legal proceedings continued, many Filipinos became increasingly convinced that Contemplacion was innocent or insane and became furious with their own government for offering her minimal consular protection and support. Her trials and tribulations were depicted in a number of documentaries and in a prize-winning film. President Ramos and his wife were slow to sense the mood of the country, though they ultimately called Contemplacion "a heroine".

Ramos's relative indifference to Contemplacion's fate left the political field open to Rodrigo Duterte, then the mayor of Davao City, who publicly burned the Singapore flag and led protests. His assiduous cultivation of the OFWs and lavish praise of their contribution to the country played an important part in later elevating Duterte to the presidency of the country. His image now appears on the OFW identity card.

Above: Official poster of the *Flor Contemplacion Story*. The film, directed by Joel Lamangan and starring Nora Aunor, won the best picture in the Cairo Film Festival in 1995.

26

The Trade in Sex Workers

The trade in sex workers is part of the more general phenomenon of human trafficking, involving supplying unpaid or low-paid household workers (this is called domestic servitude), forced labourers (working in fields, factories or workshops) and those destined for sex work, with whom we are principally concerned here.

Although we know the profits in human trafficking are very large, estimates vary greatly. In 2014, the International Labour Office assessed the annual profits from all forms of human trafficking at US$150 billion.[1]

The Natasha trade

Regarding sex workers in particular, for decades the primary source of supply was Asia, particularly from Thailand and the Philippines, but the collapse of the Soviet Union opened up a new source of workers. Alluding to the popular Russian name, this is colloquially known as "the Natasha trade". Donna M. Hughes argues that as the independent states emerged from the disintegration of the Soviet Union, they lacked the organizational capacity and regulatory agencies to tackle criminal conduct, allowing trafficking for sex to flourish.[2] The dominance of "Natashas" is particularly evident in Israel, where 70 per cent of female

Number and type of forced labourers including sex workers, 2014

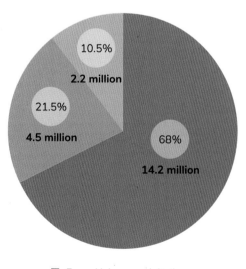

10.5%
2.2 million

21.5%
4.5 million

68%
14.2 million

- Forced labour exploitation
- Forced sexual exploitation
- State imposed forced labour

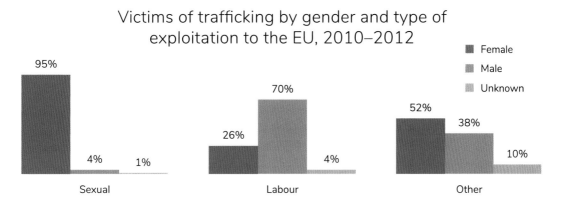

Victims of trafficking by gender and type of exploitation to the EU, 2010–2012

Female
Male
Unknown

95%
4%
1%
Sexual

70%
26%
4%
Labour

52%
38%
10%
Other

The "other" category include recruitment for forced begging, selling of children and forced marriage.

prostitutes are thought to be Russian, a number driven by strong diaspora connections and easy entry to the country, provided a Jewish origin can be plausibly claimed.

Although children and men are also trafficked for sexual purposes, women are overwhelmingly in the majority. This is in marked contrast to labour exploitation, which is dominated by men.

The story of Natalie

Natalie was born in Southeast Asia but lived in New Zealand. When she was 20 years old, she moved to the city, with her daughter. "That's when my life changed forever", she said. Her subsequent journeys show a mix of naiveté and exploitation as she struggled to escape the sex industry,

She was living rough for a while but managed to get a job in a Japanese factory and a place in a hostel. One night she was taken to dinner with a man and his friend, who took her to a "hotel". That turned out to be an illegal brothel. She ended up moving to Australia where she continued to be exploited, though this time in a legal brothel. (Brothels are legal in New South Wales under provisions of the Summary Offences Act, 1988.) She continues her story in her own words.

"Australia was worse than my home country. I was told when I got to Sydney that I had a debt of AU$6,000 plus commission per job, plus rent, plus transport, plus cleaning, and everything else they charged for. If you were five minutes late they charged you $50. It all adds up. And this was in a 'legal' brothel. I could not say no to clients – no way! I couldn't even stop and sit for a minute. I had to do it as many times in one hour as the client could do it. Three months felt like 30 years. We could sleep for maybe three hours a night, starting work at noon, finishing at 6 a.m. Eventually, I managed to run away from there too.

"I was in the sex industry for seven years, on and off. I wanted to leave for a long time. For three years I tried to get another job to support me and my daughter."[3]

Attempts to control the trade

Early attempts to control sex trafficking were highly racialized and, as Laura Lammasniemi explains, constructed around a narrative involving evil foreign men from "the Barbary Coast" (today's Morocco, Algeria, Tunisia and Libya) capturing and enslaving innocent white women.[4] In August 1885, tens of thousands of people attended a rally in Hyde Park, London, and demanded that "white slavery" be outlawed and the age of consent for girls be raised. A series of treaties adopted the racial trope, including the International Agreement for the Suppression of the White Slave Traffic in 1904. The term "white slavery" disappeared in international law in 1921, when the International Convention to Combat the Traffic in Women and Children was passed.

Contemporary attempts to regulate sex trafficking culminated in a UN Convention adopted in 2000 known, in short, as the Palermo Protocol, and signed by 171 states. The definition included "at a minimum, the exploitation of the prostitution of others or other forms of sexual exploitation, forced labour or services, slavery or practices similar to slavery, servitude or the removal of organs". Members were asked to make the provisions of the Palermo Protocol criminal offenses in their own legislation. With many variations, that has taken place. Crucially, the Palermo Protocol discounted the consent of the victim if force, the threat of force, and any means of coercion, including abduction, fraud, deceit, the abuse of power or giving or receiving payments were involved. The question of choice, consent or agency continues to dominate debates concerning sex trafficking.

The question of agency

There was no doubt in the minds of the Victorian crowd in Hyde Park that white women were taken by force by Barbary slavers – anything else would be unthinkable. Nowadays there is a more sophisticated understanding of who sex workers are, and how to understand the complicated relationship between choice and victimization. For a start, there are many women for whom sex work is not the first source of income. "They may work as waitresses, hairdressers, tailors, massage girls, street vendors, or beer promotion girls and supplement their income by selling sex on a regular basis or occasionally. They do not consider themselves as sex workers and often work outside of known venues for sex work."[5]

Again, there are a significant number of studies that show a high level of informed choice. A study of 100 Vietnamese sex workers in Cambodia found only six who had been duped – the remaining 94 knew that they were being recruited for work in a brothel. After they were freed by "rescue" organizations, the women "returned to their brothel as quickly as possible".[6] Similar findings have been reported in Europe. For example, a study of 72 East European sex workers in Holland found that few had been forcibly trafficked and most had been recruited by friends, acquaintances and even family.[7] While it may be thought that agency is demonstrated in the cases discussed, the important point to grasp is that the criminal offence of sex trafficking may have none-the-less occurred if the *means* involved to recruit sex workers involved coercion or fraud.

Above: Lithographs and paintings reinforced stereotyped assumptions about Barbary Coast white slavery. This painting by Ernest Normand was exhibited in 1885.

THE TRADE IN SEX WORKERS

27
Exiles
Dying Abroad or Returning to Power

The idea of "exile" as a poignant and painful form of migration has its roots in the biblical story of the expulsion of Adam and Eve from the Garden of Eden. To be forced to leave one's home was also a woeful fate decreed by rulers and assemblies in ancient Greece.

———

Subsequently, a similar misfortune befell numerous political figures, dissenters and military leaders in many countries. The fate of these exiles varied greatly. Some adjusted to their new lives abroad, some languished and died unhappy, some triumphantly returned to lead their countries.

Ancient Greece

In Athens, "ostracism", which has passed into our general vocabulary, was devised as a grave punishment. Someone who was seen to threaten society was banished from the city for 10 years, before being allowed to return. Among the more famous people who were ostracized were Themistocles, Cimon and Aristides the Just. Those who were ostracized should be distinguished from voluntary exiles like Solon the lawgiver who voluntarily exiled himself after drafting the city's constitution so he could not be pressured to change it.

Perhaps the most famous exile of ancient Greece was the philosopher and political theorist, Aristotle, who had founded the Lyceum school in Athens where he studied, taught and wrote. He went into voluntary exile in response to anti-Macedonian sentiments with which he was assumed to disagree. (He had spent seven years at the Macedonian court, though it is almost certainly a myth that he taught Alexander the Great of Macedonia.) For the rest of his life, Aristotle lived in his family home in the city of Chalcis.[1]

The meaning of exile

At an individual level, the key nature of the punishment is that the exiled person's connection to home – the material building, loved ones, family, community and a familiar environment – is suddenly ruptured. This form of emotional deprivation can be every bit as traumatic as physical punishment or

imprisonment. The Italian poet Dante described the pain of exile in *The Divine Comedy* (Paradiso XVII: 55–60):

You will leave everything you love most:
this is the arrow that the bow of exile
shoots first. You will know how salty
another's bread tastes and how hard it
is to ascend and descend
another's stairs

Exile of their political opponents has also commonly been used by rulers as a means of excluding them from power without turning them into martyrs, around whom popular protest and another leader espousing a similar cause might galvanize. This often works. Some 150,000 French people were expelled or went into voluntary exile in the wake of the successful French Revolution of 1789, constituting "the first instance of political emigration on a European, if not indeed a global, scale".[2]

Above: *Dante in esilio (Dante in exile)* by Domenico Peterlini, circa 1860.

Famous exiles

Napoleon Bonaparte

After his military defeat, the French Emperor Napoleon Bonaparte, was sent into exile on the Mediterranean island of Elba in 1813. In March 1815, he managed to escape and wrest back power, but he was defeated again at Waterloo and exiled again. This time the British victors were taking no chances and he was exiled to the remote island of St Helena in the South Atlantic, where he died, aged 52 on 5 May 1821. He probably succumbed to stomach cancer, but there has been a persistent story in France that he was poisoned with arsenic by his English jailers at his house on St Helena.[3]

Leon Trotsky

Of the remarkable leaders of the Russian Revolution in 1917, Trotsky was, perhaps, the most extraordinary. When the revolution nearly collapsed under the weight of its internal enemies and their external allies, Trotsky founded and led the Red Army, which finally triumphed in 1922. Trotsky was not only an outstanding military commander, he was a lucid writer, agitator and

Map of St Helena, from c.1820, showing the area where Napoleon was allowed to ride unrestricted

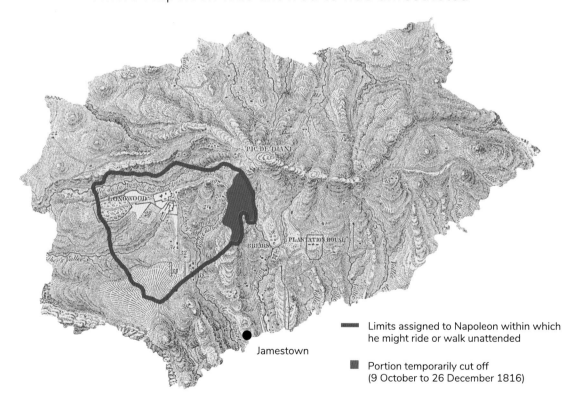

Jamestown

▬▬▬ Limits assigned to Napoleon within which he might ride or walk unattended

■ Portion temporarily cut off (9 October to 26 December 1816)

EXILES: DYING ABROAD OR RETURNING TO POWER

speaker. When Lenin died in 1924, Stalin edged Trotsky out of the key roles in the Communist Party and forced him into exile in Mexico.

Trotsky refused to stay quiet, denounced the Stalinist bureaucracy and the many failings of the revolution. He became the head of the Fourth International, which expressed, as he saw it, a more authentic revolutionary tradition. His followers, declaring themselves to be Trotskyists, grew in number and Stalin decided to silence his opponent forever. On his instructions, a Russian agent, Ramón Mercader, infiltrated Trotsky's household, posing as a friend, and assassinated him with an ice axe on 21 August 1940.

Vladimir Lenin

Like his fellow revolutionary Trotsky, Lenin spent a long time in exile, though before the revolution they both helped to make. He was exiled by the Tsarist regime to eastern Siberia for three years before leaving for London, Bern, Prague, Munich and Geneva, writing revolutionary tracts in each place. He flitted back to Russia to connect with revolutionary circles then scurried back to exile.

Finally, he seized the moment, leaving Zurich by train in April 1917 with 31 comrades. They crossed the Baltic Sea by ferry, then undertook an onward journey by rail from Stockholm to a remote corner of Sweden, bordering Finland. Horse-drawn sleds and a further train journey took him to St Petersburg. There he made a series of incendiary speeches, culminating in the resounding call, "Power to the Soviets".

Lenin's return from exile to lead the Bolshevik Revolution

■ By train
▨ By ferry

Haparanda
Tornio
Tampere
Stockholm
Helsinki
St Petersburg (Petrograd)
Moscow
Trelleborg
Sassnitz
Rostock
Berlin
Warsaw
Prague
Vienna
Kiev
Zurich
Munich
Budapest

Above: Police display the murder weapon used in Trotsky's death, Coyoacán, Mexico City, Mexico, 1940.

EXILES: DYING ABROAD OR RETURNING TO POWER

28

The Politics of Cold War Migration

The Cold War is generally considered to have begun in 1946, with escalating tensions between the Soviet Union and the West following the Second World War. It ended, at least formally, in 1991, with the collapse of the communist regimes in the Soviet Union and Eastern Europe, though some of the contemporary manifestations of Russian power carry echoes of the Cold War.

———

So far as migration is concerned, the character and scale of the process were not primarily shaped by the normal demographic, economic and social determinants but by political considerations, which inhibited emigration from the communist regimes and permitted a selective open-door policy on the part of a number of western countries. The migration barriers between East and West Germany were particularly notable and came to symbolize the overall character of the Cold War.

The defectors

Perhaps one of the most telling political taunts made of the communist regimes was that they forbade the free emigration of their citizens who, it was argued, were trapped by the communist leaderships against their wills. The riposte was, generally, not very convincing – the West was luring them with promises of

fame and money, or that would-be emigrants were involved in sensitive scientific or military projects, which would endanger the motherland.

Although at first the numbers involved were small, the political kudos the West gained by parading prominent "defectors" was considerable. The newspapers and other media lavished attention on the "escapes" of ballet stars such as Rudolf Nureyev, Mikhail Baryshnikov, Natalia Makarova and Alexander Godunov. The chess grandmaster Viktor Korchnoi defected as did Boris Spassky, though the latter sought to depoliticize his emigration to France. Sports people, intellectuals, gymnasts and the MiG-25 pilot, Viktor Belenko, followed.

It did not always go so smoothly in the case of all defectors, who included Joseph Stalin's own daughter, Svetlana Alliluyeva. She asked for, and received, political asylum in the USA in 1967, returned to the Soviet Union in 1984 and then abandoned her mother country again. She was clearly a complicated and troubled person who was not acting out of a single political motive. Perhaps it did not help her state of mind that her mother, Nadezhda, shot herself in the head in 1932 following a public disagreement with Stalin.

Above: Rudolf Nureyev at ballet rehearsal in 1970, nine years after his defection.

Opposite: Svetlana Alliluyeva, daughter of Joseph Stalin, on Long Island after seeking political asylum in the USA, 1967.

A second nonconforming example is the Nobel Laureate, Aleksandr Solzhenitsyn, famous for his excoriating exposure of the Soviet labour camps. He was expelled from the Soviet Union in 1974, only to return to Russia 20 years later. While in the West, Solzhenitsyn did not articulate the expected narrative. At a commencement speech at Harvard, he criticized the USA, among other things, for its "lack of manliness", "hasty capitulation" in the Vietnam War, intolerable music and unfettered press.[1]

The refuseniks

A group known as "refuseniks" challenged the restrictions of emigration from within the Soviet Union. In 1978, Vladimir and Maria Slepak displayed a banner protesting that for eight

Right: Soviet passport with an Israeli immigration visa, 1966.

Opposite above: Aleksandr Solzhenitsyn, with his family, on arrival in Zurich after he had left the Soviet Union.

Opposite below: Vladimir and Maria Slepak, prominent refuseniks, in Moscow, 1987.

years they had been refused a visa to join their son in Israel. For his pains, Vladimir and another activist, Ida Nudel, were arrested, charged with malicious hooliganism and sent to Siberia for several years. The Slepaks eventually ended up in Israel.

After communist control ended in 1989, the protests of the refuseniks were heard and the trickle became a flood. By 2006, about 1.6 million Soviet Jews had left the former Soviet Union. Most, over 60 per cent, migrated to Israel where the Law of Return, guaranteeing admission to Israel for Jews, was often extended to non-Jewish spouses or relatives of a Jewish immigrant. Some 325,000 migrated to the USA while, perhaps surprisingly in the light of the Holocaust, 219,000 migrated to Germany. The German government granted residence and work permits to Jews from the former Soviet Union and, again, applied a generous definition of Jewishness – only one parent had to be Jewish.

The Mariel boat lift

One of the most graphic Cold War encounters hinged around the Cuban Revolution, which started in July 1953 and ended with the replacement on 1 January 1959 of General Fulgencio Batista, who was closely allied to the USA, with a revolutionary socialist state led by Fidel Castro. As the revolution gained ground, emigrants left Cuba in considerable numbers. Many Cubans settled in Miami, 402km (250 miles) north of Cuba's capital, Havana.

A highly publicized surge in Cuban emigration arose from what was called the Mariel boat lift when Castro suddenly proclaimed on 20 April 1980 that "the revolution is voluntary" and anyone who cared to leave was free to do so from Mariel harbour. Some 125,000 took advantage of the offer. In the USA, the arrival of family members in tiny vessels was, at first, played out as a great victory demonstrating the superiority of the capitalist West.

THE POLITICS OF COLD WAR MIGRATION

There was, however, more than one sting in the tail. The sudden arrival of the "Marelitos", many of whom were unskilled, led to a drop in the wages of low-skilled locals, who were often African Americans,[2] and to consequent inter-community tensions. Moreover, media reports suggested that the Cuban government had taken the opportunity to empty inmates from jails and mental health institutions. Subsequent investigations suggested that only a small percentage were common criminals, though a larger number encouraged to leave were seen as guilty of "dangerous behaviour" – including public displays of homosexuality, which the regime did not tolerate.

Instead of being met by loving families, some Marelitos were sent to refugee camps, while 1,700 were jailed pending deportation hearings for violating US immigration laws, including having prior criminal convictions. But where were they to go, given that Cuba did not want them back? Eventually, the detainees were released or found sponsors. A 1981 Gallup poll showed that Americans placed Cubans at the bottom of a list of least-desirable neighbours, beaten only by members of a religious cult.

Cold War conflicts were often framed in personal terms, and many Americans believed that Fidel Castro had "pulled a fast one" on President Jimmy Carter. This contributed to a loss in confidence in his leadership and to the election in 1981 of Ronald Reagan, who immediately restored the Cold War rhetoric aimed at the Soviet Union and Cuba.

Left: Cuban refugees leaving the port of Mariel in Cuba.

29
Global Diasporas

The original Greek word "diaspora" evokes the dispersal or scattering of seeds. In human migration, the idea of a diaspora initially implied the forcible movement of a population (usually defined in ethnic or religious terms) to many destinations.

Because of the trauma of their displacement, a diasporic population tended to long for "home" (often a romanticized version of it) and saw its fate as linked to members of the same diaspora dispersed to other places. By the end of the 1980s, the word had expanded to include not only those who experienced forcible dispersion (designated a "victim diaspora") but also others, which were classified as labour, trade, de-territorialized, and imperial diasporas.[1] All but the last subtype are discussed below and, in some cases, the focus is on one ethnic group.

Victim diasporas

Much of the original discourse about diasporas stems from the destruction of the Temple of Solomon in 586 BC by the Mesopotamian King Nebuchadnezzar, and the forcible removal of the leadership and prominent members of Judean society to Babylon. Even though Jewish life survived and even thrived for centuries, the word "Babylon" became a code word for exile,

Above: Fanciful fifteenth-century depiction of the destruction of the Temple of Solomon in Jerusalem in 586 BC by King Nebuchadnezzar II's troops. Many Jews were taken in chains to his capital, Babylon.

The Armenian Genocide, 1915–1923

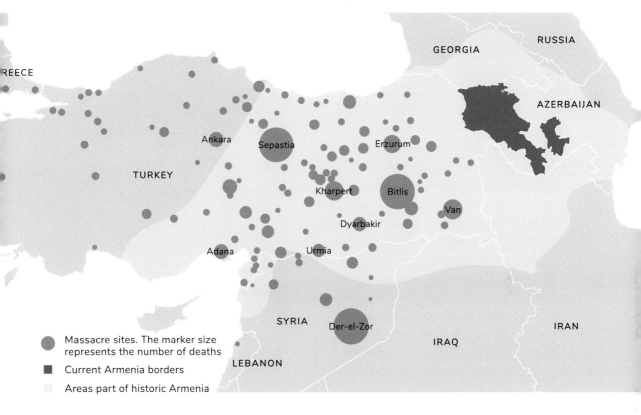

Massacre sites. The marker size represents the number of deaths

Current Armenia borders

Areas part of historic Armenia

estrangement and displacement, an antonym for the word "Zion", the place of home and contentment. This meaning was explicit in the lyrics of a 1978 hit song by the Caribbean group Boney M called "The Rivers of Babylon", and derived from the biblical Psalms 137 and 19. The opening lines of the song are:

By the rivers of Babylon, there we sat down
Ye-eah we wept, when we remembered Zion

The African diaspora recalled Atlantic slavery as the traumatic event that brought their diaspora into being. Echoing the spiritual connection with biblical Jews, Jamaican Rastafarians describe their island as "Babylon". Other victim diasporas evoke comparable events in their histories. For the Irish it is the Great Famine (see Chapter 11), for the Armenians the massacres of 1915–16 by Turkish troops (see map above). For the Palestinians the foundational ordeal is the *Nakba* ("catastrophe") of 1948, when 700,000 Palestinian Arabs fled the emerging state of Israel (see Chapter 16).

Above: Successive Turkish governments have bitterly denied that the forced relocation of Armenians to Syria and Palestine can be described as genocide. Armenians in the diaspora have mounted a relentless war of words to affirm the description. By 2017, governments and parliaments of 29 countries, as well as 48 of the 50 US states, had recognized the events of 1915–23 as genocide.

Labour diasporas: Italians

Compared with other West European countries, Italian migration started later, but persisted for much longer and was considerably greater in volume. According to Rudolph Vecoli, over the 100-year period, 1876–1976, some 26 million people left, "giving Italy the dubious honour of having registered a larger number of emigrants than any other country".[2] They travelled or migrated permanently to other parts of Europe, to North and South America (particularly over the years 1876–1915) and also established a significant community in Australia. There are few adult Italians who do not have family members abroad or have a migrant experience themselves.

Not only are there enormous cultural and geographical gulfs separating different parts of the country, unification as a nation-state came late to Italy by comparison with its European neighbours. This meant that, in addition to international migration, internal migration from less to more developed parts of the country was common – some 9 million of the country's total of 45 million moved from the south to the north between 1945 and 1975. Their movement reflected both the shattered war economy and the lack of opportunities in the rural areas of the south. Naturally, given the very large numbers involved, not everyone moved for the same reason, but most moved to sell their labour, even if their ultimate aim was to set up on their own.

What made those who moved abroad a "diaspora" were the strong links retained with "home" over generations. "Home" needs to be understood in a distinctively Italian way. It

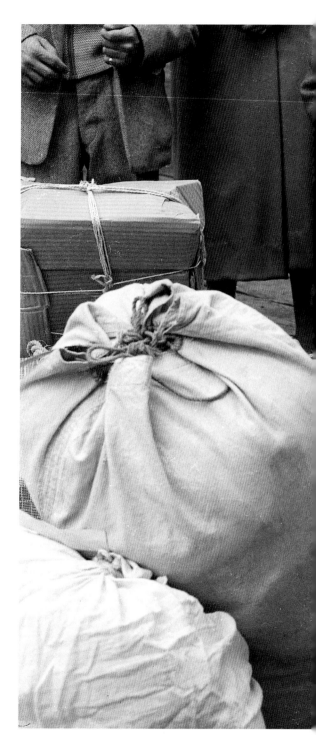

Right: Italian migrants at Circular Quay, Sydney, after arriving on the ship *Flaminia*, March 1960.

did not generally refer to the country at large, which remains rather fragmented, but to webs of transnational connections between migrants and their particular *paese* (village) or *patria* (hometown). The Italian love of a small locality is poetically described as *campanilismo*, a word meaning "attachment to one's own bell tower". It is therefore more accurate, as Donna Gabaccia has argued, to speak not of a single Italian diaspora but of multiple diasporas.[3]

Trade diasporas: Lebanese

One of the famous trade diasporas is that of the Lebanese, with putative roots in the Phoenician seafarers and traders who spread across the Mediterranean between 1550BC and 300 BC. The Lebanese diaspora included people

Left: A Lebanese peddler in Birmingham, Alabama, in 1917. He would have been described as a "Syrian" at the time, because Lebanon was once a province of Greater Syria.

Opposite: Steel-band players. The instrument was fashioned in Trinidad using discarded oil drums and spread to other Caribbean islands and to Caribbean communities in Europe, often marking the carnival season.

The Lebanese in the world, principal destinations

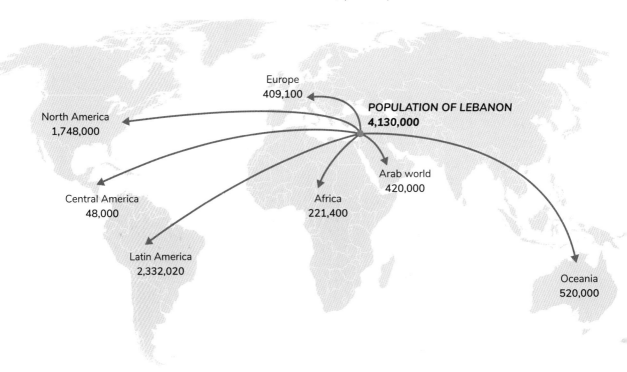

Europe
409,100

North America
1,748,000

POPULATION OF LEBANON
4,130,000

Central America
48,000

Arab world
420,000

Africa
221,400

Latin America
2,332,020

Oceania
520,000

from a range of religious and occupational backgrounds emigrating for various purposes to Africa, Arabia, Europe, Australia and the Americas. While there was no single cause for their departure, the disruption of trade patterns in the Middle East arising from the opening of the Suez Canal in 1869, is believed to be an important precipitant. Most had little capital and started out as petty traders. As the reputed Lebanese historian Albert Hourani recounts:

> The stereotype of the Lebanese newly arrived in North or South America is that of the pedlar, walking the roads from one village to another with his load of fancy goods or hardware carried on his back or on a pack animal. This was not the only way of entering the new life, but it was common enough to serve as an authentic image of the newly arrived immigrant.[4]

Those who were successful went into the retail or wholesale trade and established powerful economic niches in several countries. Some went into politics. Over the last two decades, people of Lebanese descent have become heads of state in Colombia, Ecuador (twice), Honduras, Argentina, Belize and Jamaica.[5]

Deterritorialized diasporas: the Black Atlantic

Paul Gilroy advanced the idea of a Black Atlantic to describe the complex cultural interactions that take place between African and African-diasporic populations in oceanic space, across, as he pithily put it, the waves and airwaves.[6] African sounds and rhythms, tastes and languages, crossed the Atlantic with slavery, diffused across the Caribbean and Brazil, and re-crossed to Europe and Africa in the form of reinvented cultures and traditions borne by migrants and travellers, and now also through digital connections. The movement of different genres of music, including Highlife, Calypso, Soca, Zouk, Oldschool Jungle, Dancehall, Dub and Reggae, provide a few good examples.

The consequence is a complex and partial rupture from conventional territorial reference points. The incomplete process of deracination together with the embrace of modernity, hybridity and creolization, has led to a form of double consciousness for African and African-descended migrants. To plot this shift in consciousness, as this adage by Gilroy has it, it is more important to understand routes than roots.

30
Migration to the Gulf

The Gulf countries are generally understood to be the seven Arab states that border the Persian Gulf – Bahrain, Iraq, Kuwait, Oman, Qatar, Saudi Arabia and the United Arab Emirates (UAE). They also happen to be where fabulous oil reserves have been found.

While it is true that the fossil economy is on the wane as green technologies kick in, the world still needs oil, and a lot of it. The profits from oil, which were massively accelerated after a fivefold increase in the price of oil after 1973, have fuelled massive infrastructural development in the Gulf states. Historically, a few hundred Indian pearl divers were recruited for seasonal work along the Gulf coastline. By the 1980s, millions of contract workers, generally from Asia, were hard at work building roads, hospitals, apartment blocks, schools, stadiums and public buildings – everything that a modern state could want.

So large is the volume of imported workers that in a number of the Gulf countries the number of migrant workers exceeds the indigenous population, sometimes by a large margin. The most dramatic case is the UAE where, in 2015, 89 per cent of the total population of 9.3 million were migrant workers, mostly unskilled labourers from Asia.

While the spectacular cities rising from the desert are there for all to see, social and political life have become distorted in a number of less obvious ways. Tribal societies have mutated into modern oligarchies based primarily on citizenship. Employment in the public sector is largely reserved for locals, with migrants

Opposite: Migrant contract workers in the UAE.

The proportion of nationals to non-nationals in six of the seven Gulf countries

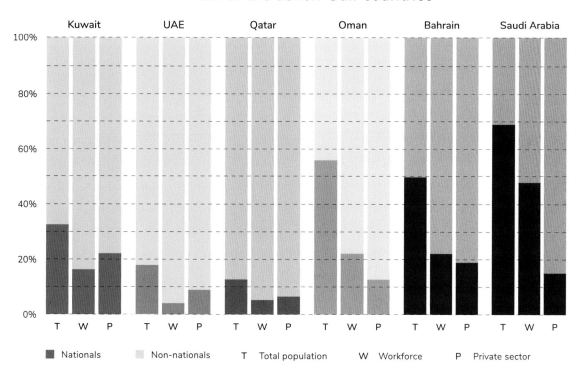

Nationals ■   Non-nationals   T   Total population   W   Workforce   P   Private sector

dominating the private sector. Wealth cascades to the political leadership and accrues also to the citizenry, while contract workers have to take what they are offered – more, to be sure than they can get at home, but only a small fraction of the income and privileges enjoyed by the citizenry. With few exceptions, contract workers are firmly cut off from access to permanent residency and citizenship.

The politics of recruitment

As the building boom commenced, the Gulf countries turned away workers from nearby Arab countries. This was to avoid opening the doors to fellow Muslims and Arabs who might exercise their claims to citizenship and social security payments, and bring their wives and families with them. Gulf state leaders were particularly resistant to recruiting Palestinian workers who, they reasoned, would drag them into the protracted Israeli-Palestinian struggle. Expressing occasional solidarity with the Palestinians was one thing, but taking on the Israelis, who were so closely allied to their customers, was bad for the oil business.

Turning to Asia made economic sense – Asian workers were cheap and could be offered limited work contracts (usually three years).

Migrant deaths in the Gulf states

When Qatar was awarded the contract to host the FIFA 2022 World Cup, massive construction works commenced, involving 800,000 migrant workers, many of whom were expected to work in the scorching heat. The outcome has been disastrous. One investigation in 2014 claimed that Nepalese migrants constructing infrastructure for the games were dying at a rate of one every two days.[1] Another report, published by the International Trade Union Confederation in September 2017, claimed that since the award of the World Cup contract in 2010 approximately 1,200 workers had died.[2]

For purposes of comparison, the highest number of deaths previously recorded in building the facilities for big sporting events were from the 2014 Winter Olympics at Sochi (60 deaths) and the 2004 Athens Olympics, with 40 killed. Ten workers died in the build-up to the 2010 Beijing Olympics and seven were killed while building the stadiums and other facilities for the 2014 Brazil World Cup. There were no fatalities recorded in the construction of the 2012 Olympics in London.[3]

Nor are migrant deaths confined to Qatar. Using an Indian government Right to Information law, in a report published in November 2018 campaigners in India revealed that 24,570 Indian workers had died in Gulf countries since 2012. They calculated that over the six years covered by the report, an average of more than 10 Indian workers had died every day in six Gulf countries. Saudi Arabia recorded the most deaths at 10,416 while Bahrain, at 1,317, had the fewest.[4] The Qatari government suggested that more than 80 per cent of the deaths of Indians working on the World Cup buildings and infrastructure could be attributed to natural causes. Given that the Indian work force comprised fit young men, it would seem that exhaustion and dehydration are regarded as natural causes.

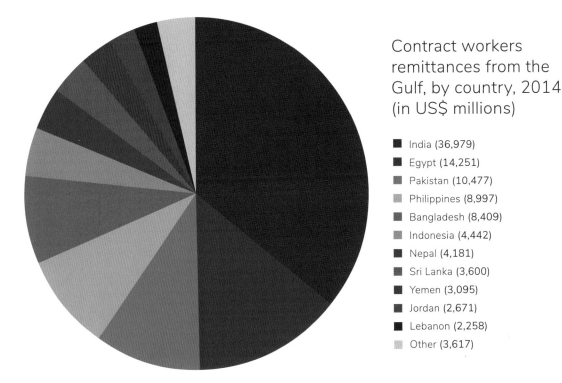

Contract workers remittances from the Gulf, by country, 2014 (in US$ millions)

- India (36,979)
- Egypt (14,251)
- Pakistan (10,477)
- Philippines (8,997)
- Bangladesh (8,409)
- Indonesia (4,442)
- Nepal (4,181)
- Sri Lanka (3,600)
- Yemen (3,095)
- Jordan (2,671)
- Lebanon (2,258)
- Other (3,617)

However, the decisions about where to recruit were primarily political. Although some historical recruitment from Egypt persisted, the new supply of labour was rapidly shifted to India, Pakistan, Bangladesh, Sri Lanka, the Philippines, Nepal and Indonesia.[5] Source countries could be rotated at whim and non-Muslims were sometimes preferred because they could not claim to be part of a worldwide *ummah* ("community").

The whole distasteful mechanics of recruitment could be outsourced to non-state actors through the *kafala* system. These labour brokers were often allied to the ruling families who collected fees from the workers (a tidy additional source of income) and guaranteed their good conduct. Using the *kafala* system allowed the authorities to hold migrant workers at arm's length. As the *kafala* system kept them isolated, the authorities rarely stepped in either to protect workers' rights, or to enforce health and safety regulations (see opposite).

Given the difficult and dangerous conditions facing contract workers in the Gulf, perhaps it is to be expected that the governments of source countries would be vigilant in protecting the interests of their citizens abroad. Except in the case of the Philippines and in a few other isolated cases, this protection has not materialized. The reasons are not difficult to find – where there are high levels of unemployment and poverty, it is difficult to intervene at the point of recruitment. Moreover, despite low wages, the collective remittances returned by workers to their countries provide significant flows of much-needed income and investment.

31
Mediterranean Migrations

For centuries the Mediterranean has been a crucial meeting point between travellers from the continents of Asia, Africa and Europe. Sea journeys of settlers to Crete date back 11,000 years. Perhaps the most visible signs of early cross-Mediterranean movements are the many Greek colonies such as Miletus, Ephesos, Smyrna, Cyme and Rhegium established along the edges of all three adjoining continents in the seventh and eighth centuries AD. Many tourists still explore the ruins of these settlements.

Less visible are the journeys of the Phoenicians, Semites from the eastern Mediterranean, who were renowned maritime traders by 1200–800 BC, even being described as "princes of sea" in the Bible. Though material evidence of Phoenicia outside its great cities of Byblos, Tyre and Sidon on the Levant is scant, there is at least one symbolically important residue of Phoenician dominance of the Mediterranean, namely the expression "Europa". Europa was the high-born mother of King Minos of Crete after whom the continent of Europe was named.

Cultural influences criss-crossed the Mediterranean from Greece, the Middle East and Africa. The Greek stories of Zeus, for example, were based on Cretan tales. While ancient Greece has often been depicted as the fount and heartland of western civilization,

there are strong links to non-European cultures. Though his work has been strongly disputed, Martin Bernal's three-volume work *Black Athena* adds African and Asiatic influences to the story of the origins and development of Greek civilization.[1] Bernal's work has been particularly well received by those seeking to document the movement of African ideas and people to Europe in ancient times. It is also relevant to remember that North Africa was intimately connected to southern Europe for centuries. The famous Carthaginian, Hannibal, crossed the Mediterranean with his African elephants, while Islamic invaders entered Spain, Portugal, South Italy and Malta from the eighth century. Their influence was only abated by forcible conversion or expulsion at the end of the fifteenth century.

Phoenician trade routes and colonies

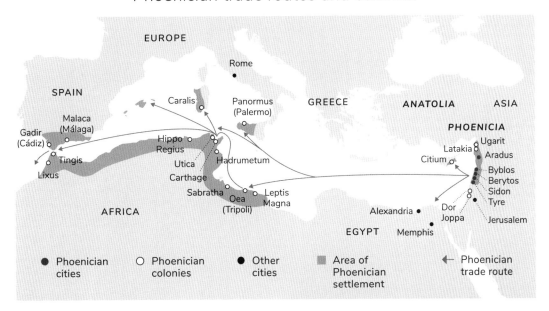

EUROPE

Rome

SPAIN

Gadir (Cádiz)
Malaca (Málaga)
Tingis
Lixus

Caralis
Panormus (Palermo)
Hippo Regius
Utica
Carthage
Hadrumetum
Sabratha
Oea (Tripoli)
Leptis Magna

AFRICA

GREECE

ANATOLIA

ASIA

PHOENICIA
Ugarit
Latakia
Aradus
Citium
Byblos
Berytos
Sidon
Tyre
Dor
Joppa
Jerusalem

Alexandria
EGYPT Memphis

● Phoenician cities   ○ Phoenician colonies   ● Other cities   ▨ Area of Phoenician settlement   ← Phoenician trade route

The sea of death

The movements of traders, settlers, scholars, missionaries, fisherfolk and warriors across the Mediterranean over many centuries generated perhaps one of the most influential works of history by the French scholar Fernand Braudel who, in his influential book, *La Méditerranée* (1949), argued that a single zone had emerged uniting the littorals around the sea, the islands within it and the sea itself. Slow environmental changes and long-term shifts in empires, civilizations and social structures had fashioned a panoramic, interlacing and complex sea of life.[2]

Braudel was interested in very long-term movements, rather than short-term fluctuations, but one suspects that he would

Right and following pages: Syrian refugees arrive on the island of Lesbos, Greece, having crossed the Aegean Sea from Turkey, 2015.

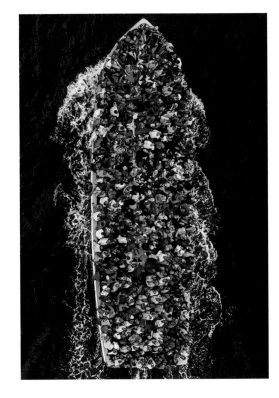

Recorded deaths, using International Organization of Migration data, 2014–19 (2019 figures between 1 January and 15 April)

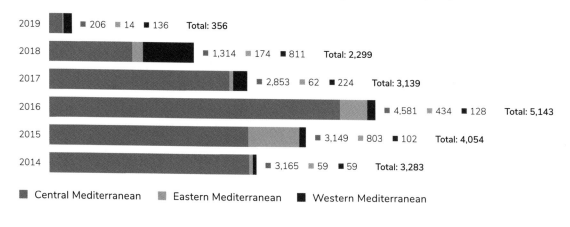

2019 ■ 206 ■ 14 ■ 136 Total: **356**

2018 ■ 1,314 ■ 174 ■ 811 Total: **2,299**

2017 ■ 2,853 ■ 62 ■ 224 Total: **3,139**

2016 ■ 4,581 ■ 434 ■ 128 Total: **5,143**

2015 ■ 3,149 ■ 803 ■ 102 Total: **4,054**

2014 ■ 3,165 ■ 59 ■ 59 Total: **3,283**

■ Central Mediterranean ■ Eastern Mediterranean ■ Western Mediterranean

Arrivals in Europe by sea, using UN Refugee Agency data, 2015–18

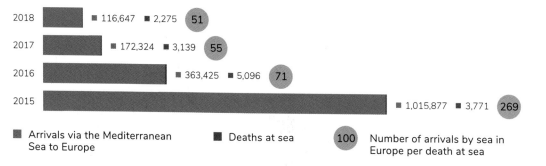

2018 ■ 116,647 ■ 2,275 **51**

2017 ■ 172,324 ■ 3,139 **55**

2016 ■ 363,425 ■ 5,096 **71**

2015 ■ 1,015,877 ■ 3,771 **269**

■ Arrivals via the Mediterranean Sea to Europe   ■ Deaths at sea   **100** Number of arrivals by sea in Europe per death at sea

be shocked at how comprehensively the sea of life has transmuted into a sea of death since 2014, as migrants from Africa and the Middle East frantically scramble to find security and opportunity by undertaking perilous boat journeys across the Mediterranean. The recorded deaths, often involving children, peaked in 2016, but still remain significant.

At first sight, it is difficult to understand why migrants would continue to attempt the sea crossing to Europe, often paying large sums to smugglers to facilitate their journeys. The answer lies partly in their desperation and partly in their calculations. For example, in the most hazardous year, 2018, of those who attempted to cross to Europe by sea, many were intercepted, but 116,647 were successful, and "only" 2 per cent died. Even one death is morally unacceptable, so the word "only" simply signifies how migrants might have assessed the risks they faced.

Ceuta: Spain in Africa

Ceuta is a small (18.5km² / 7 sq. miles) enclave on the north coast of Africa ceded to Spain in 1668. It is a short distance from the Spanish mainland across the Strait of Gibraltar and is surrounded by Morocco. Because it is Spanish, and so close to the mainland, African migrants see it as a means to enter Europe. All that separates the two jurisdictions is a 20ft (7m) fence laced with barbed wire.

The fence is regularly stormed, cut with bolt-cutters, or climbed by determined migrants. Dozens, and on some occasions hundreds, of migrants have broken through, but incursions have been contained by the defenders of "Fortress Europe" using both technical means and brute force. Motion detectors, spotlights and cameras quickly locate the migrants and they are, according to one report, "usually beaten back by policemen using sticks and fists".[3]

Even if migrants are able to scale or penetrate the fence, that is not the end of their troubles.

A detention centre in the hills has been established which, effectively, cages migrants for increasingly lengthy periods. As Ruben Andersson puts it:

> Temporality ... has become a multifaceted tool and vehicle – even a weapon of sorts – in the "fight" against illegal migration. ... Having finally breached the EU frontier, [migrants] thought fortune was smiling at them, yet here they would face a state of "stuckedness" every bit as despairing as that of Bamako or their home countries. This was so because Spain's North African enclaves were gaps in the border's landscape of time – liminal spaces with their own warped temporal logics. Yet in these gaps, the times of control and migration would also come to clash openly with each other.[4]

Below: From time to time migrants rush the fence separating Morocco from Spain.

32

Health Workers Worldwide

The demand for healthcare worldwide is on an exponential curve upwards. Poor people need healthcare interventions (infectious diseases and malaria are common), but so, too, do affluent populations as they succumb to the diseases of the rich (such as heart disease, cancer and diabetes).

———

Most people are conscious of advances in medicine and would like access to new drugs, advanced treatments and to loving care as they live into old age. To meet these rising expectations, there will have to be a significant increase in the supply of healthcare workers. One authoritative estimate is that by 2030 there will be a worldwide shortfall in excess of 4 million certified health workers (1.2 million doctors, 3.2 million nurses and over 70,000 midwives).[1]

The need for additional healthcare workers is demand-driven and universal, whatever the income-level of the country or the region, though there are particular shortfalls expected in the Americas and the Western Pacific (including Australia, Brunei, Cambodia, China and Japan.

Estimates of labour market demand (millions) for health workers, 2013 and 2030 (projected), covering 165 countries

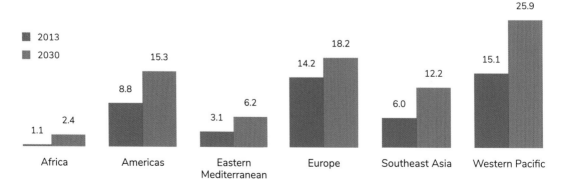

- 2013
- 2030

	Africa	Americas	Eastern Mediterranean	Europe	Southeast Asia	Western Pacific
2013	1.1	8.8	3.1	14.2	6.0	15.1
2030	2.4	15.3	6.2	18.2	12.2	25.9

Recruiting nurses in the UK for work abroad

An authoritative report issued in March 2019 suggested that, by 2029, the UK's National Health Service (NHS) will be short of 108,000 full-time equivalent nurses. Even filling half the demand would require 5,000 more nurses to start training each year by 2021, radically reducing the drop-out rate during training, and ensuring that more nurses actually join the NHS once they qualify. What makes these figures so stark is that in 2018 some 33,000 left the NHS, many leaving the healthcare profession altogether, some moving into the private sector, but a significant number also moving to work abroad. The international "portability" of UK nursing qualifications has meant that there is a constant out-migration of trained nurses and midwives for work abroad.

Many agencies are active in recruiting UK nurses and it is not difficult to spot what benefits they emphasize to support their advertising campaigns. For example, Medacs Healthcare suggests that nurses coming to Qatar will find limited shifts, modern hospitals, safety, friendliness and professionalism. The clear purpose of the pitch is to contrast conditions in Qatar with the understaffed and overworked conditions found in the NHS.

Another company, Jobs4Medical, asks, "If there seems to be little room for manoeuvre in your current workplace, then why not head somewhere where your skills will be more valued?" The company then spelled it out: "The current disillusionment clouding the NHS is prompting many professional nurses to do just that. Thousands of nurses have begun to look for jobs overseas, where working conditions and pay tend to be better."

A third site is nurses.co.uk, which advertises nursing vacancies in Australia, the Middle East, New Zealand, the United Arab Republic, the USA and Ireland. Those attracted to Australia are offered a sponsorship visa and "an excellent relocation package".[2]

Multi-directionality

Meeting the demand for healthcare workers is complicated by the multi-directionality of the flows with healthcare workers going from rich to poor, rich to rich and poor to rich countries. It is perfectly possible to imagine any one country working out its staffing needs for community practices and hospitals and training the appropriate numbers. However, the key problem in realizing this strategy is that medical certification has become increasingly portable – so, for instance, nurses trained in the UK or Australia can choose to work in Qatar or Saudi Arabia, and many do (see above). Migration agents often supply services to all comers. So, for example, a multi-located company called RPS, whose founder describes himself as a rock star of migration services, advertises on the same site that it places Australian nurses in other countries and "knows the best visa options" for experienced nurses or skilled workers wanting to work in Australia.[3]

The bulk of medical personnel move from low- and medium-income countries to high-income countries. According to the Organization of Economic Co-operation and Development (OECD), the 36 OECD countries (nearly all of them rich) have received the bulk of foreign-trained doctors, more than 200,000 of whom were working in the USA and the UK.

Supply-side issues

The supply of healthcare workers from poor countries to rich countries can cause enormous strains to the origin country's economy, though this varies greatly depending on the size of the country and its migration strategy. For example, despite having poor doctor–patient ratios, India and the Philippines produce doctors and nurses for export, judging that their remittance income will outweigh the cost of their training.

Elsewhere, the picture is much bleaker. In 2011, the overall loss in return from South Africa's investment in training doctors who have migrated to high-income countries was US$1.41 billion.[4] The loss of healthcare workers has been particularly difficult for a small country like Jamaica, which lost 41.4 per cent of its medical school graduates in 2001. Each year, Jamaica loses 8 per cent of its registered nurses and 20 per cent of its specialist nurses, most to the USA and UK. In 2003, the overall vacancy rate on the island for nurses had reached 58 per cent.[5] Another negative example is the case of Kenya where, according to data collected between 2009 and 2012, the number of Kenyan-born doctors working abroad was twice the number working in the country's public hospitals.

Opposite: A Senegalese doctor working in a cardiology unit in Vietnam.

Foreign-trained doctors working in the USA and UK, 2013 and 2014

United States, 2013

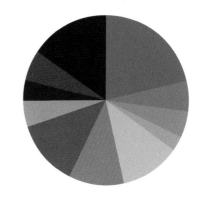

ASIA (48%)
- India (22%)
- Philippines (6%)
- Pakistan (5%)
- China (3%)
- Other Asia (11%)

- EU countries (10%)
- Caribbean islands (13%)
- Mexico (5%)
- Canada (4%)
- Africa (6%)
- Other (15%)

United Kingdom, 2014

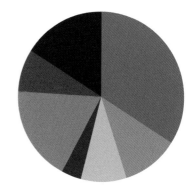

ASIA (54%)
- India (34%)
- Pakistan (11%)
- Other Asia (9%)

- Ireland (4%)
- Other EU countries (18%)
- Africa (8%)
- Other (16%)

Kenyan-born doctors working abroad

doctors graduate
every year from
Kenyan universities

the number of Kenyan-born doctors that work abroad
is twice as many as the doctors working in the national
referral hospitals and ministries of health

Kenyan doctors living abroad, 2000

2733
UK

865
USA

180
Canada

110
Australia

81
South Africa

6
Other

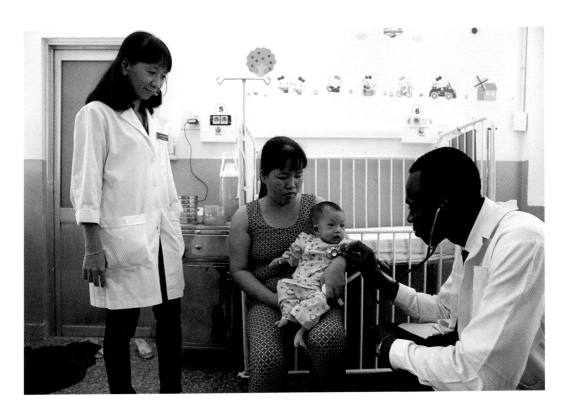

33
Syrian Refugees
The Lebanese Case

The war in Syria started in March 2011 when pro-democracy demonstrations in the southern city of Deraa were suppressed by the regime of President Assad. It is finally winding down some eight years later.

What was initially a civil war has turned into a multi-sided conflict involving Russia, Iran, Lebanon's Hezbollah movement, the USA, UK, France, Turkey, Saudi Arabia, Qatar and Kurdish forces and, until it was routed in eastern Syria in 2019, the Islamic State. For the people of Syria the outcome of the conflict has been devastating. Of the pre-war population of 22 million, nearly 55 per cent have been internally displaced or fled the borders of Syria.

Considering only those Syrians who left the country, most found themselves in neighbouring countries, particularly Turkey and Lebanon, but also Jordan and Iraq. Anyone reading much of the European press in 2015–16, during the height of the displacement crisis, might be forgiven for assuming that most of the Syrian refugees walked to Germany or came ashore on one of the Greek islands. This is not to minimize the extent of the emigration across the Mediterranean or along the land route through the eastern Balkans. Nor is it to disparage the political courage of Chancellor Merkel, who was

More than half of Syrians have been displaced since 2011

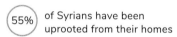

55% of Syrians have been uprooted from their homes

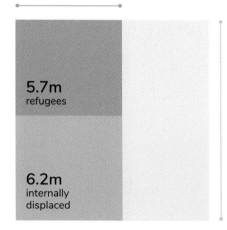

5.7m
refugees

6.2m
internally
displaced

22m
pre-war
population

aware that there was considerable opposition in Germany to extending an open door to Syrians. However, the volume and distribution of Syrians abroad in 2018 in the map opposite clearly shows how contiguous countries were in the front line.

Destination countries of Syrian refugees, up to December 2018

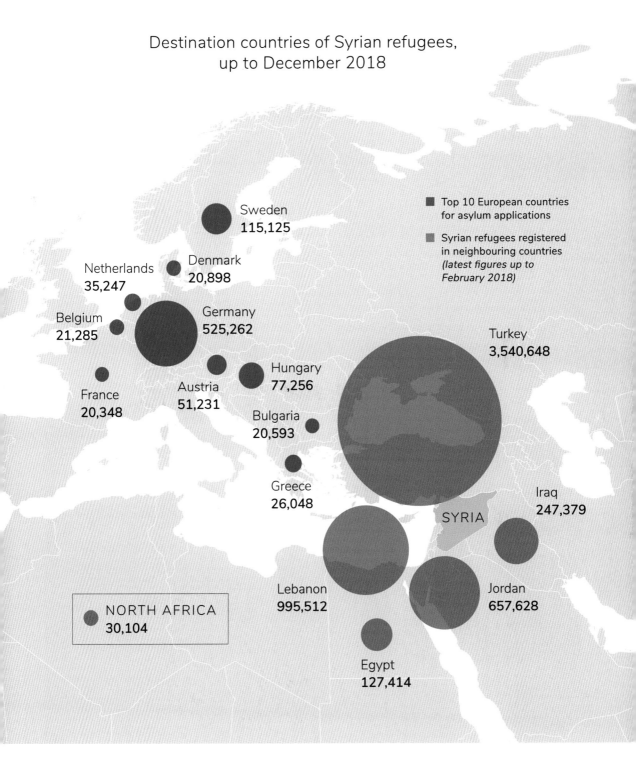

Sweden
115,125

Netherlands
35,247

Denmark
20,898

Belgium
21,285

Germany
525,262

France
20,348

Austria
51,231

Hungary
77,256

Bulgaria
20,593

Greece
26,048

Turkey
3,540,648

SYRIA

Iraq
247,379

Lebanon
995,512

Jordan
657,628

Egypt
127,414

NORTH AFRICA
30,104

■ Top 10 European countries
for asylum applications

■ Syrian refugees registered
in neighbouring countries
*(latest figures up to
February 2018)*

Syrians in Lebanon

Lebanon has hosted about one million Syrians fleeing to neighbouring countries, an astonishing one in six of its total population. For a country with complex multi-confessional splits (Sunni, Shia, Druze, Alawi, Ismaili, Maronite and Eastern Orthodox) and deep political divisions, the sudden arrival of so many Syrians threatened the precarious political and social order. Throughout the war, the political class has been riven, with about half the parliament aligning itself with President Assad of Syria, and half against him. Hezbollah, an armed Shia group based in Lebanon, crossed the frontier in support of Assad's troops. Refugees have also created a huge financial burden for the country.

Syrian refugees in Lebanon are found in many areas

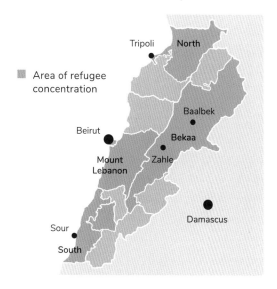

■ Area of refugee concentration

SYRIAN REFUGEES: THE LEBANESE CASE

At first sight, it is difficult to understand why Lebanon opened its borders so widely to Syrian refugees. This partly reflects the long historical relationship between the two countries. In Ottoman times, Lebanon was part of Greater Syria and there are continuing family and kinship links in many local areas. As Cameron Thibos explains, this has meant that 85 per cent of Syrians have been dispersed across the country, among some 1,600 communities. Only around 15 per cent (155,000) of Syrian refugees are located in tented camps and refashioned informal settlements.[1]

Although the Lebanese government has been praised for refusing to countenance tented camps, under the pressure of numbers some have been erected. Those in tents and elsewhere live precarious lives – most do not have residence rights and live in considerable poverty. In the Bekaa Valley, many Syrian refugee children are exploited as labourers, while young women have been pressured into early marriage or "survival sex" (exchanging sexual favours for goods or money) to avoid poverty.[2] About 300,000 children are not in school. Perhaps it is not surprising that, with somewhat more settled conditions returning to Syria, a steady stream of Syrians are returning home, regardless of the continuing danger.

Opposite: Syrians in a bus taking them home from Lebanon, January 2019.

Following pages: Syrian children play on a hillside above a refugee camp in Bar Elias in the Bekaa Valley, Lebanon, 12 March 2019. Most Syrians are not housed in tented camps.

Noha's Story

"Noha", a 40-year-old woman, has been living with her family in the Shatila camp in southern Beirut for three years, after escaping Syria in 2012. Shatila is a notable place in Lebanon's population history. It was founded as a refugee camp for Palestinians in 1949 and was the site of a notorious massacre of up to 3,500 civilians, mostly Palestinians and Lebanese Shias, by the Kataeb militia in 1982. Invading Israeli troops stood by while the massacre took place. Although Noha refers to it as a "camp", it is now an informal settlement with permanent structures laced with electric wires.

"Even though we were in poverty, we were happy. I never thought I'd be a refugee," Noha lamented. She had suffered verbal abuse and sexual harassment from Lebanese soldiers, complaining that "they touched the privacy of our bodies".

At the time of interview, Noha and her family had lived in Shatila for two and a half years with little access to healthcare, safety and basic needs. She looks after her seven children and her husband, who has had a stroke. With the help of a charity she opened a small shop selling flooring in Shatila to make money. Noha is concerned when her children go outside due to harassment and the electric wires.

She still reminisces about life in Syria: "In the village, we had a clean environment, clean bread; we planted our food and knew it was healthy. Our children were at home, not in the streets. Here, if they are late, we are worried … I feel unsafe in the camp."[3]

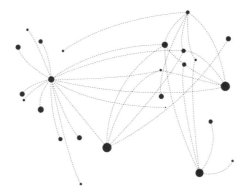

FOUR

Controversies
and Developments

34
Musical Roots and Routes

This book is about human migration, but in their hearts and heads people carry the sounds of their pasts. Sometimes they also travel with the instruments that replicate the resonances of their youth, so tracing the movement of music and instruments is often an indicative way of understanding migration flows.

———

Music is also made "on the move" and we are able to trace the changing styles and lyrics reflecting the new experiences that migrating people encounter, thus giving a texture and sense of their encounters, aspirations and difficulties. Here we draw mainly on African music on both the continent and in the African diaspora.

The movement of musical instruments

The xylophone
The difficulties associated with using the movement of instruments as a gauge of migration are twofold. There is always the possibility of simultaneous discovery, and only a small number of travelling musicians can generate a significant level of imitation. Nonetheless, ethnomusicologists have been able to map out broad areas signifying human movement or deep cultural interaction. Roger Blench, for example,

argues that the spread of the frame xylophone in Africa can be plotted from Senegal to Southern Mozambique and across much of West Africa. Gourds were utilized as resonators under each key, though occasionally cow horns were used instead of gourds. The similar ways in which the instruments were constructed and tuned, as well as playing techniques and the form of melodies, lend further support to the likelihood of diffusion through migration.[1]

Banjos
It is especially difficult to trace a single source for banjos, which are essentially drums with strings stretched out across them and are found in various configurations in the Far East, Africa and the Middle East. However, there is a clear record of a banjo-like instrument in the diaries of Richard Jobson, who explored the River Gambra (now called Gambia) in 1620 and described an instrument that was "made of a great gourd and

The spread of the xylophone in Africa

MALI NIGER CHAD
SENEGAL
THE GAMBIA
GUINEA-BISSAU GUINEA
BURKINA FASO
SIERRA LEONE GHANA NIGERIA
CÔTE CENTRAL SOUTH
D'IVOIRE AFRICAN SUDAN
LIBERIA REPUBLIC
CAMEROON
TOGO BENIN UGANDA
GABON CONGO KENYA
EQUATORIAL DR CONGO
GUINEA
TANZANIA
MALAWI
ANGOLA
MOZAMBIQUE
ZAMBIA
ZIMBABWE MADAGASCAR

- ▦ Frame xylophone,
  Western African style
- ▦ Frame xylophone,
  Central African style
- ■ Cow-horn resonator
  (North-east Nigeria)

a neck, thereunto was fastened strings"[2]. There is also documentary evidence of the re-creation of such instruments in African slave communities in the Caribbean and American South, which provided them with a means to retain some of their sense of dignity and cultural integrity.

The design of the banjo evolved in the Americas, with the gourd being replaced by the rounded wooden belly, and a fifth string being added to the original four. In this form, the banjo was adopted as a "white" instrument, spread by white minstrels parodying blacks, and later by bluegrass musicians in the Appalachian region. However, the instrument retained some of its association with popular resistance and was used in the late twentieth century by the folk singer Pete Seeger as a way of articulating the voices of the excluded and to protest against the Vietnam War.

Above: *The Banjo Player* (1856) by William Sidney Mount, a white American artist who was known to depict African American people with dignity and sensitivity.

The relationship between migration and music

John Baily and Michael Collyer argue that like film, dance and literature, music is a form of cultural production that illustrates and situates migration. However, unlike literature, which is produced by a small elite, music is often generated from below and plays a major part in the production and consumption patterns of migrants. They further remind us that while a lot can be gleaned from the lyrics of popular songs, beyond these lyrics, music has the capacity to "evoke memories and capture emotions"[3]. It is this aspect of music that has the most potent connection to migration.

The music of military bands accompanying marching soldiers was meant to raise the morale of the invaders and to cow the colonized. However, building on their own traditions of shawms and hornpipes, the Indian, Pakistani and Kashmiri army bands developed colourful adaptations of tartans and Scottish bagpipes, thus absorbing the traditions of their British opponents. For migrants arriving in more humble capacities than imperial soldiers, music became a way of recalling their homelands and re-establishing their identities in the new settings in which they found themselves. For example, English, Irish, and Scottish ballads survived in their countries of destination.

As well as romanticized songs of the past, the laments of folksingers recalled bitter memories. This one, called the "Fields of Athenry", recounts the tale of the Irishman "Michael" who was sent to Botany Bay in Australia on an English convict ship after stealing food for his family. It is still sung at sporting events in bitter memory of the Great Famine:

Michael they have taken you away
For you stole Trevelyn's corn
So the young might see the morn
Now a prison ship lies waiting in the bay
Low lie, the Fields of Athenry
Against the famine and the crown
I rebelled, they brought me down

Music on the move

The end of slavery in the American South in 1865 left many former slaves scratching out a precarious living on marginal land. They grew cotton or worked land planted with cotton as tenant farmers. The great threat to their crops was the boll weevil, about which they had heard through songs, long before the insect crossed the Mississippi river from Mexico[4]. The fear and effect of weevil infestation, combined with the attraction of factory employment in the industrializing North, caused what is known in the USA as "the Great Migration", the movement of 6 million African Americans over the period between 1900 and 1970 from the rural South to the urban North. They developed their songs en route.

The American South was also the heartland of an extraordinary burst of creolized music led by African Americans. African banjos, drums and rhythms, European trumpets, clarinets and saxophones, and upright pianos used in churches as well as bars combined to create a new art form – jazz. As African Americans moved north, the optimistic sounds of ragtime, gospel and marching bands, which centred on New Orleans, gave way to "the blues", a peculiar and beguiling music combining fear, melancholia, hope and nostalgia and usually plucked out on a guitar, a cheap and easily transportable instrument.

Three Blues styles spread by the Great Migration

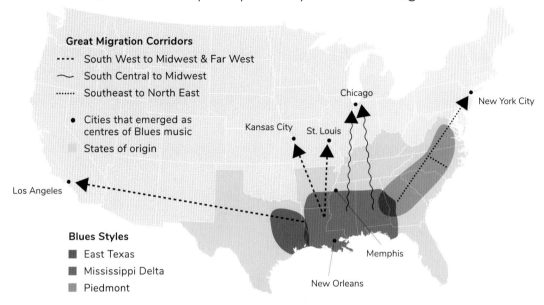

Great Migration Corridors

---- South West to Midwest & Far West

∼ South Central to Midwest

...... Southeast to North East

● Cities that emerged as centres of Blues music

States of origin

Chicago

New York City

Kansas City

St. Louis

Los Angeles

Memphis

New Orleans

Blues Styles

■ East Texas

■ Mississippi Delta

■ Piedmont

Above: Blues singers in Chicago, 1947.

35

In Search of Knowledge
International Students

In medieval Europe, wandering scholars – *scholares vagantes* (in German *fahrenden Schüler*) – were a common sight. Sometimes dissolute and usually impoverished, they moved from town to town listening to lectures and staying in run-down lodgings.

For today's scholars, the contrast could not be greater. A fiercely competitive market and high fees help to finance upmarket teaching spaces, expensive sporting facilities and comfortable accommodation. International education takes place at various ages and educational levels, but the demand is particularly notable in higher education, where some universities have become critically dependent on the recruitment of overseas students.

While the rise in the international mobility of students is apparent in all countries, India and China are the two giants of the supply side, together constituting about half the number of foreign students in the USA in 2017. Despite having many poor people who are unlikely to benefit from international educational opportunities, the number of middle-class and rich people in China and India is very large. Using a wide definition, China's statistical department claims that 400 million Chinese people are "middle class", while a stricter US measure taken in 2015 estimated that 109 million

Chinese owned wealth between US$50,000 and US$500,000. By 2017, there were, in total, 4.8 million international students, with numbers growing roughly at 12 per cent a year.

International students, 2011–17

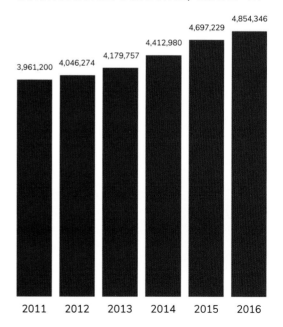

Year	Students
2011	3,961,200
2012	4,046,274
2013	4,179,757
2014	4,412,980
2015	4,697,229
2016	4,854,346

Receiving countries

Countries that recruit international students have historically been in the anglophone world, notably the USA and UK, but Canada and Australia are also significant English-speaking destinations. More recently, many continental European countries have recruited successfully, sometimes by having to offer courses in English. In the Netherlands, 850 Master's courses are taught in English, even allowing the country to recruit students from the UK. Canada has greatly boosted the number of its international students by offering various routes to permanent residency.

International students in Canada, 2018

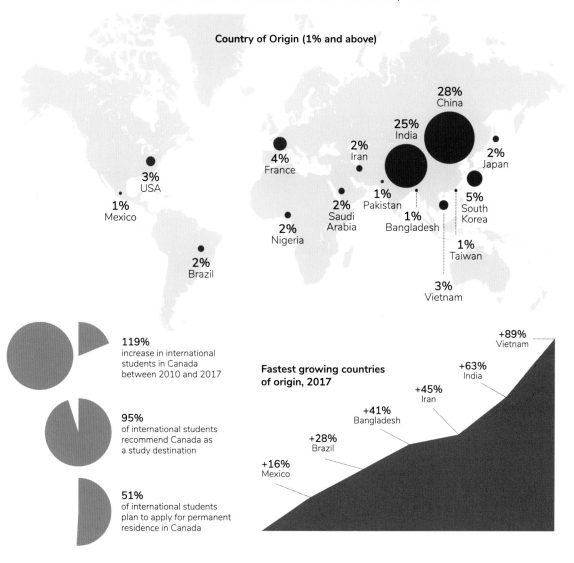

Country of Origin (1% and above)

28% China
25% India
2% Iran
4% France
2% Japan
3% USA
1% Mexico
1% Pakistan
2% Saudi Arabia
2% Nigeria
1% Bangladesh
5% South Korea
2% Brazil
1% Taiwan
3% Vietnam

119% increase in international students in Canada between 2010 and 2017

95% of international students recommend Canada as a study destination

51% of international students plan to apply for permanent residence in Canada

Fastest growing countries of origin, 2017

+16% Mexico
+28% Brazil
+41% Bangladesh
+45% Iran
+63% India
+89% Vietnam

Canada has also benefited from Green Card (work visa) delays in the USA. In response to the more onerous immigration rules that President Trump initiated in the USA, students started to switch destinations. Putting a positive face on this development, Allan Goodman, president of the US Institute of International Education, said that "everything matters from safety, to cost, to perhaps perceptions of visa policy. ... We're not hearing that students feel they can't come here. We're hearing that they have choices. We're hearing that there's competition from other countries."[1] This was confirmed by a survey of Indian students in the USA. In 2019, 70 per cent of highly skilled Indian immigrant respondents in the USA were "seriously thinking" about moving on to a more visa-friendly country. As the author of the survey noted, if all 70 per cent acted on their intentions, the USA would "stand

Above: International students graduating from Keele University, Staffordshire, in the UK.

to lose between US$19 billion and US$54 billion from this loss of talent and the costs associated with having to replace it".[2]

While the US study focuses on the more speculative opportunity costs that may be lost, a

Bogus colleges[5]

Fake colleges are not new, but they have proliferated recently, as they are significant money-makers for crooked operators and also provide a means of evading immigration controls. Many students are innocently duped, but some are fully aware that they are participating in a bogus scheme. An official body in the UK, the Higher Education Degree Datacheck lists 471 recognized and 243 bogus institutions offering degree qualifications on the date of consultation (12 April 2019). Some bogus institutions are easy to spot, such as:

University of England at Oxford
Oxford International University
Oxford College for PhD Studies

Others are much more plausible, having tantalizingly close names to the real thing, such as:

International University Robert Gordon (not the genuine Robert Gordon University); Manchester Open University (not the genuine University of Manchester or the Open University); and Wolverhamton University (not the genuine Wolverhampton University).

The fake Manchester Open University advertised degrees costing up to £35,000 and claimed to operate a non-existent campus in Oxford Road, with 2,000 students from 90 countries.

study for Universities UK by Oxford Economics centres on direct financial benefits, finding that, in 2014–15, "on-and off-campus spending by international students and their visitors generated a knock-on impact of £25.8 billion in gross output in the UK". Further, the report notes that international students supported 206,600 jobs in university towns and cities and accounted for £10.8 billion of UK export earnings.[3]

By focusing so much on the utilitarian value of international students to their hosts, we of course risk diminishing the wider cultural, scientific, educational and practical benefits of education for the students themselves and for their countries of origin.

The benefit to the countries of origin depends greatly on how many students return. The pattern is very varied, but most are happy to contribute their newly acquired skills to their home countries provided there are jobs and opportunities awaiting them. One Dutch study found that 80 per cent of foreign students returned (this is exactly the average found for all OECD countries). One important factor influencing the decisions of the 20 per cent who stayed is whether they had found a local partner during their period of study.[4]

New developments

Universities in Asia are beginning to compete successfully with the more established centres of learning in Europe, North America and Australia. There are notable advances in both teaching and research by some universities in Singapore and China/Hong Kong, which score well in international rankings. There are also quantitative leaps in China where expanding existing facilities and opening new institutions are equivalent to opening one average-sized new university every week. While the size of the age group 18–24 is slowing, provision is leaping ahead, the government declaring that it will provide full coverage of the population in the next few years. China has also joined the race to recruit international students, aiming to reach half-a-million (the size of Canada's cohort) in 2020.

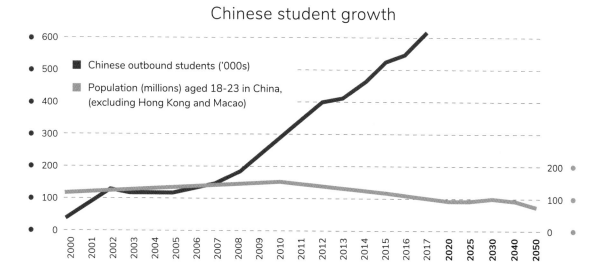

Chinese student growth

- Chinese outbound students ('000s)
- Population (millions) aged 18-23 in China, (excluding Hong Kong and Macao)

IN SEARCH OF KNOWLEDGE: INTERNATIONAL STUDENTS

36
Marriage
and Migration

Although this is a limited view, one common image of an international migrant is a male crossing a border for the purpose of seeking work. Before the 1950s, female migrants were rather shadowy figures in the background, simply accompanying their husbands and acquiring their residential or visa statuses as a result of that attachment.

Married or affianced women were usually not primary migrants but were "sent for" by their partners after they had established themselves. Where immigrant men had no continuing attachments back home, it was common for women to be remotely paired, either as "picture brides" or as subjects of arranged marriages. Such long-distance pairing arrangements continue but are now supercharged by the internet. Once women started independently migrating for work on a significant scale, the migration prism became more gender-neutral, but there are still significant and complex connections between marriage and migration.[1]

Japanese picture brides

The expression "picture brides" derived initially from the experiences of the approximately 200,000 Japanese indentured labourers who were recruited to work in the sugar and pineapple plantations in Hawaii between 1885 and 1924. Earning less than they were promised, they were forced to extend their three-year contracts. They wrote to their families to find them wives and included photographs flattering both their appearance and circumstances. Some 20,000 Japanese women responded positively, often reciprocating with a "picture". Over a 40-year period ending in the early 1990s, Barbara F. Kawakami collected 250 oral interviews recounting their experiences, which were often distressing.[2] One reported: "my husband, he drink too much, so I suffer. ... He used to beat me when he get drunk. The children used to be so afraid. They run out to the outhouse an' hide, till the beating stop." Another said: "I thought if there was a way to walk across the ocean [back] to Japan, I would have done so."

Opposite: Japanese picture brides board a liner to join their future husbands, whom they have never seen before, in South America, 1931.

Proxy marriages: Italians in Australia

Although the case of picture brides in Hawaii has been extensively documented, similar practices are, in fact, common in many migrant communities where there is a gender imbalance or where exclusionary or self-exclusionary practices inhibited marriage across class, racial, ethnic or religious lines with the locals. One unusual variation concerned approximately 12,000 Italian women who married their Australian-based Italian husbands by "proxy",

before emigrating to Australia to commence their marriages. Marriage by proxy is the legal union of two people in which one of the two spouses is absent at the time of the ceremony and is symbolically represented by a proxy. One account of the arrangement was provided by 16-year-old "Carmela", whose neighbours asked her to marry their son "Vincenzo" who had emigrated some years earlier. She at first said "no" but later changed her mind when she saw his photograph and married by proxy before joining him in Australia.[3]

Spousal and total grants of settlement in the UK, 1995–2009

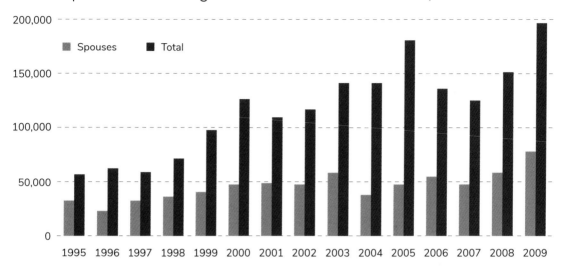

Spousal migration: UK and Japan

Perhaps because of the high status given to the family unit in many cultures and societies, it is common for immigration rules to allow family unification, usually involving spousal migration. There are notable exceptions to this rule – perhaps the most well-known are the restrictions imposed by the apartheid regime in South Africa to prevent black families settling in the designated "white areas" of the country.

In the case of the UK, spousal migration has always formed an important proportion of the "grants of settlement", though the exact number of spousal ones in relation to overall grants of settlement has varied over time in response to various administrative changes. One complicated legal issue revolved around immigrant men in polygamous marriages who are normally prevented from bringing a second or subsequent wife into the UK and also prevented from claiming benefits for more than one wife.

The extent and diversity of international marriages is also a useful index of migration in Japan where, it is often assumed, little international migration takes place. However, the extent of foreign immigration is revealed in marriage data issued by the Ministry of Health, Labour and Welfare. In 2013, about one in every 30 Japanese marriages was to a foreign national (21,488 of the 660,613 marriages). There are some marked and interesting national differences between the selection of husbands and wives.

"Bride deficits" and the commodification of brides

There are three common reasons for "bride deficits" – the lack of availability of local women for marriage.

First, the preference for sons in rural India and in "one-child" China has led to bride deficits. Using 2010 data, in India the sex ratio was 109 boys to 100 girls, while in China 118 boys were born for every 100 girls. Tens of millions of female

Nationalities of foreign wives and husbands in Japan, 2017

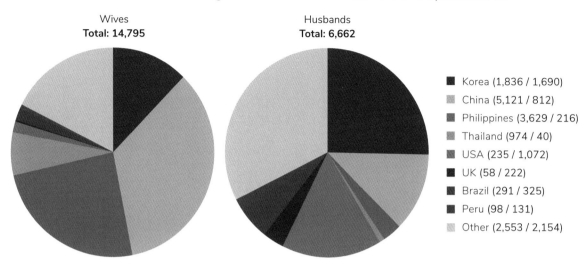

Wives
Total: 14,795

Husbands
Total: 6,662

- Korea (1,836 / 1,690)
- China (5,121 / 812)
- Philippines (3,629 / 216)
- Thailand (974 / 40)
- USA (235 / 1,072)
- UK (58 / 222)
- Brazil (291 / 325)
- Peru (98 / 131)
- Other (2,553 / 2,154)

foetuses have been aborted by parents using pre-natal screening to identify the sex of the foetus.[4]

Second, men tied to the land in rural settings often find that local women baulk at the isolation of rural life and, rather than marrying, leave the land to find opportunities elsewhere.

Third, women from both rural and urban areas are increasingly not committing to marriage at all. The change is most evident in Asia, where it was historically rare for women not to get married. Hong Kong, Taiwan and Japan show particularly high rates of non-marriage among women.

Some non-marrying women are, of course, independent migrants in their own right, but the main effect of the bride deficit is to propel men to seek brides online, often transnationally. For example, Malagasy women are persuaded to go to rural France while Japanese farmers look out for Filipino brides. Such marriages have historically been arranged by marriage brokers, who are still very much part of the system of turning "mail-order brides" into commodities.

Non-marriage among Asian women, 1970–2005

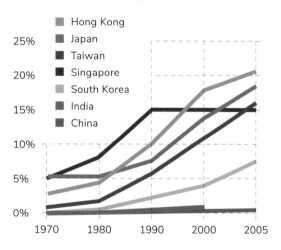

- Hong Kong
- Japan
- Taiwan
- Singapore
- South Korea
- India
- China

With the development of the internet, such transactions have become digitized and globalized. India's Shaadi.com, Jeevansaathi.com and BharatMatrimony.com are just three of India's many matrimonial sites, claiming millions of successful matches.

37

Retirement and Lifestyle Migration

Migration at the time of retirement started growing considerably in the 1970s. It is driven by a number of factors, but demographic and employment patterns are two salient underlying causes.

—

Retirement in OECD countries

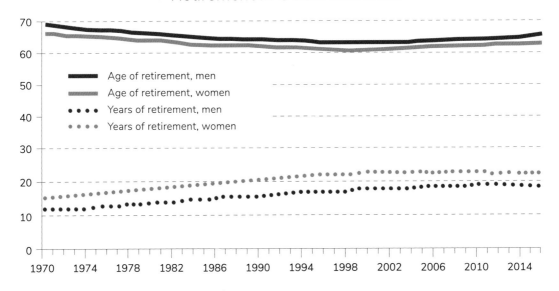

There is a significantly greater number of over-65s, particularly in the richer countries, where longevity increased over the period 1970–2005. Over the same period, the age of retirement from work and self-employment went down, leading to a rise in the number of "retirement years" from about 14 to 20 years. The enhanced number of years available for retirement not only statistically increased the number of retirees who might choose to migrate, but also encouraged that choice in the first place.

The wider picture

While demographic and employment factors underpin retirement migration, there are a number of other causal factors associated with this choice.

- The lower costs of transport have allowed much greater opportunities to travel. For example, the cost of air travel in Europe decreased by about 50 per cent in real terms between 1992 and 2010, exposing many more places to tourism and thereby suggesting previously unfamiliar sites for possible retirement.
- Contemporary retirees are relatively affluent, measured both against the retirement incomes of their parents and the likely retirement incomes of their children.
- Retirement migration is becoming closely entangled with lifestyle migration, as over-65s and early retirees make conscious choices to seek safer, sunnier, less polluted, less stressful places to enjoy "the good life", freed from the competitive pressures often found in crowded, unfriendly, colder cities.[1]
- A large number of immigrants who sought work in Europe and North America from the 1950s onward have entered, or are about to enter, their post-employment years and are faced with the choice of retiring in their countries of settlement or re-migrating to their countries of origin.[2]

Where do retirees and lifestyle migrants go?

USA

In general, retirees moving away from their homes move "south" towards sunnier climates, sometimes reversing historic trends. One

Top 10 US states for retirees, showing net migration for people over 60

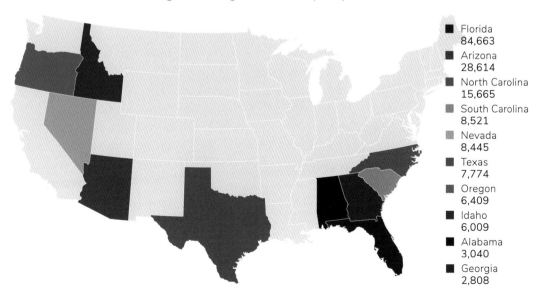

- Florida 84,663
- Arizona 28,614
- North Carolina 15,665
- South Carolina 8,521
- Nevada 8,445
- Texas 7,774
- Oregon 6,409
- Idaho 6,009
- Alabama 3,040
- Georgia 2,808

Net migration, over 60s, and the changing population profile of the Channel region

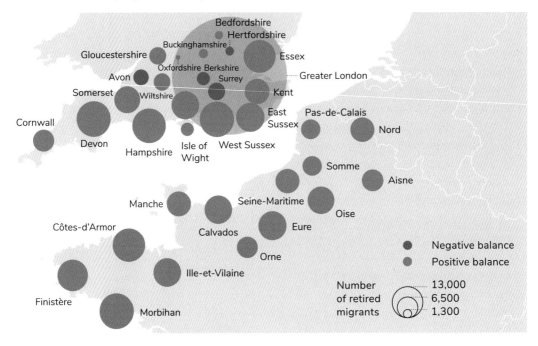

good example is the migration to the American South by African Americans deserting the de-industrializing areas of the northeast in favour of Texas, Georgia, Florida, and North Carolina, despite the legacy of poor race relations. The top 10 states in the USA for all retirees are shown in the map on page 181. Although most are marked by benign weather throughout the year, there are other powerful incentives determining location – the most important being the relative cost of living, the availability of affordable housing in favoured areas and the tax incentives offered by state and local authorities to attract retirees.

UK and France

French demographers have helped to define a distinctive "Channel region" marked by population shifts in the UK and France.[3] They were already aware of the long-standing retirement migration by British, mainly English, people to England's south coast – to coastal towns such as Brighton, Poole and Bognor Regis. What was less expected was that in addition to, or substituting for, France's expensive Côte d'Azur, French retirees were also populating Normandy and Brittany. There they were joined by British retirees who were attracted by the comparatively low property prices (compared both with the English south coast and with fashionable French regions such as the Dordogne). The demographic shifts towards an older population, one that gets older towards the west, is shown in the map above.

Lifestyle migrants

The quest for a better life has motivated many migrants, but lifestyle migrants are characterized not so much by a desperate need to move in order to find work or a livelihood, but rather by their desire to express themselves and find self-realization in an unfamiliar setting. As Michaela Benson and Karen O'Reilly argue, this has resulted in an emphasis on migrant subjectivities (what people feel and want), somewhat at the expense of the structures, institutions and industries that support their choice of residence. In this more complex understanding of lifestyle migration, property markets, airport connections, the encouragement of foreign investment (including off-shore investments to evade taxes), pension transferability and more generalized structures of power and privilege all intersect with the decision to find another life elsewhere.[4]

Adios amigos

That retirement and lifestyle migration should be set within an appreciation of the wider economic, social and political forces at work can be discerned from the slowdowns in retirement migration to European destination countries bordering the Mediterranean. As pointed out in an article titled "Adios amigos", the price of a house in Spain fell by a third between 2008 and 2016, leaving "concrete skeletons littering the country's southern coast" and British expatriates in negative equity (when the market value of a property falls below the amount of a mortgage secured on it).[5] By 2017, retirement migration to European countries from the UK had all but collapsed.

To this picture of decline in retirement migration to certain European countries should be added two other factors. In a number of places, the trends described at the beginning of the chapter have now plateaued or reversed. For example, longevity has stalled in the USA, UK and other countries, and there is increased pressure to work for longer to enhance state-supported pensions, which themselves are under threat. It is also likely that the flows of retirees across the Channel will shrink in the light of the UK referendum result in 2016 to leave the European Union. It is possible that a large number of UK nationals on the European continent will find themselves in a legal limbo, with declining assets. If they return to the UK in substantial numbers, they will amplify pressures on stretched social and health services.

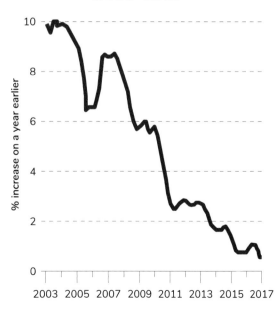

Number of residents in Spain, France, Germany and Italy receiving UK Pensions, 2003–2017

38

Climate-driven Migration

A casual search of the internet reveals that tourists are routinely being warned that if the Pacific island nations of Tuvalu and Kiribati are on their lists of "must see" places, they should not wait until their retirement years to make their bookings.

———

If sea levels rise at the current rate, all the people of Tuvalu will have to be evacuated by 2050. Kiribati will be completely submerged by 2100. In 2008, President Mohamed Nasheed of the Maldives decided to use funds from a tourist levy to purchase land in India, Sri Lanka and Australia for evacuees from his country. The adverse effects of rising sea levels in Venice are well-known. While slowly rising sea levels and other long-term climate changes will have important effects on migration over the coming years, at the moment climate-related migration is much more driven by sudden and unexpected natural disasters.

Sudden displacements

Despite reluctance and indifference by some politicians, climate scientists have established beyond doubt that a warming planet has led to biodiversity loss, declining crop yields, more frequent heatwaves, more extreme weather events and heavy rainfall.[1] Typhoons, floods, hurricanes and landslides have led to a significant loss of lives and large displacements of people. In 2016, the 10 largest displacement events were climate-related.

In the middle of March 2019, Cyclone Idai devastated large parts of south-eastern Africa. Early estimates suggest that this has led to the displacement of more than 600,000 people, particularly in the low-lying areas of Mozambique, Zimbabwe and Malawi. One family of five was forced to leave Beira when the bamboo walls of their home collapsed, and the zinc roof was torn off by winds. They fled to a neighbour's house, but the fierce winds blew that away too. Housed temporarily at a school, the family has no prospect of return to normal life. When interviewed, members of the family were very anxious about their uncle – a fisherman who had gone out to sea – whom they feared had been killed in the cyclone.[2]

Ten climate-related displacement events in 2016

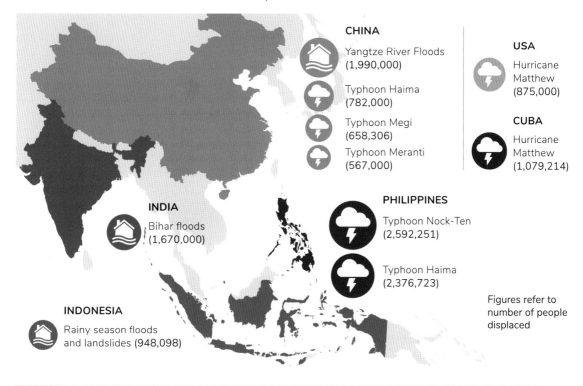

CHINA
Yangtze River Floods
(1,990,000)

Typhoon Haima
(782,000)

Typhoon Megi
(658,306)

Typhoon Meranti
(567,000)

USA
Hurricane
Matthew
(875,000)

CUBA
Hurricane
Matthew
(1,079,214)

INDIA
Bihar floods
(1,670,000)

PHILIPPINES
Typhoon Nock-Ten
(2,592,251)

Typhoon Haima
(2,376,723)

Figures refer to
number of people
displaced

INDONESIA
Rainy season floods
and landslides (948,098)

Extent of flooding in Mozambique and Zimbabwe following Cyclone Idai

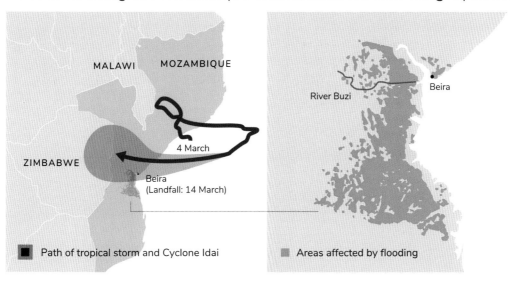

MALAWI   MOZAMBIQUE

4 March

ZIMBABWE

Beira
(Landfall: 14 March)

River Buzi

Beira

■ Path of tropical storm and Cyclone Idai

■ Areas affected by flooding

Climate, food security, conflict and migration

While the direct link between dramatic weather events and the displacement of populations is visible on our television screens, we need a more subtle analysis of the longer-term causal links between climate, food security, conflict and migration. Desertification, erratic rainfall, global warming and the poor storage of water (for example, there are only 980 large dams in sub-Saharan Africa, of which 589 are in South Africa) lead to falling yields and the death of ruminants. Richer farmers may be able to ride out a couple of bad years, but disputes over grazing land and access to fresh water, can easily turn into conflict.[3]

One example of the potential for a transboundary conflict over water is the construction of the Grand Ethiopian Renaissance Dam on the Blue Nile by Ethiopia in defiance of Egypt's historic claims to the water (the pharaohs of ancient Egypt even accorded the Nile religious significance). While this is a possible cause for future inter-state conflict, there is already ample evidence of localized armed conflicts over the supply and access to fresh water in India, China and much of Africa. Migration is an adaptive response to restricted access to water, lower levels of food security and the consequent conflicts that then arise. Disputes over watered land between nomadic livestock herders and those who practise settled agriculture have been a major source of the conflict in Darfur, Sudan, where many lives have been lost. As people migrate to seek water and arable land, they often precipitate further conflict.

Assessment

There are two major difficulties in assessing the level of migration that will result from climate change. The first depends on whether policies and actions by governments and other political actors will seriously mitigate the effects of climate change. Because this is largely an unknown variable, projections to the year 2050 of the number of migrants likely to be affected by adverse environmental conditions vary from 200 million up to 1 billion.[4] The World Bank has produced somewhat more conservative projections for 2050 covering three regions and using three scenarios – a pessimistic one in which nothing changes, an intermediate one in which more inclusive development is promoted, and a third one in which environmental issues are at the forefront of policy decisions. Numbers for the pessimistic scenario range between 117 and 143 million displaced people (see map opposite).

The second difficulty in assessing the impact of environmental change on migration is that, whereas environmentalists tend towards single-cause explanations, most migration scholars insist that the migration decision is complex, involving, for example, the opportunities on offer, collective family obligations and strategies, whether a migratory culture is abnormal or habitual, as well as a score or more of personal motivations and inhibitions. So, unless we are discussing a fast-onset event like a flood or hurricane, we need to be cautious about attributing a specific migration flow solely to environmental change.[5]

Previous spread: Aerial view of a neighbourhood in Beira, Mozambique, hit by Cyclone Idai, 24 March 2019.

Opposite: Visit by a US official to a USAID-sponsored water-pump project in the war-torn town of Golo in central Darfur, 2017.

Internal displacements due to climate change by 2050

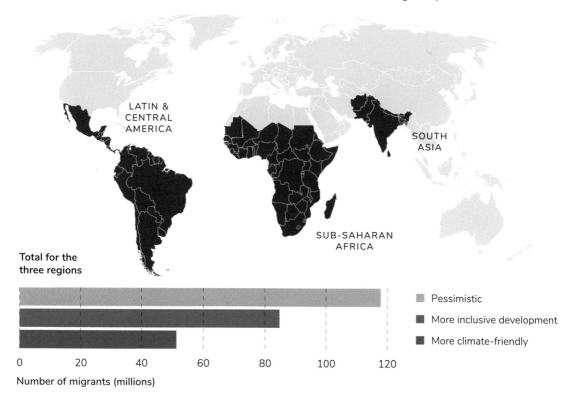

LATIN &
CENTRAL
AMERICA

SOUTH
ASIA

SUB-SAHARAN
AFRICA

**Total for the
three regions**

Pessimistic

More inclusive development

More climate-friendly

0   20   40   60   80   100   120

Number of migrants (millions)

39
Tourism
Mobility and its Discontents

In this book, the strict definition of migration (movement of people for the purpose of settlement and employment) has been relaxed to allow the examination of other aspects of mobility. Seen in this light, tourism is one of the largest, and fastest growing, movements of people, changing from a relatively insignificant global phenomenon just after the Second World War (about 15 million) to a projected figure of 1.8 billion tourist arrivals in 2030.

—

Growth in International Tourism (1945–2030)

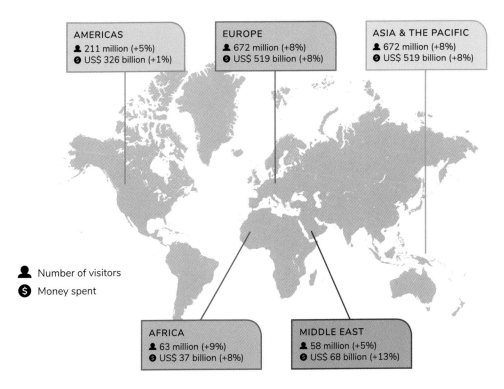

AMERICAS
- 211 million (+5%)
- US$ 326 billion (+1%)

EUROPE
- 672 million (+8%)
- US$ 519 billion (+8%)

ASIA & THE PACIFIC
- 672 million (+8%)
- US$ 519 billion (+8%)

- Number of visitors
- Money spent

AFRICA
- 63 million (+9%)
- US$ 37 billion (+8%)

MIDDLE EAST
- 58 million (+5%)
- US$ 68 billion (+13%)

Tourism is also one of the world's largest legitimate industries, alongside digital media platforms, oil and car manufacturing. According to the World Tourism Organization, it accounts for 1 in 10 jobs worldwide and a similar percentage of the world's GDP. There have been regional downward blips following security scares in North Africa and a global downturn during the world recession in 2008. However, the growth in tourism has been otherwise remorseless, reaching over 1.3 billion arrivals in 2017.

Many aspects of tourism are positive. It gives visitors the opportunity to combine their leisure activities with increasing their awareness of unfamiliar sights, cultures and cuisines. They can bring much-needed foreign exchange to poor countries, which gives local people jobs and opportunities in the hotel and leisure industries. Before the Second World War, tourism was essentially confined to rich, educated members of society but, with increased affluence and rising aspirations, the opportunities for mass tourism escalated from the 1950s, particularly in Europe and the USA. Package tour companies and cheap airlines thrived in Britain and Germany, particularly opening up southern Spain as a major tourist destination. For the relatively prosperous workers of northern Europe, foreign holidays in warm, bright Iberian resorts replaced the domestic holidays in caravan parks and holiday camps with uncertain weather.[1]

For a while, package holidays seemed to work for everybody. The tour operators flourished, the airlines filled their seats, the visitors escaped their routine lives, and the local hoteliers and staff working in the hospitality industry profited from seasonal or near year-round work. As the number of tourists rapidly escalated, however, some of the more negative aspects of the movement became apparent. With limited community input, weak or corrupt local authorities authorizing excessive hotel building, and governments desperate to enhance employment opportunities, the travel companies, property developers and foreign airlines increasingly called the shots.

Tourism and sustainability

The growth of cruises, backpacking and cheaper independent travel, together with the rise of rental companies like Airbnb, have accelerated the unsustainable ratios between travellers and locals. Spain reported having an eye-watering 82 million overseas visitors in 2017 alone (and its own population is not quite 47 million), while Venice's 55,000 permanent residents have to adjust to having 20 million extra people visiting their city each year. Tourism on this

Below: The cruise ship Crown Princess arrives in Venice.

scale presents massive challenges to the local population. It is perhaps not surprising that, since around 2014, graffiti and anti-tourist demonstrations have started to spring up in a number of popular destinations.

Planners and development experts have been aware of the dangers of unconstrained tourism since the 1970s and had recommended the use of local guesthouses in village settings in favour of resort hotels.[2] There are many positive examples of "sustainable tourism", "ecotourism" or "heritage tourism". One of the pioneers of these initiatives has been Taiwan, where "community-based tourism is linked to both sustainable development and environmental conservation. Moreover, the development of community-based tourism, especially in rural villages, fishing villages and aboriginal

communities, is a national policy of Taiwan's current government."[3]

Nonetheless, the progress towards sustainable tourism seems Sisyphean. Accompanying the country's economic boom were very large numbers of middle-class Chinese tourists who joined the throng and spent big money to see the sights and travel the routes that their European and American predecessors had traversed.

With the apparently unstoppable volume of tourists, iconic destinations are being damaged. Footfall erosion and littering are affecting Machu Pichu in Peru, while suntan lotion adds to the deterioration of the Great Barrier Reef in Australia. To make things worse, some cynical operators are promoting "last-chance" packages by inviting tourists to visit the

Chinese tourists spend more than any other nationality by a long way

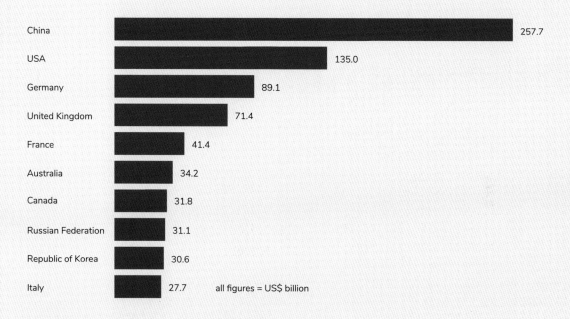

China	257.7
USA	135.0
Germany	89.1
United Kingdom	71.4
France	41.4
Australia	34.2
Canada	31.8
Russian Federation	31.1
Republic of Korea	30.6
Italy	27.7

all figures = US$ billion

Opposite: Locals put up banners on a beach in Barcelona in protest at apartments being used to house tourists.

Above: Chinese tourists snapping photos in Chinatown, London, with the incongruous "Tokyo diner" in the background.

Amazon rain forest or the Florida Everglades before they disappear, or to travel to the Maldives before the islands sink into the sea.[4] In addition to threatening fragile ecosystems and "spoiling" national sites and treasures, tourists also often threaten long-held cultural values and customs. Conservative societies are confronted by nakedness and drunkenness. By contrast, sex tourism, notably in Thailand, "has become a tourist attraction in itself, with red light districts being recommended in several reputable guidebooks".[5] Reliable and up-to-date figures are difficult to come by, but a common estimate is that there are between 200,000 and 300,000 sex workers in Thailand, mainly servicing the foreign trade. Tourism is truly agathokakological (that is comprising both good and evil).

40

Children
and Migration

Children form a significant part of refugee migration and, though
a minority, constitute a sizeable share of all migrants. Because
they are often voiceless, the challenges and experiences
of over 30 million migrant children are largely unknown.

———

Conscious of the potential for human rights abuses that may be experienced by child migrants, much of the limited discussion of their situation has been undertaken by lawyers, investigative journalists and social policy experts. The question of how to deal with unaccompanied and separated children raises particular concerns for welfare agencies and for the authorities in the receiving countries. Even where children are not themselves migrants, they are profoundly affected by migration, particularly when their parents seek work in far-off places, leaving other family members to bring them up. Also considered here is the situation of children who arrive as minors or are born in a country of settlement to migrant parents who are undocumented or deemed illegal.

A global profile
of child migrants

In 2017, according to UN figures, 30 million of the 258 million international migrants were children.

However, this gives a misleading picture of the extent of the phenomenon. In 2013, in China alone, 36 million of the country's 245 million internal migrants were children. The number of children among India's cohort of internal migrants is also considerable – the last time this was reliably estimated was in 2007–8, when 15 million children were internal migrants.[1]

Most children, naturally, move with one or both their parents, but they are particularly affected by having to abandon their homes, undertake difficult journeys, and find their feet in a new environment. These pressures are massively magnified in refugee situations. The plight of Middle Eastern refugee children on the island of Lesbos, Greece, has been examined by a Harvard psychologist, Vasileia Digidiki.[2] She found that many children were affected by insomnia and experienced bedwetting and nightmares, which are all "strongly indicative of post-traumatic stress disorder". Many children had to face the loss of family members who had been left behind

International migrants by age 1990–2017, indicating proportion of those under 18 (in millions)

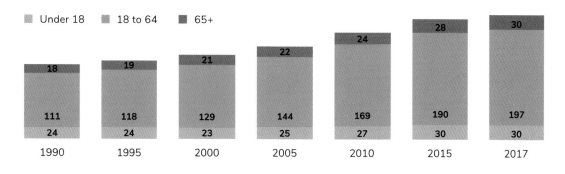

Under 18   18 to 64   65+

	1990	1995	2000	2005	2010	2015	2017
65+	18	19	21	22	24	28	30
18 to 64	111	118	129	144	169	190	197
Under 18	24	24	23	25	27	30	30

Demographic profile of migrants arriving in Greece, Italy, Spain and Bulgaria, showing proportions of accompanied, unaccompanied and separated children, 2017

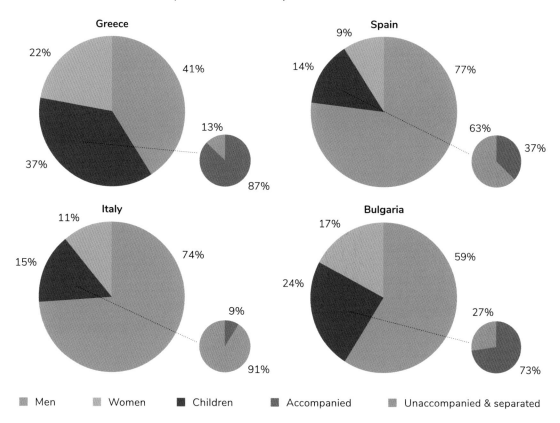

Greece — 41%, 22%, 37%; 13% / 87%

Spain — 9%, 14%, 77%; 63% / 37%

Italy — 11%, 15%, 74%; 9% / 91%

Bulgaria — 17%, 24%, 59%; 27% / 73%

Men   Women   Children   Accompanied   Unaccompanied & separated

or had died during the journey. In some cases, the children felt responsible for their parents' trauma.

It was notable that there were some positive experiences to report. Open camps in lieu of detention centres allowed a degree of normalcy and made it possible to educate the children in their native languages, alongside those of their transit country and that of their intended final destination (Greek, German and English). Enabling migrant children to join local children in recreational activities both helped the migrant children heal and reduced xenophobia and stigmatization among the host population of the island.[3]

The migration crisis across the Mediterranean and through the Balkans, involving African and Middle Eastern migrants, peaked in 2015–17; a remarkable number of unaccompanied and separated children were affected, and they often have to face acute emotional and legal problems.

The children left behind

Even if children are not themselves part of the migration flow, the migration of their parents may affect them profoundly. Take the case of China. Because the *hukou* system (see Chapter 23) restricts the access of rural migrants to urban social services, including healthcare and education, most children, 70 million in 2013, are left behind in the villages to be looked after by family members, usually grandparents, who are often unable to provide them with any access to educational opportunities. In 2013, nearly 4 in 10 children in rural areas were living without one or both parents due to migration.

The separation of parents from their children "left behind" can be particularly difficult in the case of transnational migrants. In a study of Twi Ghanaian children with parents abroad, Cati Coe found that they openly expressed sadness at the scattering of their family, using the English word

Opposite: Chinese "left behind" children in a rural school. The children are prone to anxiety and perform poorly, even where they have access to schooling.

Right: Members of the Catholic community hold rosary beads as they pray during a protest demonstration in support of the DREAM Act, Capitol Hill, Washington DC, 27 February 2018.

"family", rather than the Twi near-equivalent, which refers to a lineage. It seems the children had accepted a Western or Asiatic model of a small nuclear family and were often highly critical of the care they received from members of their extended family. Some even accused their carers of diverting remittances destined for them to the carers' own children.[4]

DREAMers in the USA

The strange appellation "DREAMers", describing children in the USA who are legally "aliens", derives from the Development, Relief, and Education for Alien Minors (DREAM) Act, which two Democratic Party senators proposed in 2001. Offering recognition to children born in the USA whose parents were not legally resident there, the Act failed to pass and, despite being reintroduced several times, has never come into force. With the anti-immigrant rhetoric running high during Donald Trump's presidency, it is

doubtful that it will pass in its original form in the foreseeable future.

In 2019, the estimated number of DREAMers was 3.6 million, compared with a total of 11.3 million undocumented immigrants. During the Obama administration, 1.8 million DREAMers were protected from deportation under a programme called the Deferred Action for Childhood Arrivals (or DACA). At the time of writing, there are continuing negotiations between representatives of Congress and President Trump to find a permanent solution for the DREAMers in exchange, so President Trump proposes, for authorizing payment for his wall (see Chapter 41). Fortunately, undocumented children are well organized, and have considerable public support for their campaign for recognition. Many Latin American immigrants are Catholics and for this and other ethical reasons the Catholic Church has expressed strong support for the DREAMers.

41
Do Walls Work?
Borders and Migration

The idea that building a wall can prevent migration was given enormous publicity in the 2016 presidential election campaign in the USA when Donald Trump fired up his supporters by getting them to chant the phrase "Build that wall", a reference to migrants illegally crossing the Mexican–US frontier.

———

Building fences, barriers and walls has become part and parcel of the revival of nationalism in many parts of the world. Defended in the name of security and targeting the cross-border movements of drugs, goods and people, similar obstacles have appeared on the 4,096km (2,545-mile) boundary between India and Bangladesh, along Hungary's Croatian and Serbian borders (in 2015) and in Israel–Palestine. The genre includes exotic barriers such as the sand wall (called a *berm*) peppered with mines bulldozed between Morocco and the Western Sahara. The tiny Spanish enclaves of Ceuta and Melilla in Morocco form the European Union's only land frontiers with Africa and have been forbiddingly fenced. One author has calculated that by 2016 the number of walls had quadrupled since the fall of the Berlin wall in 1989, rising from 15 to 65 and covering 40 countries.[1]

Many of these "walls" (to use a generic term) cover a crazy patchwork of geographical and social anomalies. For example, in 2015 India and Bangladesh exchanged 162 parcels of land, which happened to lie on the "wrong" side of the border. These territories include "the *pièce de résistance* of strange geography: the world's only 'counter-counter-enclave': a patch of India surrounded by Bangladeshi territory, inside an Indian enclave within Bangladesh".[2] The Israeli–Palestinian "separation barrier" also does not simply demarcate the legally defined 1967 border, which only covers 15 per cent of its length. As it weaves between settlements, encircles villages and isolates communities it doubles the length of the Green Line, the demarcation between Israel and its neighbours established after the 1948 war.

Trump's wall

Although part of this general movement towards enclosure, President Trump's wall has captured the imagination of his supporters and attracts continuous press coverage. Some of his earlier extravagant boasts were scaled back. His most recent promise is to wall off just over half of the 3,145km-long (1,954-mile) frontier between Mexico and the USA, leaving the rest to the Rio Grande River and the mountainous terrain. There are many practical objections to Trump's wall. The estimated cost has escalated from US$4 billion to over five times that sum; it is doubtful that it could be built in the president's first term of office; and it is highly unlikely that Mexico will pay for the wall, as Trump has announced on many occasions.

However, the key issue is whether the Trump wall will make a significant difference to the flow of illegal (others prefer the term "undocumented") migrants moving across the Mexican border. There are many reasons to be sceptical that significant reductions will arise. First, although it is widely accepted that the overall number of illegal residents in the USA is about 11 million people, fewer than half that number are from Mexico.[3] Second, it is a common misapprehension that all undocumented migrants enter the USA illegally. In fact, "overstayers" – migrants who have entered the country *legally* but stayed beyond the expiry of their visas – counted for 42 per cent of the cumulative historical total of all undocumented persons in 2014. Moreover, the trend is accelerating. Of

Opposite: The building of the Berlin Wall, 6 June 1961, was meant to deter migration from East Germany to the West. The Berlin Wall, which survived for 28 years, anticipated many of the current attempts to build walls between peoples.

those who joined the ranks of the undocumented population in the same year (2014), 66 per cent were overstayers.[4]

These figures alone suggest that even if Trump's wall is built it will be of limited effectiveness. It is relevant also to point out that he is not starting from "zero wall" but proposing the augmentation of existing barriers. We can therefore observe what the consequences of the gradual fencing and militarization of the border have been over the last two decades. These have been carefully documented by Douglas Massey.[5] One notable effect has been to displace migrants from their traditional crossing points at El Paso and San Diego to the Sonoran Desert. This crossing still presented a good chance of success but was more dangerous and more expensive, thus adding to the coffers of the "coyotes", the people smugglers, and making the migrants less likely to return to Mexico and re-cross the border. Why would migrants wish to cross, return and re-cross? Simply because the wider region has formed a single economic zone since the nineteenth century. The circulation of people was common, as Mexicans returned for retirement, to look after a relative or simply to go to a family wedding. By further inhibiting labour circulation, the likely outcome of Trump's wall will be to increase the number of permanent South–North crossings and, in effect, trap illegals in the USA, rather than keep them out. Massey was able to measure this deterrent against homecoming, from the probability of returning from a first trip within 12 months at 48 per cent in 1980 to zero in 2010.

DO WALLS WORK? BORDERS AND MIGRATION

President Trump's Border Wall

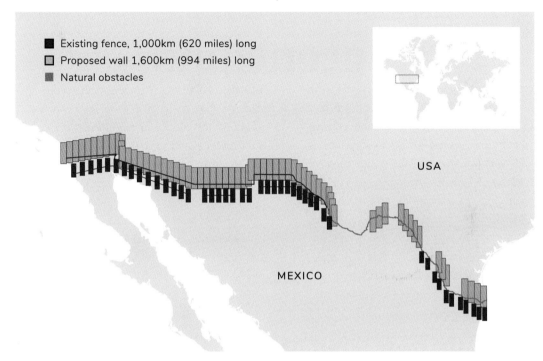

■ Existing fence, 1,000km (620 miles) long
□ Proposed wall 1,600km (994 miles) long
▨ Natural obstacles

USA

MEXICO

Why build a wall?

It would be an exaggeration to say that walls and similar barriers have no effect on inward migration flows, but their potency is often vastly exaggerated. For the USA–Mexico situation, there is a good case to be made that facilitating return through easy remittance of earnings, tax breaks and working with the Mexican authorities to enhance returnees' investments would be far more effective than barrier controls. This suggests that walls are being erected for other reasons, principally as a way of assuaging long-standing residents' angry reactions to foreigners. Trump's "big, beautiful wall" as he calls it, is a visible and concrete reminder of the phrase "we here, they there". In observing a similar phenomenon in Israel–Palestine, Rachel

Busbridge suggests that a wall is a "performance of sovereignty", a way of bombastically declaring a physical space to be "ours". She explains that a wall also "reflects deep power asymmetries ... with its materiality holding profound discursive and affective implications for the subjectivities and psyches of the respective nations".[6] So a wall is sending a powerful message – not only saying "you can't come here", but also that "we can enforce our will because we are stronger", which is precisely the message that Trump's supporters wish to hear. In short, controlling migration is far less important to populist leaders than appearing to control migration.

Opposite: The barrier separating Palestinians and Israelis on the West Bank.

42

Detentions and Deportations

The German philosopher Immanuel Kant (in *Perpetual Peace: A Philosophical Sketch*, 1795) is generally credited with developing the argument that states should willingly open their borders to strangers if their intentions are peaceful, for example, engaging in trade. However, nation-states have increasingly assumed the right to police their frontiers with greater and greater vigilance.

———

Not only do they seek to stop migrants crossing national borders without permission, but they also claim the legal right to detain or deport them if they have violated their entry conditions. The most common violation is the practice of "overstaying"; that is, entering a country legally but staying on after the period allowed on a visa or entry permit has expired. Other violations include concealing a criminal record prior to entry or committing a crime before citizenship or the right to permanent residence has been granted. Deportation, or at least the threat of deportation, frequently follows.

Detention

Migrants are detained for a number of reasons. They may have used forged papers or deemed to have lied about their intentions at the port of entry. Sometimes they are asylum seekers, waiting for their claims to be processed. Sometimes they are convicted criminals; sometimes

they are overstayers awaiting removal. In the last two decades, detaining and processing immigrants for removal has been scaled up to industrial proportions. By 2019, the Global Detention Project, a non-profit organization based in Geneva, had recorded the existence of 1,251 detention centres worldwide. They sometimes have fanciful names – "holding centre", "migrant facility" or "special removal centre for administrative arrested people" – but what they have in common is that they are hidden from public scrutiny. Detainees are held in limbo and are not part of each country's normal protective legal processes. An indication of the large number of people held in such facilities can be gleaned from the average daily population of detainees in the USA, which has grown sevenfold since 1994.

Two major sources of complaint by concerned campaigners have accompanied the rise in the number of immigration detainees in many countries. The first is that the facilities, many of

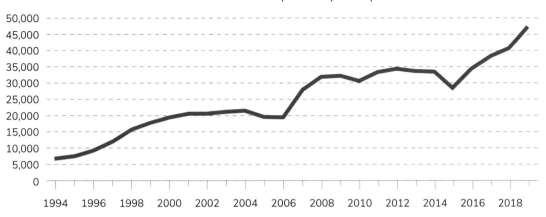

Average daily population of detainees in the USA, 1994–2019 (fiscal years)

Above: Protesters march to the South Australia parliament demanding closure by the Australian government of the offshore immigration detention centres on Manus and Nauru, Adelaide, Australia, 9 April 2017.

which are actual or former prisons, are unsuitable for families, nursing mothers or asylum seekers. The Australian offshore detention centres on the islands of Manus and Nauru have been a particular target for protestors.

The second concern is that, either under fiscal pressure or through ideological preference, the management of detention centres has been assigned to private sub-contractors with too little public oversight or legal accountability. This issue has been explicitly addressed in a revealing paper by Dora Schriro, former director of the US Immigration and Customs Enforcement's Office of Detention Policy and Planning during the Obama administration. Although critical of the immigration policies of President Trump, she by no means exculpates the regime tolerated by President Obama, arguing that for-profit detention centres should not be used to house families and should be closely supervised by ICE (the Immigration and Customs Enforcement, Department of Homeland Security) to prevent human rights abuses.[1]

Deportation

The sheer scale of the deportation of migrants would probably surprise many observers, including migration scholars. Matthew Gibney reminds us that more than 2 million non-citizens were deported from the USA between 1997 and 2007; in 2009 alone 400,000 non-citizens were deported. In the case of the UK, more than

Flight map for ICE Air, where the passengers wear handcuffs

In addition to chartering international flights, ICE Air Operations flies immigration detainees within the USA. This map displays the typical domestic weekly routes.

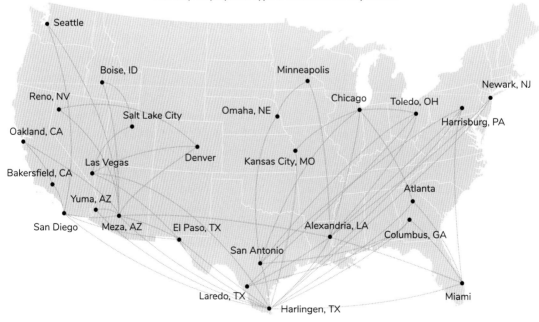

400,000 people were deported between 1997 and 2007 while Germany deported more than 130,000 (by air alone) between 2000 and 2005.[2] In the case of the USA, the shocking 9/11 (11 September 2001) events propelled the creation of the Department of Homeland Security, which has developed an Automated Biometric Identification System now containing more than 100 million prints. If a match is found on a suspected immigration case, ICE issues a "detainer", a prelude to removal. At that moment, the "industrial model" kicks in. People about to be deported are flown by specially charted aeroplanes from city to city, then gathered in sufficient numbers to be flown home or taken to a border town for bussing out of the USA. Aircraft, fuel, security and medical support ramps up the costs of removal – US$1,978 per person in 2016.

Above: The mobile billboard campaign to encourage voluntary return, described on Twitter as #racistvan.

The United Kingdom

In the UK, the management of deportation has, historically, largely been "under the radar", but as numbers increased the Home Office (the country's ministry of the interior) found it more and more difficult to administer the system of removal without creating major political scandals and negative publicity. Where overstayers were rooted in the community with their children at neighbourhood schools, local campaigners were often successful in stopping their removal. Residents of Caribbean origin with an entitlement to stay in the UK were summarily deported (see Chapter 21) and the Home Office now finds itself having to pay compensation to the deportees. The Home Office also ran a disastrous publicity campaign from mobile trucks to encourage illegal migrants to turn themselves in. Community police forces complained that the vans were inflaming inter-ethnic tensions and the scheme was quickly abandoned.

43

Solutions to Mass Displacement

The legal bedrock protecting refugees is the 1951 Convention Relating to the Status of Refugees. It enjoins states to offer asylum to individuals with "a well-founded fear of being persecuted for reasons of race, religion, nationality, membership of a particular social group or political opinion".

———

While the Convention remains indispensable, particularly in the principle of "non-refoulement" (not returning refugees or asylum-seekers to "unsafe" countries where they might face persecution), many observers have concluded that the provisions of the 1951 Convention need updating to cover contemporary mass displacement. Accompanying family members and children are poorly protected, while the sheer number of displaced people means that group determinations will have to supplement individual decisions. The receiving state is the crucial legal gateway in implementing the Convention, which is now becoming a serious impediment to fair consideration, as many politicians are under pressure to resist all immigrants, however deserving of protection they might be. The growing gap, some would say chasm, in protection has led to a demand for radical and imaginative solutions to solve the issue of mass displacement.

The scale of the displacement problem

The massive growth in the number of refugees and displaced people since the 1951 Convention can be seen in the data provided by the UNHCR (see graph opposite).

While the expression "persons of concern" includes 40 million internally displaced people, who remain the responsibility of the home states, there remains a large number of refugees whose fate is in the hands of other states, where anti-immigrant parties may be in the ascendant. Without providing a worldwide list, suffice to say that support for anti-immigrant parties across 13 European countries has doubled from 12.5 per cent of the electorate in January 2013 to 25 per cent in September 2018 (although it is concentrated in Poland, Germany, Italy and Hungary).[1] Probably the most explicit hard-liner is the Hungarian prime minister, Victor Orbán. In response to an EU request to admit a

Refugees and other "persons of concern", 1950–2017

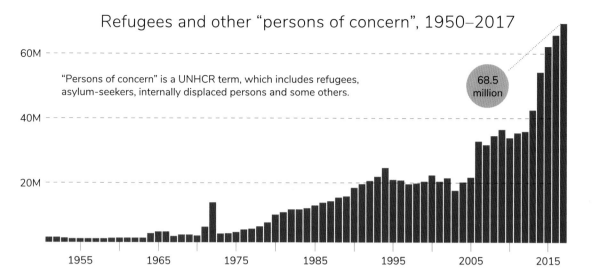

"Persons of concern" is a UNHCR term, which includes refugees, asylum-seekers, internally displaced persons and some others.

68.5 million

60M

40M

20M

1955   1965   1975   1985   1995   2005   2015

The world's top 10 refugee host countries

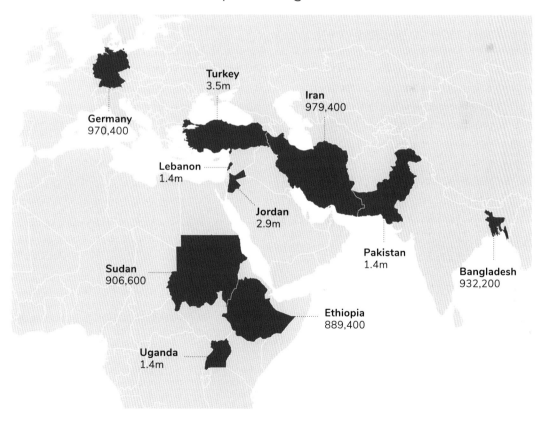

Germany
970,400

Turkey
3.5m

Iran
979,400

Lebanon
1.4m

Jordan
2.9m

Pakistan
1.4m

Bangladesh
932,200

Sudan
906,600

Ethiopia
889,400

Uganda
1.4m

reasonable share of migrants, he said, "who can decide who they wish to live with? Can you force groups of aliens on them or should you allow them to decide on who they want to adopt?"[2]

Contrary to much of the conventional wisdom broadcast in western European countries, it is untrue that Muslim-majority countries have turned a blind eye to the fate of their co-religionists. Amnesty International's 2017 report reveals that Muslim countries are, by a long way, hosting the most refugees, constituting 6 of the top 10 host countries (see map, page 207).

Alternative visions

Despite some countries showing generosity to refugees, provision and support still remains way short of the need. This has led to a number of imaginative and wide-ranging proposals, including building dedicated spaces for refugees on islands, developing refugee camps into proto-cities and promoting a new transnational polity, or political organization, called Refugia, where refugees will largely govern their own affairs.[3]

A refugee island

The most elaborately worked-out island solution for refugees is to create a "Europe-in-Africa" city-state on the Tunisian Plateau – a thin strip of seabed in the Mediterranean between Tunisia and Italy. According to this plan, which it is hoped the European Union would fund, the level of the seabed would be lifted, and the resultant land rented from Tunisia and Italy on a 99-year lease, thereby creating a new country, with its own passport, constitution, economy and social system. Theo Deutinger, a respected Dutch architect, has modelled the concept in detail. The design will incorporate elements from Europe and Africa – a mosque like Casablanca's, a church like St Peter's in Rome, a university like Oxford, an urban fabric like Timbuktu's, and so on. Initially, EIA would cater for 150,000 people, but it could be expanded by pouring more sand onto the shallow shelving.

Tents into cities

A second set of solutions recognizes that the temporary shelters and tents thrown up in the emergency period following a mass displacement are unsustainable. As the time spent in camps grows ever more protracted, tents are simply inappropriate – tearing easily, inadequate in adverse weather, and providing poor levels of security and privacy. The race is on to improve

SOLUTIONS TO MASS DISPLACEMENT

the standard-issue tent. An early runner, one that had to be modified because of fire risk, is a flat-pack solution for a modest house, made by the famous Swedish furniture company, Ikea.

Beyond the simple provision of better shelter, more far-sighted policy makers have advocated site-and-service schemes, setting shelters on a basic infrastructure (marked plots, with water, sewerage and electricity at the ready). As residents self-improve their dwellings, new cities will emerge from the tents of old.

Opposite: Flat pack shelters that can be assembled by refugees.

Above: The self-organization of refugees includes a flag of the Refugee Nation designed by the artist Yara Said, a Syrian refugee who found asylum in Amsterdam. The black and orange design is a tribute to those wearing life jackets in those colours as they crossed the Mediterranean. These Congolese refugees in Brazil hold up the Refugee flag and one from the Democratic Republic of the Congo.

Refugia: a transnational polity

Robin Cohen and Nicholas Van Hear, who take the principle of self-organization much further, suggest that a new transnational entity ("Refugia") can be fashioned in the hundreds of sites where refugees have "washed up". Neither a new state nor a transnational social movement, Refugia would be refugee-led and democratically governed. Refugees would be able to join at will or leave, taking their chances with existing states. Sites would be digitally connected and mobility within Refugia and beyond negotiated through visas and agreements. Benefits to "Refugians" would be delivered through a chip or app called a "Sesame chip". This is obviously a somewhat utopian idea, and has prompted a good deal of discussion, some critical, on the web.[4]

44

Migration Futures

As we have seen in this book, migration is as old as human society. As humans have populated, some would say overpopulated, the world, migration has taken many forms – from nomadism, to the exploitation of labour, to a flight from conflict, to opportunity seeking. Much of the early understanding of migration derives from the movements of nomadic peoples following their herds, traders following their nose for a good bargain, and coerced and free unskilled labour put to work in the fields, factories and service sectors, often on a one-way ticket to their new destinations. Some of these dynamics and forms of migration will continue and some will mutate, but as we peer into the future, we see three broad trends, which are discussed below.

- Insofar as the richer states can manage migration flows, we are likely to see an increase of selectivity. While low-skilled and family migration will continue, boosting semi-skilled and especially skilled migration will be the preferred immigration policy.
- There will remain considerable numbers of migrants generated by sudden-onset events (such as fleeing from natural disasters and political conflict) as well as millions who will be moving in response to long-term climate and demographic changes.
- For many citizens in migrant-receiving societies, the detailed dynamics and patterns of migration are of less significance than whether migrants will "fit in" and whether cultural differences can be surmounted. The

fear of difference fuels nativist and nationalist movements, but there is hope for a more harmonious future too.

Selective migration management

Three countries that have historically received large numbers of immigrants are the USA, Canada and Australia, so their migration histories and trajectories provide a good litmus test for the future forms of immigration control. For many years, selection of migrants to these countries was based on racial or cultural criteria, which, since the 1970s, have been discarded in favour of choosing skilled migrants or those who fill employment gaps. Canada and Australia have gone furthest

Stock of migrants by skill (percentage of total population), 1975–2015

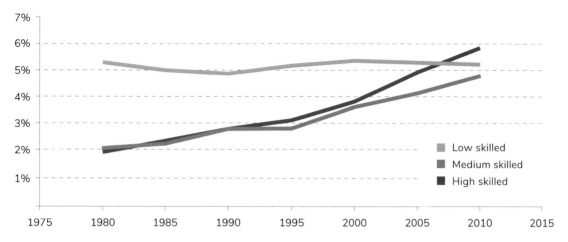

in what is sometimes called "immigration shopping". For example, one of the Australian visas, the Regional Skilled Migration Scheme, only applies to low-population growth areas of Australia where employers are unable to fill skilled positions from the local labour market. If you (a fictional intending migrant) want a job in Brisbane, Gold Coast, Newcastle, Sydney, Wollongong, Melbourne or Perth do not bother to apply, but if you are a certified dentist who is younger than 45, speaks English, and is prepared to work in the Northern Territory, sign here![1]

Such carefully crafted forms of selection are likely to increasingly mark migration policy in the OECD countries (broadly the 36 most developed nations). It is already apparent that the numbers of low-skilled migrants, many family migrants and care workers, are flatlining or declining, while high-skilled migrants are growing significantly. As we have seen in Chapter 35, richer countries will also increasingly use post-study visas as a means of persuading highly-skilled international

students to stay, particularly in the high-tech, engineering and medical sectors. For many poor countries, the "brain-drain" of skilled workers will be difficult. However, as we have seen in Chapter 25, highly populated countries such as India and the Philippines have trained millions of their workers to take advantage of skill shortages in rich countries in exchange for enhanced remittance income.

Above: Graphic representation of the "brain-drain" from poor countries.

MIGRATION FUTURES

Unmanaged migration

A long way away from the world of selective immigration control in OECD countries, is the near certainty that migrant numbers elsewhere will grow significantly in reaction to climate change, political conflict and regionally specific demographic change. Sudden-onset events like hurricanes or floods seem to be increasing in intensity and frequency as warmer seas power higher wind speeds. Managing the consequent displacements of people is made more difficult as infrastructural damage becomes more extensive and more expensive to replace.

With increased news coverage of events as far apart as Venezuela, Syria and the Sudan we are also much more conscious of the swirl of populations arising from civil conflict. The UNHCR predicts that by the end of 2019, 5.3 million Venezuelans (one in six of the population) will have fled their country.[2] A similar number took flight from Syria during the last eight years of civil war, though 250,000 are expected to return in 2019. There are perhaps as many as 3.2 million internally displaced people in the Sudan.

The number of migrants generated by sudden natural disasters and political conflict is large, but it is perhaps important to emphasize that there are slower climatic and demographic changes that are likely to propel the movement of tens of millions of people over the longer term. Let us take the issue of desertification alone. The Gobi Desert is overtaking grassland at the rate of 3,600km² (1,390 sq. miles) each year, while the Sahara has grown by 10 per cent since 1920. Drought, together with the loss of livestock and arable land threaten livelihoods and promote conflict,

making more and more people calculate that the only way they can survive is by migration. Coastal erosion due to rising sea levels is, of course, also important and headline-grabbing when islands have to be evacuated, but this phenomenon will generate fewer migrants than the gradual loss of arable land.

Demographic shifts are often "under the radar", but regional demographic contrasts allow us to spot where the major migration pressures are likely to arise. Starting from a similar number of live births in 1950, the discrepant fertilities between Africa and Europe provide one striking example (see chart).

Number of live births, Africa and Europe (millions)

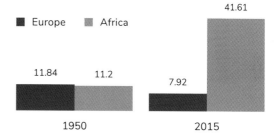

With its relatively high fertility rate, high vulnerability to climate change, low scores on the human development index and significant (though, it has to be emphasized, declining) levels of political conflict, Africa is already experiencing large migration flows, which are unlikely to abate. Most migration will be within the continent but alongside significant movement to other continents, particularly Europe.

Opposite: Desperate Venezuelans, fleeing their country's economic and political crisis, cross illegally into Colombia.

Migrants within Africa and from Africa, 1990–2017

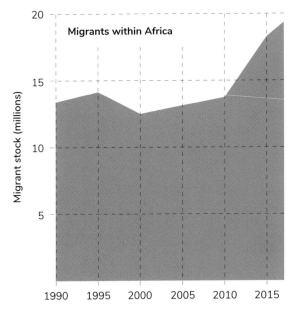

Migrants within Africa

Migrant stock (millions)

1990 1995 2000 2005 2010 2015

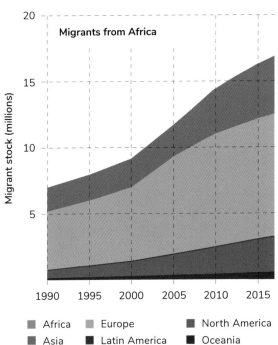

Migrants from Africa

Migrant stock (millions)

1990 1995 2000 2005 2010 2015

■ Africa ■ Europe ■ North America
■ Asia ■ Latin America ■ Oceania
& the Caribbean

Reactions to migration

While the patterns and dynamics of migration are of enduring interest to scholars, employers and governments, many people in settled populations are more interested in the social consequences of migration. In particular, they ask whether they will get along with the newcomers or whether differences of religion, ethnicity, colour and culture will create barriers to integration and acceptance. Logically and empirically, we can map out three kinds of social interaction ("three Cs") arising from migration:

- Conflict (often inducing separation and demands for restrictions on further immigration);
- Cohabitation (when people of different cultures rub along with each other, but without much enthusiasm); and
- Creolization (where, often slowly, they learn from each other and merge differing cultures through a process called hybridization or creolization).

Conflict

We live in an era when the suddenness, speed, diversity and volume of migration has activated and publicized the first possibility, conflict, and there is little doubt that populist and nationalist politicians in many parts of the world (notably in Italy, Hungary and the USA) have profited from the fears of long-resident populations. This anxiety takes many forms, but one index of the level of concern is the consistent exaggeration of the numbers of migrants in any given population.

Perceived and real migrant shares of population (selected countries)

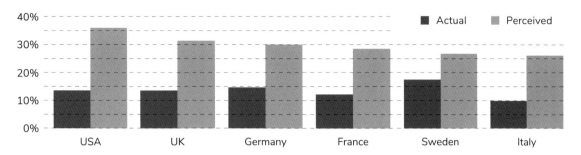

Cohabitation

Despite lots of contemporary examples of conflict arising from migration, seen over the longer term the remaining variations are more common. Historical contacts between disparate peoples show how cultural boundaries were imagined and constructed, usually in racial language, but also transgressed through the human capacity for mimicry, curiosity, sexual desire and empathy. In societies where "secular-rational values" predominate over "traditional values" there is less emphasis on religion and family values. Likewise, where "self-expression values" trump "survival values", there is an increasing tolerance of foreigners.[3]

In both cases, however, interaction might comprise quite superficial forms of co-habitation between people of different origins and cultural heritages. Minor economic transactions, polite greetings and tentative smiles are, of course, a whole lot better than outright hostility or hate crimes. However, in these prosaic everyday forms of encounter the bubbles barely meet. In deeper forms of interactions, the bubbles overlap significantly and a "creolized space" emerges that is clearly and visibly different from the parent cultures.

Creolization

In the case of creolization, we are talking about deep and incremental encounters. We are not observing one-way assimilation or integration into a dominant culture. Nor do we find a wholly harmonious or equal blending of identities and cultures. In creolizing settings, shared spaces and intercultural exchanges are normally asymmetrical and hierarchical. Yet creolization shows how encounters may be creative, productive and often subversive of the dominant order. Beneath the appearance of impenetrability between ethnicities are the music to which we listen (jazz, reggae, rock), the moves we make (samba, salsa), the invention of syncretic religions (Christianity, Buddhism),[4] the food we eat (not just fusion food but the deployment of new ingredients) and many other creolized practices, from dub poetry, to capoeira and modern yoga.

Because creolization is diffused and hidden from the headlines, we often fail to notice how shared social and cultural practices slowly change existing power structures and social relations. Creativity from below subtly but pervasively undermines the supposedly impermeable boundaries of race, culture and identity. This suggests that migrants and locals can gradually evolve a shared future.

Notes

Introduction

1 Mimi and John Urry Sheller, "The new mobilities paradigm", *Environment and Planning* A: *Economy and Space*, 38 (2) 2006, 207–26, doi: 10.1068/a37268.

1 Out of Africa: Early Humans

1 Yuval Noah Harari, *Sapiens: a brief history of humankind*, London: Vintage Books, 2011, p.56.

2 James Suzman, *Affluence without abundance*, London: Bloomsbury, 2017.

3 George Busby 'Here's how genetics helped crack the history of human migration' The Conversation, 13 January, 2016. https://theconversation.com/heres-how-genetics-helped-crack-the-history-of-human-migration-52918

2 Explorers: Arabic, Chinese and European

1 Al-Futuhat website, "The Islamic role in nautical discoveries: reassessing mainstream modern history', 2018. http://alfutuhat.com/islamiccivilization/Nautical%20science/Role.html

2 Khaliq Ahmad Nizami, "Early Arab contact with South Asia", *Journal of Islamic Studies*, 5 (1), 1994, p.53, citing J.H. Kramers. See also Ross E. Dunn, *The adventures of Ibn Battuta: a Muslim traveler of the fourteenth century*, Berkeley: University of California Press, 2012.

3 Mariners' Museum and Park website, "Zheng He", 2018. https://exploration.marinersmuseum.org/subject/zheng-he/

4 Mariners' Museum and Park website. 'The ages of exploration', 2018. https://exploration.marinersmuseum.org/type/age-of-discovery/

3 Early Religions and Migration

1 Daniel Lovering, "In 200-year tradition, most Christian missionaries are American", *Reuters*, 21 February 2012. https://www.reuters.com/article/us-missionary-massachusetts/in-200-year-tradition-most-christian-missionaries-are-american-idUSTRE81J0ZD20120221

2 Linda Learman, *Buddhist missionaries in the era of globalization*, Honolulu: University of Hawai'i Press, 2005, p.6.

3 Dirk Hoerder, *Cultures in contact: world migrations in the second millennium*, Durham, NC: Duke University Press, 2002, pp.87, 89–90.

4 Nomads: From Acephalous Societies to Empires

1 New World Encyclopedia, "Nomad", 7 December 2018. http://www.newworldencyclopedia.org/entry/Nomad

2 Ajay Saini, "The lesson from this missionary's death? Leave the Sentinelese alone", *Guardian*, 27 November 2018. https://www.theguardian.com/commentisfree/2018/nov/27/missionary-death-sentinelese-andaman-islands

3 Quoted in Patrick Daley and Dan O'Neill, "'Sad is too mild a word': press coverage of the *Exxon Valdez* oil spill", *Journal of Communication*, 41 (4), 1991, pp.42–57, doi: 10.1111/j.1460-2466.1991.tb02330.x.

4 Walter Meganack, "The day the water died", June 1989. https://jukebox.uaf.edu/site7/speech-written-chief-walter-meganack

5 Thomas T. Allsen, *Culture and conquest in Mongol Eurasia*, Cambridge: Cambridge University Press, 2004, pp.17–23.

5 The Romani and Travellers

1 New World Encyclopedia, "Nomad", 7 December 2018. http://www.newworldencyclopedia.org/entry/Nomad

2 Dean Nelson, "European Roma descended from Indian 'untouchables', genetic study shows", *Telegraph*, 3 December 2012. https://www.telegraph.co.uk/news/worldnews/europe/9719058/European-Roma-descended-from-Indian-untouchables-genetic-study-shows.HTML

3 James A. Watkins, *History of the Gypsies*, Owlcation, 2016. https://owlcation.com/humanities/The-Gypsies

Drawing on Angus Fraser, *The Gypsies*, Oxford: Wiley-Blackwell, 1995 (second edition).

4 P. Lane, S. Spencer and A. Jones, "Gypsy, traveller and Roma: experts by experience", National Federation of Gypsy Liaison Groups and the Joseph Rowntree Foundation Trust, 2014.

5 Alexandra Nacu, "The politics of Roma migration: framing identity struggles among Romanian and Bulgarian Roma in the Paris region", *Journal of Ethnic and Migration Studies*, 37 (1), 2011, pp.135–50, doi: 10.1080/1369183X.2010.515134.

6 Sharon Bohn Gmelch and George Gmelch, "The emergence of an ethnic group: the Irish Tinkers", *Anthropological Quarterly*, 49 (4), 1976, 225–38.

6 Liquid Continent: Pacific Islanders

1 Paul D'Arcy, "The people of the sea", in Donald Denoon (general editor) *The Cambridge History of the Pacific Islanders*, Cambridge: Cambridge University Press, 1997, p.75.

2 Sandra Bowdler, "The Pleistocene Pacific", in Donald Denoon (general editor) *The Cambridge History of the Pacific Islanders*, Cambridge: Cambridge University Press, 1997, pp.45–6.

3 Lilomaiava-Doktor Sa'iliemanu, "Beyond migration: Samoan population movement (*Malaga*) and geography of social space (*Vā*)", *The Contemporary Pacific: A Journal for Pacific Island Affairs*, 21 (1), 2009, pp.1–32, doi: 10.1353/cp.0.0035.

7 Atlantic Slavery

1 Eric Williams, *Capitalism and slavery*, Chapel Hill, NC: University of North Carolina Press, 1944, pp.34, 35.

2 Philip Curtin, *Atlantic slave trade: a census*, Madison: University of Wisconsin Press, 1972, p.87.

3 Clare Midgley, "Slave sugar boycotts, female activism and the domestic base of British anti-slavery culture", *Slavery and Abolition: A Journal of Slave and Post-Slave Studies*, 17 (3), 1996, pp.137–62, doi: 10.1080/01440399608575190, poem quoted on p.144.

8 Indian Indentured Workers

1 Hugh Tinker, *A new system of slavery: the export of Indian labour overseas, 1830–1920*, London: Oxford University Press, 1974, pp.126–35.

2 Tinker (1974: 176, citing Thakur Gajadhar).

9 Empires: Their Labour and Military Regimes

1 Miroslav Verner, *The Pyramids: the mystery, culture, and science of Egypt's great monuments*, London: Grove Press, 2001, pp.75–82.

2 See New World Encyclopedia, "Potosí", 27 May 2015. www.newworldencyclopedia.org/entry/Potosí and Atlas Obscura, "Potosí Silver Mines", 2019. https://www.atlasobscura.com/places/potosi-silver-mines

3 For estimates, see Ranjith MR, "Dark history of Congo rubber exploitation", 7 March 2017. https://www.rubberasia.com/2017/03/07/dark-history-congo-rubber-exploitation/ Note: there is a credible challenge to the often-repeated guestimate of "10 million deaths". See Ryan Faulk, "Mythologies about Leopold's Congo Free State", 24 July 2016. https://thealternativehypothesis.org/index.php/2016/07/24/mythologies-about-leopolds-congo-free-state/ Quotation cited in Robin Cohen, *The new helots: migrants in the international division of labour*, Aldershot: Gower, 1987, p.11.

4 Cohen 1987, p.11.

5 Jacques Chirac, "Allocution de M. Jacques Chirac, Président de la République, à l'occasion du 90ème anniversaire de la bataille de Verdun", 25 June 2006. http://www.jacqueschirac-asso.fr/archives-elysee.fr/elysee/elysee.fr/francais/interventions/discours_et_declarations/2006/juin/fi000721.html

10 The *Hajj*: The Fifth Pillar of Islam

1 Seán McLoughlin, "Hajj: how globalisation transformed the market for pilgrimage to Mecca", *The Conversation*, 15 August 2018. http://theconversation.com/hajj-how-globalisation-transformed-the-market-for-pilgrimage-to-mecca-97888

2 Ben Flanagan, "Hajj 2014: warnings over UK 'rip off' agents", *Al Arabiya News*, 3 October 2014. http:// english.alarabiya.net/en/perspective/features/2014/10/03/Hajj-2014-Warnings-over-UK-rip-off-agents.html

3 Marie Dhumieres, "The Bosnian who made the pilgrimage to Mecca – on foot", *Independent*, 24 October 2012. https://www.independent.co.uk/news/world/middle-east/the-bosnian-who-made-the-pilgrimage-to-mecca-on-foot-8225227.html

4 Surinder Bhardwaj, "Non-Hajj pilgrimage in Islam: a neglected dimension of religious circulation", *Journal of Cultural Geography*, 17 (2), 1998, p.70, doi: 10.1080/08873639809478321.

11 The Irish and the "Famine Exodus"

1 Mike Dash, "How Friedrich Engels' radical lover helped him father socialism", Smithsonian.com, 1 August 2013. https://www.smithsonianmag.com/history/how-friedrich-engels-radical-lover-helped-him-father-socialism-21415560/#uXmxb33qTOeKiCV6.99

2 Robert Scully, "The Irish and the 'famine exodus' of 1847", in Robin Cohen (ed.) *The Cambridge survey of world migration*, Cambridge: Cambridge University Press, 1995, pp.80–4.

3 Noel Ignatiev, *How the Irish became white*, London: Routledge, 1995.

12 Workers in South Africa's Mines

1 Robin Cohen, *Endgame in South Africa? The changing structures and ideology of apartheid*, Trenton, NJ: Africa World Press, 1988, p.40.

13 From Convicts to "Ten Pound Poms": British Migration to Australia

1 Deborah Oxley, *Convict maids: the forced migration of women to Australia*, Cambridge: Cambridge University Press, 1996, p.3.

2 Oxley (1996) p.9.

3 Robin Cohen, *Global diasporas: an introduction*, London: Routledge, 2008, p.72.

4 *The Southern Cross*, "First Catholic boy migrants arrive in West Australia", Adelaide, 19 August 1938. See also Geoffrey Sherington, "Contrasting narratives in the history of twentieth-century British child migration to Australia: an interpretive essay", *History Australia*, 9 (2), 2012, pp.27–47, doi: 10.1080/14490854.2012.11668416; Stephen Constantine, "The British government, child welfare, and child migration to Australia after 1945", *Journal of Imperial and Commonwealth History*, 20 (1), 2002, pp.99–132, doi: 10.1080/03086530208583135.

5 Steven Morris and Ellen Connolly, "Julia Gillard: the ten pound Pom who became prime minister of Australia", *Guardian*, 24 June 2010. https://www.theguardian.com/world/2010/jun/24/julia-gillard-ten-pound-pom-prime-minister-australia

14 The "Great Atlantic Migration" to the USA

1 Jon Gjerde, "The Scandanavian migrants", in Robin Cohen (ed.) *The Cambridge Survey of World Migration*, Cambridge: Cambridge University Press, 1995, p.88.

16 Palestine: Jewish Immigration and the Displacement of the Palestinians

1 Golda Meir, Interview with Frank Giles, *The Sunday Times*, 15 June 1969.

2 Thomas Friedman, "Promised land: Israel and the Palestinians see a way to co-exist", *New York Times*, 5 September 1993. https://www.nytimes.com/1993/09/05/weekinreview/promised-land-israel-and-the-palestinians-see-a-way-to-co-exist.html

3 Geremy Forman and Alexandre (Sandy) Kedar, "From Arab land to 'Israel lands': the legal dispossession of the Palestinians displaced by Israel in the wake of 1948", *Environment and Planning D: Society and Space*, volume 22 (6), 2004, pp.809–30, doi: 10.1068/d402.

4 Jalal Al Husseini, "Jordan and the Palestinians", in Myriam Ababsa (ed.) *Atlas of Jordan: history, territories and society*, Beirut: Presses de l'Ifpo, 2013, pp.230–45, doi: 10.4000/books. ifpo.4560.

17 "New Commonwealth" Migration to the UK

1 Robin Cohen, *The new helots: migrants in the international division of labour*, Aldershot: Gower, 1987, pp.127–8.

2 G.C.K. Peach, "West Indian migration to Britain", *International Migration Review*, 1 (2), 1967, pp.34–45, doi: 10.2307/3002807.

3 Muhammed Anwar, "'New Commonwealth' migration to the UK", in Robin Cohen (ed.) *Cambridge Survey of World Migration*, Cambridge: Cambridge University Press, 1995, p.277.

18 Turkish Migration to West Germany

1 Deniz Göktürl, David Gramling and Anton Kaes (eds) *Germany in transit: nation and migration, 1955–2005*, Berkeley: University of California Press, 2007, p.8.

2 Cf. the fourfold division proposed by Yunus Ulusoy, "From guest worker migration to transmigration: the German–Turkish migratory movements and the special role of Istanbul and the Ruhr", in D. Reuschke, M. Salzbrunn and K. Schönhärl (eds) *The economies of urban diversity*, New York: Palgrave Macmillan, 2013, doi: 10.1057/9781137338815_4.

3 Max Frisch, Öffentlichkeit *als Partner*, Berlin: Suhrkamp, 1967, p.100. "Man hat Arbeitskräfte gerufen, und es kamen Menschen" in original German.

4 Nermin Abadan-Unat, "Turkish migration to Europe", in Robin Cohen (ed.) *The Cambridge survey of world migration*, Cambridge: Cambridge University Press, 1995, p.281.

19 The Vietnamese Boat People

1 L. Davis, "Hong Kong and the Indochinese refugees", in S. Chantavanich and E.B. Reynolds (eds), *Indochinese refugees: asylum and resettlement*, Bangkok: Institute of Asian Studies, Chulalongkorn University, 1988, p.151.

2 Chan Kwok Bun, "The Vietnamese boat people in Hong Kong", in Robin Cohen (ed.) *The Cambridge survey of world migration*, Cambridge: Cambridge University Press, 1995, pp.382–3.

3 Christopher Parsons and Pierre-Louis Vézina, "Migrant networks and trade: the Vietnamese boat people as a natural experiment", *Economic Journal*, 128 (612), 2018, F210–34, doi: 10.1111/ecoj.12457.

4 Jill Rutter, *Refugee children in the UK*, London: McGraw-Hill, 2006, p.68.

20 Post-Soviet Migration

1 Robin Cohen, "East–West and European migration in a global context", *Journal of Ethnic and Migration Studies*, 18 (1), 1991, pp.9–26, doi: 10.1080/1369183X.1991.9976279.

2 Stefan Wolff, "German and German minorities in Europe", in Tristan James Mabry (ed.) *Divided nations and European integration*, Philadelphia: University of Pennsylvania Press, 2013. Available at http://www.stefanwolff.com/research/germany-and-german-minorities-in-europe

3 Nicholas Van Hear and Robin Cohen, "Diasporas and conflict: distance, contiguity and spheres of engagement", *Oxford Development Studies*, 45 (2), 2017, pp.171–84, doi: 10.1080/13600818.2016.1160043.

21 Caribbean Migrations

1 Tia Ghose, "Humans may have been stuck on Bering Strait for 10,000 years", Live Science webpage, 27 February 2014. https://www.livescience.com/43726-bering-strait-populations-lived.html

2 Jill Sheppard, "A historical sketch of the poor whites of Barbados: from indentured servants to 'Redlegs'", *Caribbean Studies*, 14 (3) 1974, quote from p.75.

3 B.W. Higman, *Slave population of the British Caribbean, 1807–1834*, Kingston, Jamaica: The Press, University of the West Indies, 1995, p.3.

4 Julie Greene, "Who built the Panama Canal?", *Jacobin* webpage, 21 June 2017. https://www.jacobinmag.com/2017/06/ trump-panama-canal-varela-imperialism-latin-america

22 The Overseas Chinese

1 OER Services, "Chinese dynasties: seaports and maritime trade", in *World Civilization*, Portland: Lumen Learning, 2016. https://courses.lumenlearning.com/suny-hccc-worldcivilization/chapter/trade-under-the-tang-dynasty/

2 Robin Cohen, *Global diasporas: an introduction*, London: Routledge, 2008, p.85.

3 Lydia Potts, *The world labour market: a history of migration*, London: Zed Books, 1990, p.71.

4 Ong Jin Hui, "Chinese indentured labour: coolies and colonies", in Robin Cohen (ed.) *The Cambridge survey of world migration*, Cambridge: Cambridge University Press, 1995, pp.51–6.

5 Cohen (1995) p.90.

6 Suzy Strutner, "The 10 best Chinatowns in the entire world", *HuffPost US*, 7 December 2017. https://www.huffingtonpost.co.uk/entry/chinatowns-all-over-the-world_us_4704673

23 *Hukou* and Internal Migration in China

1 T. Cheng and M. Selden, "The origins and social consequences of China's hukou system", *The China Quarterly*, 139, 1994, 644–68, doi: 10.1017/S0305741000043083.

2 John Torpey, "Revolutions and freedom of movement: an analysis of passport controls in the French, Russian, and Chinese revolutions", *Theory and Society*, 26 (6), 1997, p.857. https://www.jstor.org/stable/657937

3 Public Radio International, "China's *hukou* system puts migrant workers at severe economic disadvantage", PRI webpage, 1 May 2013. https://www.pri.org/stories/2013-05-01/chinas-hukou-system-puts-migrant-workers-severe-economic-disadvantage

4 "The rural–urban divide: ending apartheid", *The Economist*, 19 April 2014. https://www.economist.com/special-report/2014/04/19/ending-apartheid

24 Population Transfer and the Partition of India

1 Yasmin Khan, *The great partition: the making of India and Pakistan*, New Haven, CN: Yale University Press, 2007, p.17.

2 Begum, Arghwani. Oral history Interview by Fakhra Hassan (31 August 2015), The 1947 Partition Archive. Web, 15 May 2019. <https://exhibits.stanford.edu/1947-partition/catalog/sy490th7041>

25 The Export of Workers: The Philippines

1 Robyn Margalit Rodriguez, *Migrants for export: how the Philippine state brokers labor to the world*, Minneapolis: University of Minnesota Press, 2010, p.4.
2 Maruja M.B. Asis, "The Philippines: beyond labor migration, toward development and (possibly) return", *Migration Policy Institute* online article, 12 July 2017. https://www.migrationpolicy.org/article/philippines-beyond-labor-migration-toward-development-and-possibly-return

26 The Trade in Sex Workers

1 International Labour Office, *Profits and poverty: the economics of forced labour*, Geneva: ILO, 2014, p.13.
2 Donna M. Hughes, "The 'Natasha' trade: the transnational shadow market of trafficking in women", *Journal of International Affairs*, 53 (2), 2000, pp.625–6.
3 Equality Now, "Stories of survivors: Natalie and Sam". https://www.equalitynow.org/natalie_sam.
4 Laura Lammasniemi, "Anti-white slavery legislation and its legacies in England", *Anti-Trafficking Review*, (9), 2017, pp.64–76, doi:10.14197/atr.20121795.
5 J. Vandepitte, R. Lyerla, G. Dallabetta, F. Crabbé, M. Alary and A. Buvé, "Estimates of the number of female sex workers in different regions of the world", *Sexually Transmitted Infections (BMJ Journals)*, 82 (S3), 2006, iii18–25, doi: 10.1136/sti.2006.020081.
6 Study reported in Ronald Weitzer, "The social construction of sex trafficking: ideology and institutionalization of a moral crusade", *Politics and Society*, 35 (3), 2011, p.454, doi: 10.1177/0032329207304319.
7 Ibid.

27 Exiles: Dying Abroad or Returning to Power

1 J.J. O'Connor and E.F. Robertson, "Aristotle", University of St Andrews web page, February 1999. http://www-history.mcs.st-andrews.ac.uk/Biographies/Aristotle.html
2 Friedemann Pestel, "French Revolution and migration after 1789", *European History Online*, 11 July 2017. http://ieg-ego.eu/en/threads/europe-on-the-road/political-migration-exile/friedemann-pestel-french-revolution-and-migration-after-1789
3 This author has visited Longwood, St Helena, and observed flaking wallpaper, said to contain arsenic, next to Napoleon's bed. Therefore, we could be talking of accidental poisoning compounded, perhaps, by various medications ingested over the years containing the same substance. Certainly, on exhumation, his hair and body contained high levels of arsenic.

28 The Politics of Cold War Migration

1 "Expulsion from the Soviet Union", Wikipedia page, 10 March 2019. https://en.wikipedia.org/wiki/Aleksandr_Solzhenitsyn#Expulsion_from_the_Soviet_Union.
2 George J. Borjas, "The wage impact of the *Marielitos*: a reappraisal", Harvard University working paper, 2015. https://sites.hks.harvard.edu/fs/gborjas/publications/working%20papers/Mariel2015.pdf.

29 Global Diasporas

1 Robin Cohen, *Global diasporas: an introduction*, second edition, London: Routledge, 2008.
2 Rudolph J. Vecoli, "The Italian diaspora: 1876–1976", in Robin Cohen (ed.) *The Cambridge survey of world migration*, Cambridge: Cambridge University Press, pp.124–22.
3 Donna R. Gabaccia, *Italy's many diasporas*, London: UCL Press, 2000.
4 Albert Hourani, "Introduction", in Albert Hourani and Nadim Shehadi (eds) *The Lebanese in the world: a century of emigration*, London: I.B.Tauris for the Centre for Lebanese Studies, p.7.
5 Yuri Slexkine, *The Jewish century*, London: Princeton University Press, 2004, p.31.
6 Paul Gilroy, *The black Atlantic: modernity and double consciousness*, London: Verso, 1993.

30 Migration to the Gulf

1 Owen Gibson and Pete Pattisson, "Death toll among Qatar's 2022 World Cup workers revealed", *Guardian*, 23 December 2014. https://www.theguardian.com/world/2014/dec/23/qatar-nepal-workers-world-cup-2022-death-toll-doha
2 Amy Foster, "Death toll rises in the lead up to the 2022 World Cup", News.com.au, 29 September 2017. https://www.news.com.au/world/asia/death-toll-rises-in-the-lead-up-to-the-2022-world-cup/news-story/43896b31023dd6ab6ed213637fe4d3e7
3 Ibid.
4 Development News, "Data reveals 24,570 Indian workers have died in Gulf countries since 2012", 8 November 2018. www.developmentnews.in/data-reveals-24570-indian-workers-died-gulf-countries-since-2012/
5 Manolo I. Abella, "Asian migrant and contract workers in the Middle East", in Robin Cohen (ed.) *The Cambridge survey of world migration*, Cambridge: Cambridge University Press, 1995, pp.418–23.

31 Mediterranean Migrations

1 Martin Bernal, *Black Athena: the Afroasiatic roots of classical civilization*, volumes 1, 2 and 3, London: Free Association Books, 1987–2006.
2 Fernand Braudel, *La Méditerranée et le monde méditerranéen à l'époque de Philippe II*, Paris: Armand Colin, 1949.
3 Rod Norland, "'All of Africa is here': where Europe's southern border is just a fence", *New York Times*, 19 August 2018. https://www.nytimes.com/2018/08/19/world/africa/ceuta-morocco-spain-migration-crisis.html
4 Ruben Andersson, "Time and the migrant other: European border controls and the temporal economics of illegality", *American Anthropologist*, 116 (4), 2014, pp.796, 803, doi:10.1111/aman.12148.

32 Health Workers Worldwide

1 J. Buchan, I.S. Dhillon and J. Campbell (eds) "Health employment and economic growth: an evidence base", Geneva: World Health Organization. https://www.who.int/hrh/resources/WHO-HLC-Report_web.pdf (p.16)
2 RPS Migration, "Work as a nurse or as a skilled migrant in Australia". http://104.236.45.183/work-in-australia/
3 Report by the Health Foundation, The Kings Fund and the Nuffield Trust *Closing the gap: key areas for action on the*

health and care workforce, London, March 2019, p.2. https://www.medacs.com/Allied-healthcare-jobs-qatar; https://www.jobs4medical.co.uk/blog/; https://www.nurses.co.uk/jobs/nursing/rest-of-world/963/oo-ps-lf1-pp

4 E.J. Mills, S. Kanters, A. Hagopian, N. Bansback, J. Nachega, M. Alberton et al., "The financial cost of doctors emigrating from sub-Saharan Africa: human capital analysis", *The BMJ*, 343, 2011, doi: 10.1136/bmj.d7031.

5 Aisha K. Lofters, "The 'brain drain' of health care workers: causes, solutions and the example of Jamaica", *Canadian Journal of Public Health*, 103 (5), 2012, p.e377.

33 Syrian Refugees: The Lebanese Case

1 Cameron Thibos, "One million Syrians in Lebanon: a milestone quickly passed", Migration Policy Centre, Policy Briefs, June 2014. http://hdl.handle.net/1814/31696

2 Katharine Jones and Leena Ksaifi, *Struggling to survive: slavery and exploitation of Syrian refugees in Lebanon*, London: The Freedom Fund, 8 April 2016. https://d1r4g0yjvcc7lx.cloudfront.net/uploads/Lebanon-Report-FINAL-8April16.pdf (p.3)

3 "Noha's story", Global Fund for Women, 2012. https://www.globalfundforwomen.org/nohas-story/#.XIe-VfZ2uUk

34 Musical Roots and Routes

1 Roger Blench, "Using diverse sources of evidence for reconstructing the prehistory of musical exchanges in the Indian Ocean and their broader significance for cultural prehistory", 2012. http://www.rogerblench.info/Archaeology/Africa/ AAR%20paper%20Indian%20Ocean.pdf

2 Peter McKay, "Plucking heartstrings", *Spectator*, 14 April 2012. https://www.spectator.co.uk/2012/04/plucking-heartstrings/2

3 J. Baily and M. Collyer, "Introduction: music and migration", *Journal of Ethnic and Migration Studies*, 32 (2), 2006, pp.167–82, doi: 10.1080/13691830500487266.

4 D. Bloome, J. Feigenbaum and C. Muller, "African-American marriage, migration and the boll weevil in the US South, 1892–1920", September 2015, p.3. https://pdfs.semanticscholar.org/165e/72ede4c43acdd49ebed11acd3cde0daeaa17.pdf

35 In Search of Knowledge: International Students

1 Yeganeh Torbati, "Fewer foreign students coming to United States for second year in row -survey", Reuters: Technology, Media and Telecommunications, 13 November 2018. https://uk.reuters.com/article/usa-immigration-students-idUKL2N1XN161

2 P.B. Vijayakumar and C.J.L. Cunningham, "US immigration policies hamper entrepreneurial ambitions", *University World News*, 15 March 2019. https://www.universityworldnews.com/post.php?story=20190312145259472

3 Universities UK, "International students now worth £25 billion to UK economy: new research", 6 March 2017. https://www.universitiesuk.ac.uk/news/Pages/International-students-now-worth-25-billion-to-UK-economy---new-research.aspx

4 G.E. Bijwaard and Qi Wang, "Return migration of foreign students", *European Journal of Population*, 32 (1), 2016, pp.31–54, doi: 10.1007/s10680-015-9360-2.

5 Prospects HEDD, UK higher education's official degree verification service, https://hedd.ac.uk/; and Sally Weale,

"Seventy-five bogus universities shut down in past four years", *Guardian*, 8 April 2019. https://en.wikipedia.org/wiki/Bogus_colleges_in_the_United_Kingdom

36 Marriage and Migration

1 Caroline B. Brettell, "Marriage and migration", *Annual Review of Anthropology*, 46, 2017, pp.81–97, doi: 10.1146/annurev-anthro-102116-041237.

2 Randall, "The untold stories of Japanese picture brides", AsAmNews website, 24 December 2017. https://asamnews.com/ 2017/12/24/the-untold-stories-of-japanese-picture-brides/

3 Francesca Rizzoli, "Italian proxy brides: Australia's forgotten generation of female migrants", SBS, 27 September 2017. https://www.sbs.com.au/yourlanguage/italian/en/article/2017/09/25/italian-proxy-brides-australias-forgotten-generation-female-migrants

4 *The Economist*, "The flight from marriage", 20 August 2011. https://www.economist.com/briefing/2011/08/20/the-flight-from-marriage

37 Retirement and Lifestyle Migration

1 Benson, Michaela and O'Reilly Karen (eds) *Lifestyle Migration: Expectations, Aspirations and Experiences*, Abingdon: Routledge, 2009.

2 Augustin De Coulon, "Where do immigrants retire to?" *IZA World of Labor*, 297, 2016, pp.1–10, doi: 10.15185/izawol.297.

3 F. Turbout and P. Buléon, "Ageing demographic structure", *Cross Channel Atlas: Channel space*, translated by Louis Shurmer-Smith, University of Caen Normandie, 2001. https://atlas-transmanche.certic.unicaen.fr/en/page-406.html

4 Michaela Benson and Karen O'Reilly, *Lifestyle migration and colonial traces in Malaysia and Panama*, London: Palgrave, 2018, pp.10–27.

5 *The Economist*, "The sun sets on British pensioners' migration to Europe", 19 December 2017. https:// www.economist.com/britain/2017/12/19/the-sun-sets-on-british-pensioners-migration-to-europe

38 Climate-driven Migration

1 The New Climate Economy, "The science: key findings from the IPCC and the New Climate Economy reports", August 2018. https://www.un.org/en/climatechange/science.shtml

2 Carey Lodge, "Cyclone Idai tears through Mozambique: Adelino's story", 27 March 2019. https://www.worldvision.org.uk/ news-and-views/blog/2019/march/cyclone-idai-tears-through-mozambique-adolinos-story/

3 Liette Connolly-Boutin and Barry Smit, "Climate change, food security, and livelihoods in sub-Saharan Africa", *Regional Environmental Change*, 16 (2), 2016, pp.385–99.

4 M. Brzoska and C. Fröhlich, "Climate change, migration and violent conflict: vulnerabilities, pathways and adaptation strategies", *Migration and Development*, 5 (2), 2016, pp.193, 196, doi: 10.1080/21632324.2015.1022973.

5 Ibid.

39 Tourism: Mobility and its Discontents

1 Christopher M. Kopper, "The breakthrough of the package tour in Germany after 1945", *Journal of Tourism History*, 1 (1), 2009, pp.67–92, doi: 10.1080/17551820902742798.

2 Emanuel de Kadt, "Social planning for tourism in the developing countries", *Annals of Tourism Research*, 6 (1), 1979, pp.36–48, doi:10.1177/004728758001800369.

3 Lee Tsung Hung, "Influence analysis of community resident support for sustainable tourism development", *Tourism Management*, 34 (2), 2013, p.37, doi: 10.1016/j.tourman.2012.03.007.

4 Jessica Brown, "Last chance tourism: is this trend just causing more damage?", *Independent*, 7 June 2018. https://www.independent.co.uk/news/long_reads/last-chance-tourism-travel-great-barrier-reef-amazon-machu-picchu-a8363466.html

5 Krittinee Nuttavuthisit, "Branding Thailand: correcting the negative image of sex tourism", *Place Branding and Public Diplomacy*, 3 (1), 2007, pp.21–30, doi: 10.1057/palgrave.pb.6000045.

40 Children and Migration

1 Unicef data, "Child migration", December 2018. https://data.unicef.org/topic/child-migration-and-displacement/migration/

2 Vasileia Digidiki, "The experience of distress: child migration on Lesvos, Greece", in Jaccqueline Bhabha, Jyothi Kanics and Daniel Senovilla Hernández (eds) *Research handbook on child migration*, Cheltenham: Edward Elgar, 2018, pp.447–57.

3 Ibid.

4 Cati Coe, "How children feel about their parents' migration: a history of the reciprocity of care in Ghana", in C. Coe, R.R. Reynolds, D.A. Boehm, J. Meredith Hess and H. Rae-Espinoza (eds), *Everyday ruptures: children, youth, and migration in global perspective*, Nashville, TN: Vanderbilt University Press, 2011, pp.102–4.

41 Do Walls Work? Borders and Migration

1 Elisabeth Vallet (ed.), *Borders, fences and walls: state of insecurity?* 2014, London: Routledge.

2 *The Economist*, "Why India and Bangladesh have the world's craziest border", 25 June 2015. https://www.economist.com/the-economist-explains/2015/06/24/why-india-and-bangladesh-have-the-worlds-craziest-border

3 Jens Manuel Krogstad, Jeffrey S. Passel and D'Vera Cohn, "5 facts about illegal immigration in the US", Pew Research Center webpage, 27 April 2017. http://www.pewresearch.org/fact-tank/2017/04/27/5-facts-about-illegal-immigration-in-the-u-s/

4 Catalina Gonella, "Visa overstays outnumber illegal border crossings, trend expected to continue", NBC News webpage, 7 March 2017. https://www.nbcnews.com/news/latino/visa-overstays-outnumber-illegal-border-crossings-trend-expected -continue-n730216

5 Douglas S. Massey, "The counterproductive consequences of border enforcement", *Cato Journal*, 37 (3), 2017, general ref and p.553. https://object.cato.org/sites/cato.org/files/serials/files/cato-journal/2017/9/cato-journal-v37n3-11-updated.pdf

6 Rachel Busbridge, "Performing colonial sovereignty and the Israeli 'separation' wall", *Social Identities: Journal for the Study of Race, Nation and Culture*, 19 (5), 2013, p.655, doi: 10.1080/13504630.2013.835514.

42 Detentions and Deportations

1 Dora Schriro, "Obstacles to reforming family detention in the USA", working paper 20, Global Detention Project, 2017. https://www.globaldetentionproject.org/wp-content/uploads/2017/01/Schriro-GDP-working-paper-2.pdf

2 Matthew J. Gibney, "Is deportation a form of forced migration?", *Refugee Survey Quarterly*, 32 (2), 2013, pp.119–20, doi: 10.1093/rsq/hdt003.

43 Solutions to Mass Displacement

1 *The Economist*, "Right-wing anti-immigrant parties continue to receive support in Europe", 10 September 2018. https://www.economist.com/graphic-detail/2018/09/10/right-wing-anti-immigrant-parties-continue-to-receive-support-in-europe

2 Shaun Walker, "Viktor Orbán calls for anti-migration politicians to take over EU", *Guardian*, 10 January 2019. https://www.theguardian.com/world/2019/jan/10/viktor-orban-calls-anti-migration-politics-take-over-eu-matteo-salvini

3 These alternatives are discussed in Robin Cohen and Nicholas Van Hear, "Visions of Refugia: territorial and transnational solutions to mass displacement", *Planning Theory and Practice*, 18 (3), 2017, 494–504, doi: 10.1080/14649357.2017.133 0233. The idea of Refugia is discussed at book length in Robin Cohen and Nicholas Van Hear, *Refugia: radical solutions to mass displacement*, London: Routledge, forthcoming 2020.

4 The proposal and critiques can be found at the COMPAS webpage: https://www.compas.ox.ac.uk/project/the-refugia-project/

44 Migration Futures

1 For Australia, see Australian Visa Bureau, "Regional skilled migration scheme Australia", 2018. http://www.visabureau.com/australia/regional-skilled-migration.aspx. For Canada, see Global Migrate, "Canada skilled immigration program", blog, 13 October 2018. https://global-migrate.com/blog/canada-skilled-immigration-program/

2 Emma Beswick, "Venezuela crisis: by the end of 2019, 1 in 6 people will have fled the country", *Euronews*, 12 February 2019. https://www.euronews.com/2019/02/09/venezuela-crisis-by-the-end-of-2019-1-in-6-people-will-have-fled-the-country

3 These four kinds of value systems derive from the Inglehart–Welzel cultural map, which should be consulted in the original to understand its full complexity. See World Values Survey, "Inglehart–Welzel cultural map", 2008. http://www.worldvaluessurvey.org/images/Cultural_map_WVS5_2008.jpg

4 "The average Christian believes in the monotheist God, but also in the dualist Devil, in the polytheist saints, and in animist ghosts", Yuval Noah Harari, *Sapiens: a brief history of humankind*, London: Random House, 2014, p.223.

Index

Credits

The publishers would like to thank the following sources for their kind permission to reproduce the pictures in this book.

Key: t = top, b = bottom, c = centre, l = left & r = right

AKG-Images: De Agostini Picture Library/W.Buss 48

Alamy: AB Historic 92; /AF Fotografie 16; /The Africa Image Library 14; /Ancient Art & Architecture 17; /Archiv Gerstenberg/ullstein bild 133; /Art Collection: 169; /Byvalet 36; /Christophel Fine Art/UIG 34; /David Creedon 60; /De Agostini 22; /Michael DeFreitas Caribbean 103; / GL Archive 76br; /Amer Ghazzal 203; /Granger Historical Picture Archive 76tl, 140; /Interfoto 76bc; /ITAR-TASS News Agency 76tr; /M. Timothy O'Keefe 145; /Keystone 135; /Mark Phillips 174; /Science History Images 76tc; /Matthias Scholz 191

Birmingham Public Library 144

Birmingham Museum Art Gallery 43

Bridgeman Images: De Agostini Picture Library 20-21

Harvard University, Center for Geographic Analysis 13

Museum of New Zealand Te Papa Tongarewa, Wellington, New Zealand 39; /SZ Photo/Scherl 44

Eyevine: Massimo Sestini 151

Rick Findler 205

Getty Images: Bain News Service/Interim Archive 9; / Bettmann 72, 75, 177; /Ron Case/Keystone/Hulton Archive 68; /Demelza Cloke 40; /Colorvision/ullstein bild 89; / Corbis 61; /John Dominis/The LIFE Picture Collection 134; /Fine Art Images/Heritage Images 38; /Flying Camera/ Archive Photos 71t; /Fox Photos 67; /John Franks 84t; / Jill Freedman 104b; /Kevin Frayer 196; /Godong/BSIP 159; /Benainous/Tinacci/Gamma-Rapho 31; /AFP/Pinn Hans 81; /Annet HELD/Gamma-Rapho 136b; /In Pictures Ltd./ Corbis 193, 200; /Jerome Joseph/Chicago History Museum 171; /Kempff/ullstein bild 90; / Keystone-France/Gamma-Keystone 198; /Kyodo News 124t; /Leemage/Corbis 30; /Albert Llop/Anadolu Agency 192; /Saul Loeb/AFP 197; / Stefano Montesi/Corbis 208; / North Wind Picture Archives 24; /Ross Land 47; /Edwin Levick 56; /AFP/Arsis Messinis 152-153; /Josef Novy 35; /The Print Collector/Print Collector 109; /Roslan Rahman/AFP 53; /Andrew Renneisen 186-187; /AFP/Geoff Robins 166; /AFP/Ashraf Shazly 189; / Reg Speller/Fox Photos 63; /SSPL 104t; /Fred Stein Archive/ Archive Photos 76bl; /Brent Stirton 146; /The Sydney Morning Herald/Fairfax Media 142-143; /Universal Images Group 10, 113; /Veejay Villafranca 124b; /World History Archive 18t, 23; /Barbara Zanon 46b; /Zuma Press, Inc 155

Library of Congress 41

Private Collection 46t, 49, 50, 51, 108, 129, 137

Tânia Rêgo/Agência Brasil 209

Science Photo Library: Pascal Goetgheluck 12

Shutterstock: AP 2, 94-95, 121, 125; /Olmo Calvo/AP 110; / Daily Mail 85b; /Alfredo Dagli Orti 131; /Rolex Dela Pena/ EPA 112, 115; / Max Desfor/AP 118; /Martin Divisek/EPA 33; /Heinz Ducklau/AP 136t; /Eddie Adams/AP 138-139; / Granger 120; /Bilal Hussein/AP 162, 164-165; / Ratov Maxim 96; /Martin Mejia/AP 212; /Yulia Plekanova 59; /Who is Danny 211

Topfoto: Heritage-Images 77

Tropenmuseum Collection 106

University of Iowa Libraries Special Collections Department 71b

Every effort has been made to acknowledge correctly and contact the source and/or copyright holder of each picture and Carlton Publishing Group apologises for any unintentional errors or omissions, which will be corrected in future editions of this book.

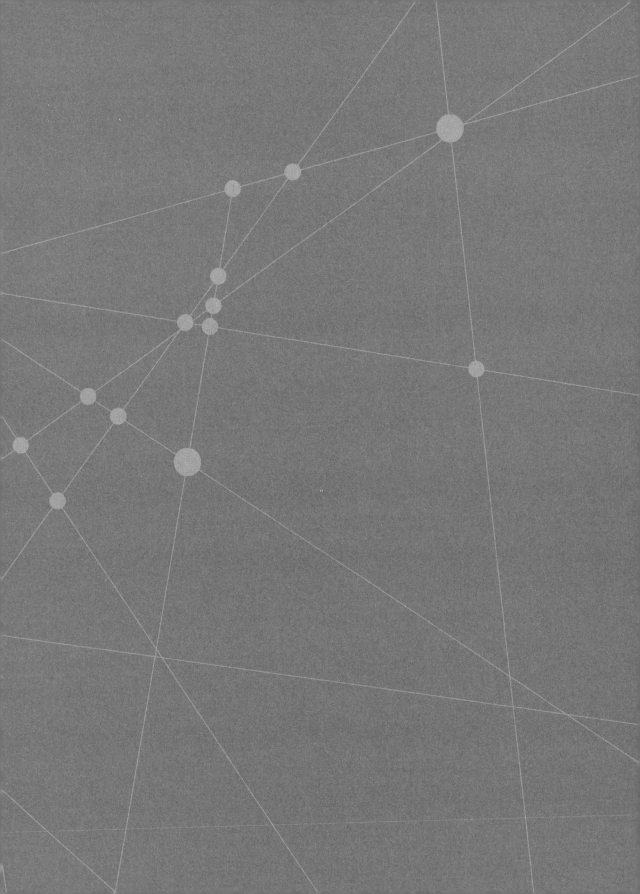